The Politics of Skin Tone

Chicago Studies in American Politics
A series edited by Susan Herbst, Lawrence R. Jacobs, Adam J. Berinsky,
and Frances Lee; Benjamin I. Page, editor emeritus

ALSO IN THE SERIES

How Politicians Polarize: Political Representation in an Age of Negative Partisanship
by Mia Costa

False Front: The Failed Promise of Presidential Power in a Polarized Age
by Kenneth Lowande

Moral Issues: How Public Opinion on Abortion and Gay Rights Affects American Religion and Politics
by Paul Goren and Christopher Chapp

The Roots of Polarization: From the Racial Realignment to the Culture Wars
by Neil A. O'Brian

Some White Folks: The Interracial Politics of Sympathy, Suffering, and Solidarity
by Jennifer Chudy

Through the Grapevine: Socially Transmitted Information and Distorted Democracy
by Taylor N. Carlson

America's New Racial Battle Lines: Protect versus Repair
by Rogers M. Smith and Desmond King

Partisan Hostility and American Democracy
by James N. Druckman, Samara Klar, Yanna Krupnikov,
Matthew Levendusky, and John Barry Ryan

Respect and Loathing in American Democracy: Polarization, Moralization, and the Undermining of Equality
by Jeff Spinner-Halev and Elizabeth Theiss-Morse

Countermobilization: Policy Feedback and Backlash in a Polarized Age
by Eric M. Patashnik

Race, Rights, and Rifles: The Origins of the NRA and Contemporary Gun Culture
by Alexandra Filindra

Additional series titles follow index.

The Politics of Skin Tone

African American Experiences, Identity, and Attitudes

NICOLE D. YADON

The University of Chicago Press
Chicago and London

The University of Chicago Press, Chicago 60637
The University of Chicago Press, Ltd., London
© 2025 by The University of Chicago
All rights reserved. No part of this book may be used or reproduced in any manner whatsoever without written permission, except in the case of brief quotations in critical articles and reviews. For more information, contact the University of Chicago Press, 1427 E. 60th St., Chicago, IL 60637.
Published 2025

34 33 32 31 30 29 28 27 26 25   1 2 3 4 5

ISBN-13: 978-0-226-84033-8 (cloth)
ISBN-13: 978-0-226-84035-2 (paper)
ISBN-13: 978-0-226-84034-5 (e-book)
DOI: https://doi.org/10.7208/chicago/9780226840345.001.0001

Library of Congress Cataloging-in-Publication Data

Names: Yadon, Nicole, author.
Title: The politics of skin tone : African American experiences, identity, and attitudes / Nicole D. Yadon.
Other titles: Chicago studies in American politics.
Description: Chicago : The University of Chicago Press, 2025. | Series: Chicago studies in American politics | Includes bibliographical references and index.
Identifiers: LCCN 2024038169 | ISBN 9780226840338 (cloth) | ISBN 9780226840352 (paperback) | ISBN 9780226840345 (ebook)
Subjects: LCSH: Colorism—United States. | Black race—Color—Political aspects—United States. | Human skin color—Social aspects—United States. | Race discrimination—Social aspects—United States. | Race discrimination—Political aspects—United States. | African Americans—Race identity—United States. | Colorism—United States—Public opinion. | African Americans—United States—Attitudes. | Public opinion—United States. | United States—Race relations—Political aspects.
Classification: LCC E185.625 .Y34 2025 | DDC 305.896/073—dc23/eng/20240925
LC record available at https://lccn.loc.gov/2024038169

Contents

List of Illustrations vii

1 Introduction 1

2 Skin Color Politics: A Brief History and Theoretical Framework 14

3 Revisiting the Link between Skin Color and Politics: Combining Observational and Qualitative Data 38

4 Examining the Connections between Skin Color, Perceptions of Policing, and Political Participation 67

5 Skin Tone Identity: A Theoretical Framework and Measurement 91

6 The Political Associations of Skin Tone Identity 128

7 Conclusion 159

Acknowledgments 177
Appendixes 183
Notes 219
References 225
Index 247

Illustrations

Figures

2.1 Growth and Change in the Non-White Population over Time   33
3.1 Massey-Martin Skin Tone Scale   43
3.2 Yadon-Ostfeld Skin Color Scale   44
3.3 Association between Skin Color and Political Attitudes (2012 ANES)   50
3.4 Association between Skin Color and Immigration-Related Attitudes (2012 ANES)   53
3.5 Support for Affirmative Action and Guaranteed Jobs by Skin Color (NSAL)   56
3.6 Comparing Policy Preferences of White Americans (by Partisanship) and Black Americans (by Skin Tone) in the 2012 ANES   60
4.1 Belief That Police Treat Darker-Skinned People Worse   75
4.2 Belief That "Many [police] officers see people like me as animals, thugs, and less than human," by Skin Tone (2020 CMPS)   78
4.3 Index of Views toward Police (2020 CMPS)   78
4.4 Belief That Discussing Skin Tone Distracts from Bigger Issue of Race, by Skin Tone (2019 AmeriSpeak)   84
4.5 Likelihood of Having Participated in a Protest, March, Rally, or Demonstration in the Last Four Years, by Skin Tone (2012 ANES)   86
4.6 Likelihood of Having Participated in a Protest, March, Rally, or Demonstration since January 2020, by Skin Tone (2020 CMPS)   87
5.1 Skin Tone Identity Importance by Skin Tone (Bivariate)   116
5.2 Skin Tone Introjection Measure by Skin Tone (Bivariate)   117
5.3 Skin Tone Identity Importance by Skin Tone (Multivariate)   120
5.4 Coefficient Plot of Skin Tone Identity Correlates   124

5.5 Skin Tone Identity Importance by Age   125

6.1 Association between Skin Tone Identity and Support for Reducing Income Inequality   136

6.2 Association between Skin Tone Identity and Support for Two Affirmative Action Propositions (2019 AmeriSpeak)   137

6.3 Belief That "Many [police] officers see people like me as animals, thugs, and less than human" (2020 CMPS)   141

6.4 Index of Views toward Police (2020 CMPS)   142

6.5 Belief That Police Treat Darker-Skinned People Worse   143

6.6 Likelihood of Having Participated in a Protest, March, Rally, or Demonstration since January 2020 (2020 CMPS)   145

6.7 Treatment Effects on Colorism-Related Items by Skin Tone and Skin Tone Identity   155

6.8 Treatment Effects on Power-Related Items by Skin Tone and Skin Tone Identity   157

A6.2A Control Condition   205

A6.2B Treatment 1A: Racial Inequities Treatment (Version 1)   206

A6.2C Treatment 1B: Racial Inequities Treatment (Version 2)   207

A6.2D Treatment 2A: Color-Based Inequities Treatment (Version 1)   208

A6.2E Treatment 2B: Color-Based Inequities Treatment (Version 2)   209

Tables

2.1 The Skin Color Politics Theoretical Framework and Roadmap of the Book   37

3.1 Skin Tone Correlates in the 2012 ANES   48

3.2 Summary of Associations between Skin Tone and Political Dependent Variables   51

3.3 Number of Interview Participants Linking Race, Color, and Gender on Two Racialized Policies   63

4.1 Perceived Relationship between Darker Skin Tone and Frequency of Worse Police Treatment   74

4.2 Summary of Associations between Darker Skin and Likelihood of Criminal Justice Contact Variables (2020 CMPS)   77

4.3 Distribution of Responses to Police Dehumanization Question (2020 CMPS)   77

LIST OF ILLUSTRATIONS ix

4.4	Perception That Discussing Skin Tone Distracts from Discussing Bigger Issue of Race	84
5.1	The Skin Color Politics Theoretical Framework and Roadmap of the Book	104
5.2	Distribution of Skin Tone Identity and Racial Identity (2020 CMPS)	119
6.1	Summary of Associations between Skin Tone Identity and Political Dependent Variables	146
6.2	Comparison of Experimental Treatment Language	151
A3.1	Descriptive Statistics from Survey Samples of African Americans	184
A3.2A	African American Policy Preferences in the 2012 ANES by Skin Tone	185
A3.2B	African American Policy Preferences in the 2012 ANES by Skin Tone	186
A3.2C	African American Policy Preferences in the 2012 ANES by Skin Tone	187
A3.3	Examining Broader Sets of Issues and Policy Opinions by Skin Tone (2012 ANES)	188
A3.4	African American Policy Preferences in the 2001–2003 NSAL by Skin Tone	190
A3.5	Distribution of Interview Participants' Self-Identified Skin Color	193
A3.6	Overview of Interview Participants' Education Distribution	194
A3.7	Domains Referenced as Associated with Skin Tone among Interview Participants	194
A4.1	Relationship between Skin Color and Reported Interactions with Police among Black Respondents	195
A4.2	Policing Battery Details	196
A6.1A	Political Views by Skin Tone, Skin Tone Identity, and Racial Identity (CMPS 2020)	197
A6.1B	Policy Preferences by Skin Tone Identity and Racial Identity (2019 AmeriSpeak)	198
A6.1C	Policy Preferences by Skin Tone, Skin Tone Identity, and Racial Identity (2019 AmeriSpeak)	198
A6.1D	Political Views by Skin Tone Identity and Racial Group Attachment (2019 AmeriSpeak)	199
A6.1E	Political Views by Skin Tone, Skin Tone Identity, and Racial Group Attachment (2019 AmeriSpeak)	200
A6.1F	Political Views by Skin Tone Identity and Racial Group Attachment (2019 AmeriSpeak)	201
A6.1G	Political Views by Skin Tone, Skin Tone Identity, and Racial Group Attachment (2019 AmeriSpeak)	202

A6.1H   Political Views by Skin Tone Identity and Racial Group Attachment (2020 CMPS)   203

A6.1I   Political Views by Skin Tone, Skin Tone Identity, and Racial Group Attachment (2020 CMPS)   204

A6.3A   Regression Estimates for Treatment, Skin Tone, and Skin Tone Identity   213

A6.3B   Regression Estimates for Treatment, Skin Tone, and Skin Tone Identity   215

A6.3C   Regression Estimates for Treatment, Skin Tone, and Racial Identity   217

A6.3D   Regression Estimates for Treatment, Skin Tone, and Racial Identity   218

1
Introduction

The Washington family had roots dating back to 1930s Georgia. Several decades later, however, the family moved to Ypsilanti, Michigan. The Washingtons settled into a middle-class area that was racially mixed; their neighborhood had many other African American families like the Washingtons but also several White families. Many of the people in the neighborhood worked at a nearby manufacturing plant. The youngest child in the Washington family was Carter,[1] a friendly and outgoing elementary school student with an infectious smile and a booming laugh. Carter took after his grandfathers, both of whom had very dark complexions. His parents and his older siblings, on the other hand, were all light-skinned like both of Carter's grandmothers.

Carter's parents showered him with love and support, which he viewed as the basis for his self-confidence and self-love growing up as a chubby, dark-skinned Black boy.[2] Still, he recognized early on that there could be stigma attached to dark skin in broader society. This revelation occurred to Carter during an otherwise typical squabble between him and his older sister. On this day, however, his sister called him a derogatory name alluding to the darkness of his skin. Carter was startled; he understood that his sister's comment was designed to be cutting and cruel, implying that her lighter complexion was somehow better than his darker complexion. Overhearing this color-based taunt from the other room, Carter's parents became uncharacteristically upset. At first, Carter thought he and his sister were both in trouble, but it quickly became clear that it was only his sister who was in trouble. *Big trouble*, as he recalled it. The combination of his sister's comment and the powerful reaction from his parents helped cement the importance of skin tone to Carter's understanding of the world. If skin tone was not important, why would his sister have mentioned it in an effort to hurt his feelings? And why would his parents have been so upset by her remark? From that moment onward, Carter was conscious that he was not only African American but a *dark-skinned* African American. He felt that his dark complexion was an important part of his identity, and he was determined to love and embrace it in all its glory.

As he grew into adolescence and eventually adulthood, Carter recognized that different value could be placed on the lightness or darkness of one's skin tone, with the associated meaning changing across time and place. For example, he noted that a lighter complexion was often associated with stereotypical portrayals of beauty among Black women, while darker complexions were associated with perceived strength among Black men. On the dating scene, Carter felt that being dark-skinned worked to his advantage. But these associations carried very different connotations in other settings—most notably, he thought, with respect to law enforcement. When dealing with police, being a dark-skinned Black man with a large stature meant that Carter had to be very careful about how he presented himself. Even though his close friends described him as a big teddy bear, other people—especially White people—could quickly feel intimidated or threatened by him given his appearance.

The attachment that Carter felt to both his race and his dark skin tone also influenced his broader views of how society operates and the potential opportunities and experiences available to him. Carter observed that people's racialized stereotypes about Black people were most strongly attributed to dark-skinned Black people; for example, he felt that darker-skinned people would more reflexively be perceived as lazy, violent, or unintelligent. Darker-skinned Black people were less likely to be cut slack or given the benefit of the doubt. Thus, Carter felt that darker-skinned people were more vulnerable to challenging experiences: they faced greater hurdles to economic advancement, they were more heavily (and frequently) scrutinized by the police, and they were even subject to social hardships from other people's snap judgments based on appearance alone. His complexion, then, influenced the way that he viewed the world, not just with respect to himself—though he had often felt discriminated against—but more broadly in terms of how he thought about the obstacles, challenges, and circumstances, both large and small, that people like him faced daily. The system was not set up in a way to create a level playing field for everyone, and it never had been. To counter these challenges, Carter tried to be more generous in giving people the benefit of the doubt; more willing to lend support to people who had fallen on hard times; more open to giving an extra boost to people who had faced obstacles but were trying to improve their station in life. As someone who loved his dark skin while also recognizing that dark skin could be stigmatized, Carter felt that it was important to support people who faced various forms of stigmatization.

My conversation with Carter was conducted during the course of this research project and reflects the perspective and experiences of one person. Yet Carter's observations closely mirror the comments made by many of the other 99 African Americans with whom my research team spoke, as well as the broader patterns found by social scientists. A substantial body of research highlights the importance of skin color gradations within and across racial categories, both historically and in the present day (Monk 2021).[3] Dating back to the institution of slavery, divisions and differential treatment based on African Americans' skin color are well documented. Both lighter- and darker-skinned Black people suffered greatly under the institution of slavery, but their suffering often manifested in different forms. Slaveholders were more likely to have lighter-skinned Black people working in the home, and this group was also more likely to receive specialized training and to be literate (Bodenhorn 2006; Frazier 1965; Reuter 1918; Russell, Wilson, and Hall 2013). Lighter-skinned Black people were also more likely to enjoy better health, have larger families, and amass greater wealth, as well as being more likely to be freed from slavery than their dark-skinned counterparts (Bailey, Saperstein, and Penner 2014; Bodenhorn 2011; Bodenhorn and Ruebeck 2007; Davis 1991; Frazier 1932; Green and Hamilton 2013; Hughes and Hertel 1990; Menke 1979; Myrdal 1944; Reece 2018b; Russell, Wilson, and Hall 2013).

The advantages afforded lighter-skinned Black people were based on eugenicist notions of "traits" associated with different racial groups, such that enslaved Black people with lighter skin were thought to be more intelligent, more attractive, and more similar to Whites. Preferencing of those with lighter skin occurred among both Black and White people (Bodenhorn and Ruebeck 2007). Were these socioeconomic associations of skin tone not actually about skin tone but about mixed-race parentage? This is undoubtedly part of the story, especially within the institution of slavery, where Black women were forced into sexual encounters to augment the slaveholders' labor force. Skin tone as a phenotypical marker has distinct associations relative to multiracialism, however. For example, contemporary research examining African Americans who report having two Black parents—and thus are not considered multiracial—finds that skin tone effects persist even among this monoracial Black group (Monk 2018). Siblings with darker skin have a higher likelihood of arrest and a greater risk of cardiovascular hypertension despite shared parental and family characteristics (Kizer 2017; Laidley et al. 2019). While mixed-race parentage undoubtedly influences people's lived experiences, opportunities, and access to resources, skin color has additional and distinct influences that are not interchangeable with multiracialism.

Although much has changed since the Civil War era, the attention paid to and value placed on skin tone has not diminished over time. Indeed, the fact that the first Black president and vice president of the United States—Barack Obama and Kamala Harris, respectively—are both lighter-skinned, multiracial Black people highlights the continued influence of what is known as colorism, or the preferencing of those with lighter skin over those with darker skin. The effects of colorism drawn from evidence in the nineteenth century not only persist in the present day but appear to have intensified. Darker-skinned Black people have worse outcomes across a variety of vitally important domains, including income, wealth, and health. They also face harsher treatment by police and in the criminal justice system: darker-skinned Black people are more likely to receive the death penalty for the same or comparable crimes than their lighter-skinned Black or White counterparts (Adames 2023; Bowman, Muhammad, and Ifatunji 2004; Burch 2015; Eberhardt et al. 2004; 2006; Goldsmith, Hamilton, and Darity 2007; Harburg et al. 1978; Hargrove 2018; Hebl et al. 2012; Hughes and Hertel 1990; Johnson, Farrell, and Stoloff 1998; Keith and Herring 1991; Krieger, Sidney, and Coakley 1998; Laidley et al. 2019; Monk 2021; Ransford 1970; Seltzer and Smith 1991; Yadon 2022). In many cases, skin tone disparities are equal to or larger than the magnitude of racial disparities (Monk 2015, 2018). These patterns should not be interpreted as implying that lighter-skinned Black people do not face discrimination based on race. Rather, they suggest that darker-skinned people face an *additional layer* of discrimination in mainstream society based on skin tone in addition to discrimination based on race.

Importantly, however, the value associated with skin tone is contextual. As Carter's experiences demonstrate, darker skin is not *always* associated with worse social outcomes or uniformly negative assessments, nor is lighter skin *always* associated with better social outcomes and uniformly positive assessments. In some contexts darker skin is assigned positive value; for example, being perceived as more racially "authentic" or physically stronger, which has advantages in certain social settings (Monk 2015). Darker-skinned people may experience a stronger sense of belonging or more authenticity, especially in majority Black contexts (Anderson and Cromwell 1977; Brunsma and Rockquemore 2001; Carter 2003; Drake and Cayton 1945; Goering 1972; Hunter 2005, 2007). Thus, efforts to counteract the negative connotations often associated with darker skin can instill a sense of pride or a perception of authenticity among darker-skinned Black people.

Qualitative evidence drawn from conversations with African Americans across a variety of contexts highlights how skin tone is commonly perceived to be associated with opportunities and experiences (e.g., Brown and Lemi 2021; Wilder 2015). Colorism is not simply an esoteric academic interest but something recognized by many African Americans as meaningfully influencing their lived experience. Complementing these earlier investigations, my research team conducted 100 in-depth interviews with African Americans in the Midwest as part of this research project to understand how people think about skin tone not only in society but specifically with respect to politics.

The conversation with Carter that opens this chapter was one such interview. Each conversation began by discussing some general questions related to race. This allowed participants to highlight potential attributes that they felt were meaningful before shifting more explicitly to discussing skin tone. Some mentioned characteristics like class, gender, or religion, while a handful of participants explicitly mentioned skin tone. One of these interview participants was Alice, a 58-year-old light-skinned Black woman who was a retired social worker. When asked what attributes are important to Black people she knew, Alice replied without hesitation, "Oh, well among Black people, honey, it's skin color and hair." She continued with candid reflections on the advantages associated with being light-skinned: "The closer you are to White, you're perceived as *better than*. And you're also not just perceived as *better than*, but that you have more *opportunities than*. And you're not looked down upon by Caucasians" (emphasis in original). Although blunter in her delivery than other interview participants, Alice was far from alone in making such observations. Indeed, it was nearly universal when explicitly asked: 95 out of 100 Black interview participants agreed that the darkness or lightness of one's skin tone within racial groups has important social implications. Clearly, then, skin tone meaningfully informs how people understand power to operate in society, even though it not frequently recognized or theorized within mainstream political science literatures.

A Color-Based Politics?

Scholars have long explored the meaning and impact of skin color on racial identity and social relations, as well as in the criminal justice system. Until recently, however, relatively little scholarly attention has been paid to understanding how skin tone may be politically meaningful (Abrajano, Elmendorf, and Quinn 2018; Brown and Lemi 2021; Hochschild and Weaver 2007; Lerman, McCabe, and Sadin 2015; Ostfeld and Yadon 2022a, 2022b; Terkildsen 1993; Weaver 2012; Yadon 2022; Yadon and Ostfeld 2020). Indeed, a primary area of focus for political scientists is to uncover the roots of inequality and to help us better understand differences between racial groups in their policy preferences, partisanship, candidate preferences, and more. Of course, race remains essential to understanding the American political landscape, and it is well documented that the Black-White divide cuts broadly and deeply throughout American society (Jackman 1994; Kinder and Sanders 1996; Kluegel and Smith 1986; Schuman et al. 1997; Sigelman and Welch 1991; Tate 1994).

Importantly, however, race is a multidimensional construct and racialized experiences hinge on the intersections of race alongside several additional forces. Black feminist theorists have argued this point for decades with respect to the unique experiences of Black women (e.g., Collins 1989; Combahee River Collective 1977; Crenshaw 1990; Hancock 2016; McCall 2005). As noted by the Combahee River Collective (1977), "the major source of difficulty in our political work is that we are not just trying to fight oppression on one front or even two, but instead to address a whole range of oppressions. We do not have racial, sexual, heterosexual, or class privilege to rely upon, nor do we have even the minimal access to resources and power that groups who possess anyone of these types of privilege have." Put differently, the experiences of Black women cannot be reduced to either those of their race or those of their gender. Appropriately, then, more scholarly attention has been paid in recent decades to theorizing and examining various forms of intra-racial heterogeneity in an effort to more fully understand Black political views and behavior (e.g., Banks, White, and McKenzie 2019; Barker, Jones, and Tate 1998; Cohen 1999; Crenshaw 1990; Davenport 2018; Davis and Brown 2002; Davis 1991; Dawson 1994, 2001; Frasure and Williams 2009; Gay 2004; Jones 2015; Philpot 2017; Phoenix 2019; Prestage 1991; Simien 2012; Simien and Clawson 2004; Smith 2014; Tate 1994, 2010; Walton 1985; Walton, Smith, and Wallace 2017).

The potential political significance of intra-racial variation in skin tone arguably merits similar attention, but such analyses are complicated by the fact that skin tone has historically served as a *marker* of race rather than being a distinct category like gender or class. Of course skin tone is one of a constellation of factors—including, for example, facial features, hair texture, hair color, accent, neighborhood—associated with how one is racialized (Ostfeld and Yadon 2022b). In this project, I focus on skin color because it is relatively difficult to change compared with other components, relatively easy to assess, and influential in shaping one's experiences and potential identities.

Because darker skin is associated with closer proximity to Blackness and thus elicits stronger applications of racialized stereotypes, the combination of one's racial categorization and one's skin tone will meaningfully influence lived experiences. Most research examining skin color in the political realm has examined Black political candidates and sought to gauge levels of support among potential voters (e.g., Brown 2014; Brown and Lemi 2021; Burge, Wamble, and

Cuomo 2020; Lemi 2020; Lemi and Brown 2019; Lerman, McCabe, and Sadin 2015; Orey and Zhang 2019; Terkildsen 1993; Weaver 2012). Outside of the realm of political candidates, two sets of scholars have sought to examine whether African Americans' skin tone is associated with views of discrimination, racial group attachment, or a small number of political views (Hochschild and Weaver 2007; Seltzer and Smith 1991). This first wave of research on skin tone and African Americans' political attitudes notes the widespread social and economic weight of African Americans' skin tone, but paradoxically finds little evidence of skin tone's political import. This, of course, runs counter to broader literatures noting consistent associations between resources and political views (McCall and Manza 2011; McCarty, Poole, and Rosenthal 2006; Stonecash 2000). Perhaps skin tone is a unique case in which disparities are subsumed under the broader fight against racial disparities (Hochschild 2006; Hochschild and Weaver 2007). Alternatively, it may be too early to draw such conclusions with respect to the political associations of African Americans' skin tone. A thorough investigation of these possibilities is inhibited by the historical scarcity of available data that includes measures of skin tone, measures of political views, and substantial numbers of African American respondents.

Even in the present day, few social scientific surveys include measures of both skin color and political opinions. In my earlier book project with Mara Ostfeld, we conducted an original, face-to-face data collection effort to examine how skin color may be linked with political attitudes across multiple ethnoracial groups. There, we created a generalized theory for skin color's importance in society and then tested this through a face-to-face survey with Black, Latino, and White respondents in the Midwest (Ostfeld and Yadon 2022b). As with any study, this research design has both advantages and disadvantages. For example, focusing on multiple groups in a given study requires constructing a generalized framework, which can be of broader impact than focusing on a single group. Indeed, there had been little examination of Latinos' or Whites' skin tone and political attitudes in the United States prior to our project. But this generalized framework and the constraints of our face-to-face data collection necessitated a very short survey with questions that we anticipated to be broadly relevant across multiple racial groups rather than being specific to a single group. While we did find that Latinos' and Whites' skin tone was associated with our handful of political attitudinal measures, we did not find similar associations among African Americans (Ostfeld and Yadon 2022b). Similar questions to those I posed about the first-wave studies apply here: Is there truly no association between African Americans' skin tone and political views? Or are there idiosyncrasies in our sample (e.g., something about the region or the specific survey sites selected) or something about the specific questions we included, that limit the potential to uncover a color-to-politics link for African Americans? Open questions remain, then, about how Black people view skin tone as potentially connected to their political views, especially on issues, such as policing, where color-based disparities are especially prominent. The lack of evidence of a correlation between skin tone and African Americans' political attitudes thus far also suggests the importance of incorporating a series of in-depth interviews to help make better sense of the phenomenon of colorism. Whether skin tone is associated with one's political views or not, it is undoubtedly valuable to hear people talk about these issues in their own words.

Consequently, this book presents a deeper investigation into the political implications of skin tone by focusing on the attitudes and experiences of African Americans. This decision is drawn partly from the prominent role that Black people's skin tone has played throughout US history; this includes not only the institution of slavery, but also the unique nature of the "one-drop rule," which created a shared racial classification for anyone with known Black racial ancestry, no matter how distant. Still, the multilayered hierarchy of racism and colorism produces inequalities by using appearance to race people even within shared racial categories. That is, darker skin among African Americans signals one's proximity to Blackness and results in a stronger application of racialized stereotypes—for example, being perceived as aggressive, intimidating, or dangerous—even among people within the shared racial group (Banks 1999; Maddox and Gray 2002; Monk 2021). While some of these stereotypes may also apply to darker-skinned members of other racial groups, the combination of historical forces, long-standing stereotypes, and positioning of African Americans within the racial hierarchy leads to colorism's unique importance within this community. In turn, this may give way to a distinct relationship between skin tone and political views for this group, as well as the potential development of a color-based identity.

This book builds on an interdisciplinary literature demonstrating the importance of African Americans' skin tone for everyday life to theorize and measure the ways in which it may also be relevant for political views. I contend that there are three primary reasons to believe that there may be a contemporary link between African Americans' skin tone, political views, and political identity. First, significant sociodemographic shifts in the last several decades have contributed to a reshaping of the American racial hierarchy. This includes growing levels of immigration, the incorporation of new and sizable ethnoracial groups into the United States such as Latinos and Asian Americans, as well as increased levels of multiracial identification. These sociodemographic shifts have increased the number of categories included within the racial hierarchy and have contributed to a blurring of boundaries around many groups. Greater variance in experiences among members of a shared racial group owing to factors such as color has the potential to influence the salience of color on lived experiences and corresponding political views.

Second, skin tone may primarily be politically meaningful in domains where skin tone disparities are especially pronounced. That is, in domains where color-based discrimination is especially prominent and well known—for example, related to education, jobs, or policing—we would expect that skin tone might be more strongly associated with political views. Limitations in the survey items included in prior studies have reduced scholars' ability to investigate this possibility. Third, it may be the case that skin tone's importance in society leads to skin tone being taken up as a meaningful social identity in addition to race. This does not mean that a color-based identity will rival or supersede racial identity in importance. Both identities can be meaningful to a person's sense of self, with varying importance or salience over time and across contexts. Thus, I posit that given the importance of skin tone in society, people may develop a psychological attachment to their skin tone. This skin tone identity should, in turn, be associated with political views in certain domains.

Building from a framework anticipating that darker-skinned Black people experience double-layered discrimination in mainstream society based on the darkness of their skin in addition to their race, I expect that skin tone will be associated with the following: (1) Black people's views of the sociopolitical world, particularly on issues or issue areas where colorism is especially salient, such as jobs or policing; and (2) Black people's political identities, including the potential for the formation of a meaningful color-based identity, particularly among darker-skinned individuals. To test these expectations, I use a mixed-methods approach that includes seven national and nationally representative surveys, a hundred original in-depth interviews with African Americans in the Midwest, and a survey experiment to provide a fuller portrait of skin tone's political import among African Americans. These varied data sources provide an opportunity to triangulate across multiple studies to more clearly understand how skin tone is perceived to operate (or not) in politics. Further, the expectation that skin tone identity may be undergirding potential associations between skin tone and political views is a novel contribution to the literature that has examined skin tone primarily as a characteristic associated with social outcomes. This is an important advancement in the colorism literature because it suggests that any potential associations between skin tone and political views may be due to a *psychological attachment* to one's skin tone. Thus, the inclusion of measures of skin tone identity in my original surveys provides a first opportunity to begin understanding this potential sociopolitical identity and its political import.

This effort builds from existing studies documenting that skin color is associated with how people are treated in society. The body of colorism literature demonstrates that, on average, people with lighter skin within racial groups receive better treatment, more opportunities, and bigger rewards, as well as gentler criticism or punishment (Monk 2021). An innovation of my work is that while it builds from these widespread manifestations of colorism, it shows that skin color influences people's sense of identity, their political preferences, and even their political participation with respect to protest activities. While of course racial identification as African American remains very important toward understanding American politics, I hope to persuade readers that being attentive to intragroup skin tone heterogeneity contributes toward better understanding African Americans' political views, behavior, and identity. In turn, focusing on the multidimensionality of race—including the influence of skin tone specifically—should not be minimized or overlooked. Studying skin tone does not diminish the importance of studying race; rather, it adds value toward understanding intragroup heterogeneity, which helps paint a fuller portrait of racialized experiences and views.

Positionality Statement

As with any research agenda, it is important for researchers to engage with questions regarding their positionality to the subject. As a White woman with fair skin, I have undoubtedly benefited from White privilege throughout my life. I have not faced stigmatization based on either my race or my skin tone. As a result, my ability to understand the ways in which skin tone and colorism operate is not informed by personal lived experiences of being dark-skinned in a majority White country, but instead by reading, listening, and observing the world and people from backgrounds very different from my own. This means that I will always be an observer and an outsider looking in on the stigmatization associated with colorism.

At the same time, my privileged status permits insight into how White people think and talk, implicitly or explicitly, about skin tone and race. Of course, White people are largely responsible for the divisions and stereotypes based on skin tone throughout US history, as well as the corresponding institutionalization of color-based biases and gatekeeping of power and resources for those with lighter skin. As a result, colorism should not be construed as primarily an *intra*-group issue within communities of color; rather, the continuing *inter*-group dynamics surrounding colorism should be acknowledged and their origins explored and articulated. While this book focuses on political views and behaviors of African Americans, the historical components and theoretical framework of the project build from a recognition that colorism has been created and perpetuated by those traditionally in positions of power—that is, Whites.

Although reasonable people may disagree, I feel strongly that drawing attention to and speaking about systemic disparities based on racism or colorism should not fall solely on the shoulders of the marginalized, as it often does. Thus, while this project contributes to an academic literature that often centers White voices and perspectives, I hope my work will be viewed as building on and amplifying, and certainly not replacing, the work of those with more direct experiences with colorism. More broadly, by dissecting race- and color-based inequities—and, specifically, the ways that colorism manifests in the political sphere—I hope that this book makes a modest contribution toward recognizing and reducing the power unjustly associated with lighter skin in our society.

Roadmap of the Book

The remainder of the book proceeds as follows. In chapter 2, I build from literatures across the social sciences to create a theoretical scaffold which argues that not only a racial hierarchy but also a more fine-grained skin tone hierarchy exists in the United States. Because this skin tone hierarchy influences experiences and opportunities in society, I argue that it also meaningfully influences political views. I theorize that darker-skinned Black Americans should hold more liberal political views than their lighter-skinned counterparts, on average, given their heightened experiences with discrimination and lower socioeconomic status.

In chapter 3, I walk through the data sources used throughout the book, including a series of national and nationally representative survey evidence. As noted earlier, 100 in-depth interviews with African Americans were conducted in the Detroit and Columbus metropolitan areas as part of this project. Given the importance of race of interviewer effects, the interviewers for this project were an inter-racial team; I conducted 43 interviews, and the remainder were conducted by four Black women research assistants. Each interviewer had distinct experiences with the intersection of race, color, and power based on her own appearance and background, which were brought implicitly into every conversation (Brown 2012; Young 2004). The substance of the conversations revealed similar patterns in responses and views regarding skin tone's importance across all five interviewers, but the style of the conversations was distinct. While I discuss this further in chapter 3, I provide a brief overview of the methodological background here given the qualitative data highlighted earlier in this chapter.

I then begin testing my theoretical expectations that skin tone is associated with Black Americans' social and political views in domains where color-based disparities are especially pronounced. I present evidence of the ways that skin tone is intimately connected with politics, from policy preferences to representation to political participation in chapters 3 and 4. Consistent with my theoretical expectations, I find that darker-skinned Black people are more liberal than their lighter-skinned counterparts on issues where color-based disparities are especially salient, such as jobs, income, and policing. These estimates reveal that, on average, the policy preferences of lighter-skinned Black people are similar to those of White Democrats, whereas darker-skinned Black people hold more liberal policy positions than either Whites or lighter-skinned Black people. Using original measures, I find that darker-skinned individuals are also consistently more likely to report that skin tone influences their treatment by police, treatment by White people, job opportunities, and social mobility. With respect to perceptions of policing and participation in political protests, a combination of qualitative interviews and multiple surveys reveals that both skin tone and gender are associated with one's opinions and protest behavior.

The evidence presented throughout chapters 3 and 4 underscores that skin tone holds a significant relationship with political views even after statistically accounting for sociodemographic factors like income, education, and racial group attachment.[4] The independent effect of skin tone above and beyond these factors suggests that something besides socioeconomic correlates or corresponding lived experiences underlies the relationship between skin tone and policy preferences. That is, perhaps it is not simply skin tone as a characteristic that is doing this work, but one's attachment to a skin tone group—that is, one's *skin tone identity*. Building from social identity theory and social categorization theory, I outline in chapter 5 how a color-based identity would operate. I anticipate that darker-skinned Black people will have, on average, a stronger sense of color-based identity given a recognition of the association between skin tone and one's experiences, treatment, and status in society. Accordingly, I present qualitative and survey evidence that skin tone is a meaningful identity for many African Americans. Across multiple surveys and two novel measures of skin tone identity, I reliably find that more than 50 percent of Black Americans report their skin tone as being important to how they view themselves. Consistent with my theoretical expectations, darker-skinned African Americans are significantly more likely to report their color as important to their identity than those with lighter skin. This suggests that skin tone identity is meaningful socially and leaves open the possibility that it may also be meaningful politically.

In chapter 6, I bring to bear a combination of survey and experimental evidence demonstrating the political associations of skin tone identity. I revisit the issue areas and, where possible, the same survey questions examined in chapters 3 and 4 to assess how skin tone identity and its intersections with skin tone itself may be associated with one's views. On issues or policy proposals that explicitly reference skin tone—including a color-based affirmative action item and perceptions of color-based disparities in police treatment—skin tone identity was meaningfully associated with political views. The largest and most consistent effects of skin tone identity were found on the policing-related items and were most often driven by strongly identified dark-skinned African American men. Further, the survey experiment revealed that reading about racial inequities had no effect on perceptions of colorism or color-based issues, whereas reading about color-based inequities did. As in the observational analyses, it was strongly identified dark-skinned African Americans for whom reading about color-based inequities provokes the strongest reaction in terms of further recognizing the influence of colorism in society and hoping for access to more positions of power.

I conclude the book by underscoring the importance and broader implications of acknowledging skin tone politics in the contemporary American racial landscape. Given that inequities between lighter- and darker-skinned African Americans are often of a similar magnitude to those between Black and White Americans—and that race-based efforts to reduce inequalities can further exacerbate color-based disparities—scholars and policymakers need to devote more targeted attention to colorism. This work adds to a growing chorus of scholarship documenting meaningful heterogeneity in lived experiences based on factors such as race, gender, class, and skin tone, among others. While this body of research does not question the importance of racial identity, it underscores that a singular focus on categorical race inhibits understanding the richness and complexity of racialized experiences based on factors such as skin tone or gender. Examining the multidimensionality of racialized experiences, such as those expressed by Carter and Alice earlier in this chapter, help provide clearer insight into the political identities, views, and behavior of African Americans living in an increasingly diversifying US population.

2

Skin Color Politics:
A Brief History and Theoretical Framework

> But just the role in general society, the darker you are, more of the fear factor. And whatever stereotype people have about Black people, the darker you are, the more likely those might be attributed to you in society.
> 47-YEAR-OLD, dark-skinned male interview participant

In her 1983 book *In Search of Our Mothers' Gardens*, novelist and activist Alice Walker coined the term "colorism" to describe discrimination associated with skin tone, specifically a preference for lightness. She noted that even among individuals identifying with the same racial group, the lightness or darkness of one's skin tone influences a combination of social and institutional aspects of daily life. Walker notes that colorism works alongside other forms of discrimination such as sexism and racism:

> Still, I think there is probably as much difference between the life of a black black woman and a "high yellow" black woman as between a "high yellow" woman and a white woman. And I am worried, constantly, about the hatred the black black woman encounters within black society. Ironically, much of what I've learned about color I've learned because I have a mixed-race child. Because she is lighter-skinned, straighter-haired than I, her life—in this racist, colorist society—is infinitely easier. And so I understand the subtle programming I, my mother, and my grandmother before me fell victim to. Escape the pain, the ridicule, escape the jokes, the lack of attention, respect, dates, even a job, any way you can. (Walker 1983, p. 291)

Within the space of a single page, Walker highlights multiple associations between skin color and lived experiences for African Americans. She notes both the personal and professional manifestations in intra- and inter-racial contexts.

A body of scholarly evidence reveals empirical support for Walker's observation that the combination of race and color exposes darker-skinned Black people to additional barriers and discrimination compared with lighter-skinned Black people and lighter-skinned people of other races. In many cases, the magnitude of color-based disparities between lighter- and darker-skinned African Americans is equal to or greater than that of race-based disparities between Black and White Americans (Monk 2015, 2018). On average, compared with lighter-skinned Black people and White people, darker-skinned Black people have less wealth, lower wages, higher levels of unemployment, lower levels of education, and lower occupational prestige; they face higher levels of social rejection, worse health outcomes, are perceived as more likely to engage in criminal activity, are more likely to be arrested or incarcerated, receive harsher criminal sentences, and are even more likely to receive the death penalty for comparable crimes (Adames 2023; Bowman, Muhammad, and Ifatunji 2004; Eberhardt et al. 2004; 2006; Goldsmith, Hamilton, and Darity 2007; Harburg et al. 1978; Hargrove 2018; Hebl et al. 2012; Hughes and Hertel 1990; Johnson, Farrell, and Stoloff 1998; Keith and Herring 1991; 1991; Kizer 2017; Krieger, Sidney, and Coakley 1998; Laidley et al. 2019; Monk 2018; 2021; Ransford 1970; Seltzer and Smith 1991; Yadon 2022; Goldsmith, Hamilton, and Darity 2006).

This pattern of evidence—observed within Black communities and corroborated empirically by social scientists—speaks to the intertwined nature of colorism and racism. These two phenomena coexist to maintain a hierarchy that defines Whiteness as the "ideal" (Banks 1999; Brown and Lemi 2021; Fanon 1952; Lemi and Brown 2020; Burch 2015). Colorism operates as a feature of anti-Blackness, with one's skin color serving as a cue for proximity to Whiteness. Specifically, darker skin signals closer proximity to Blackness and results in a stronger application of racialized stereotypes—for example, being perceived as aggressive, intimidating, or dangerous (Banks 1999; Maddox and Gray 2002; Monk 2021).[1]

Colorism stems from structures, belief systems, and forces created and perpetuated by White people. Indeed, skin tone has served as a marker helping to define racial categories in American society for centuries. Definitions of racial categories have shifted and evolved depending on the preferences of the White power structure, including determining who has access to citizenship, rights, and opportunities in the United States (Haney Lopez 1997; Harris 1993; Ostfeld and Yadon 2022b). For example, laws related to immigration, naturalization, and anti-miscegenation all influenced the racial profile of the United States and were developed with an eye toward maintaining skin color differences between racial groups (Haney Lopez 1997; Smith 1997). As discussed further below, the importance of skin tone among African Americans was codified by slavery as an institution. On the basis of eugenicist notions of "traits" purportedly associated with different racial groups, enslaved Black people with lighter skin—who were often the offspring of their enslavers—were thought by Whites to be more intelligent, attractive, capable, and similar to Whites than darker-skinned Black people.

The multilayered hierarchy of racism and colorism produces inequalities by using phenotype to race people even within shared racial categories. Within the Black community, however, these associations have been turned on their head in some cases to counteract these negative stereotypes. Among Black people, darker skin is often viewed more positively. For example, darker-skinned people can experience a stronger sense of belonging or more authenticity, especially in majority Black contexts (Anderson and Cromwell 1977; Brunsma and Rockquemore 2001; Carter 2003; Drake and Cayton 1945; Goering 1972; Hunter 2005, 2007). Messages such as "Black is beautiful" also serve to shift the narrative by emphasizing that darker skin and more Afrocentric features should be valued as representations of and connections to African heritage and culture. Thus, the composition of groups as well as the context in which they reside is meaningful in influencing the connotations associated with both race and skin tone. Of course, colorism is a phenomenon widely recognized within the Black community, but it would be a mistake to view it as a solely or even primarily an intragroup issue.

The remainder of this chapter proceeds as follows: First, I provide a brief overview of the history and context of colorism in the United States. This serves as a foundation for understanding that colorism has wide-ranging impacts in society and is worthy of study alongside racism. Second, I review previous efforts to examine the link between skin tone and political attitudes among African Americans, with an eye toward highlighting the remaining opportunities for further exploration such as those I undertake in this book. Third, I introduce my arguments for why, where, and how I expect African Americans' skin tone to be associated with political attitudes in contemporary politics. The theoretical framework underpinning the psychological attachment to skin tone groups as a meaningful social and political identity will be introduced in chapter 5.

The Legacy of Colorism in the United States

Recognizing the importance of attributes such as skin color is rooted in an understanding that access to power and opportunity stems from a combination of factors. Given that race is a social construct, many components influence the racialized experience (Omi and Winant 1994; Roth 2016; Saperstein and Penner 2012). For example, the sociologist Eduardo Bonilla-Silva (2004b; 2004a) argues that the racial hierarchy is not simply a Black-White divide, but also contains a middle tier of "honorary Whites" in which groups are jockeying to enjoy higher status based, in part, on skin tone.[2]

Building on the notion that multiple factors influence how race is experienced, fellow political scientist Mara Ostfeld and I argue that race can be understood metaphorically as the root system of a tree. Within our "Roots of Race" conceptualization, each component—such as racial identification, skin color, socioeconomic markers, religion, accent, diet, and more—serves as an individual root (Ostfeld and Yadon 2022b). Together, these roots serve as the foundation supporting the tree. While each root contributes to the structure of the tree, some roots are larger and denser, meaning they have greater influence. What determines how large a given root will be? Complementing other scholars' conceptualizations (Banton 2012; Chandra 2006), we argue that the relative durability and visibility of a given root will inform how race is experienced. This is because these components serve as clearer markers for institutions and institutional actors to use in exerting power. While someone can change their name, learn a new language, or update the clothing options in their wardrobe, there are other characteristics—such as skin color—that are not easily shifted (Chandra 2006; Horowitz 1985; Jablonski 2021). By definition, skin color is highly visible, easily assessed, and "sticky"—that is, relatively difficult and unlikely to change (Chandra 2006; Jablonski 2021). In turn, the high visibility and stickiness of skin color allows color-based hierarchies and systems to be "easier to maintain over a larger territory than a hierarchical system based on nonvisible signs of difference" (Horowitz 1985, pp. 44–45). As a result, components such as an individual's racial identification or skin color are likely to be more meaningful in the broader racial construct than other components such as accent or diet.

Because skin color is a physical marker that is easily assessed, historically it could be used as a proxy for racial categorization (Haney Lopez 1997; Hochschild and Powell 2008; Hollinger 2006; Ostfeld and Yadon 2022b). Along the continuum of skin tone, darker skin is associated with closer proximity to Blackness; this tightly woven connection between skin color and racial categorization provided the necessary foundation for those in power to segregate access to resources and opportunities. It influenced lived experiences and access to opportunities in the domains of citizenship, property rights, wealth, health, education, and more. One example of this is the 1896 Supreme Court decision in *Plessy v. Ferguson*, which upheld the practice of racial segregation in train cars in Louisiana. Albion Tourgée—the attorney for the appellant, Homer Plessy, who had one-eighth known African ancestry and an appearance resembling that of a White man—sought to exploit the ambiguities surrounding legal definitions of race and racial categories while highlighting the value of categorical Whiteness and the "damages" associated with perceptions of being non-White (Harris 1993). Indeed, Tourgée argued that the value of Whiteness was obvious: "Probably most white persons if given a choice, would prefer death to life in the United States *as colored persons.* Under these conditions, is it possible to conclude that *the reputation of being white* is not property? Indeed, is it not the most valuable sort of property, being the master-key that unlocks the golden door of opportunity?" (quoted in Harris 1993, p. 1748 [emphasis in original]). For centuries, a variety of presumed authorities—including political philosophers, religious leaders, and scholars—have perpetuated the vilification of darker-skinned people (Banks 1999; Fanon 1952; Jablonski 2021; Ostfeld and Yadon 2022b). In turn, institutions and people in positions of power have used color to define who should and should not have access to basic rights and protections.

Importantly, however, assessments of skin tone are dynamic and contextual. Darker skin is not *always* associated with worse social outcomes or uniformly negative assessments, nor is lighter skin *always* associated with better social outcomes and uniformly positive assessments. In some contexts darker skin can be assigned positive value—for example, being perceived as more racially "authentic" or physically stronger, which may have advantages for African Americans in certain social settings including with respect to dating (Monk 2015). In other contexts, however, darker skin can be assigned more negative value—for example, in police interactions or workplace settings with White colleagues, or during consideration for inclusion in certain elite Black social groups such as the Jack and Jill. Of course, how one thinks about one's own skin color is also a contextual process. Sociologist Ellis Monk observes that "as a variant of subjective social status, self-rated skin color measures individuals' dynamic and relational sense of status in the social circles and contexts they live out their lives" (2015, p. 434). Consistent with my perspective, this suggests that while assessments of skin tone may vary to some extent across contexts—for example, someone identifying as the lightest person in their family, but also one of the darker-skinned kids in school—one's self-reported skin tone provides valuable insight into how people see themselves as fitting into the world in which they live. As discussed further in chapter 5, people hold cognitive constructs associated with skin tone, and these constructs may also correspond to a sense of emotional attachment to their color-based group. Thus, capturing how people understand their skin tone or their level of skin tone identity in their local environment helps make sense of their broader experiences, views, and perceived positionality in society. Below I review some of the history related to colorism to lay a foundation for anticipating why and how skin color continues to be meaningful today.

THE ROOTS OF COLORISM: WHITES' STRATIFICATION OF AFRICAN AMERICANS BASED ON SKIN TONE

A discussion of skin tone in American society requires a recognition that slavery as an institution served as the foundation for much of the color-based variation among African Americans in the present day. Through the rape of enslaved Black women at the hands of White slaveowners, a number of mixed-race children—often with lighter complexions—were born. These lighter-skinned, mixed-race individuals had access to opportunities not available to their darker-skinned Black counterparts, both within and outside the system of slavery. Given their connection to Whiteness and Whites' belief in eugenicist views, mixed-race people were viewed as more similar to Whites and falsely stereotyped as smarter, more talented, and—given their often biological connection to White enslavers—were viewed more warmly and were kept in closer company (Bodenhorn 2011; Myrdal 1996; Reuter 1918). These perceptions often led mixed-race people to receive special attention and treatment; for example, being tasked with jobs inside the home that corresponded with valuable skills such as learning to read, write, and even skilled trades such as being a seamstress or carpenter. These skills were highly valuable outside the institution of slavery and could be passed down through generations. Indeed, mixed-race people were more likely to be freed from slavery and to hold more wealth, have larger families, live longer, and have better overall health during the nineteenth century (Bodenhorn 2011; Bodenhorn and Ruebeck 2007; Frazier 1932; Green and Hamilton 2013; Hughes and Hertel 1990; Myrdal 1996; Reece 2018b; Russell, Wilson, and Hall 2013; Saperstein and Gullickson 2013). Thus, the institution of slavery—and specifically White people in positions of power—helped enshrine the value placed on African Americans' skin tone. I expand below on some specific ways that the combination of race and skin tone has been made important by Whites historically, as well as how Whites continue to do so in the present day.

Despite an amorphous definition that has shifted and evolved over time, categorization as White provides opportunities to act as gatekeepers of power and property (Haney Lopez 1997; Harris 1993). The haziness around definitions of "Whiteness" has allowed for the combination of race and skin tone to structure American society throughout history. Prior to the Civil War, there was an emphasis placed on distinguishing between free and enslaved Black people. Free Black people—who were predominantly mixed-race—largely had physical characteristics appearing to blend the two races, and in many cases, the social characteristics of Whites given their closer proximity and greater access—for example, being literate, wealthier, and living a lifestyle more similar to that of Whites (Berlin 1974; Frazier 1930; Reece 2021; Toplin 1979). In some cases, Whites developed tenuous alliances with free Black people because they were seen as a buffer between White and Black people (Allen, Telles, and Hunter 2000; Davis 1991; Menke 1979). Free Black people were even sometimes able to become racially White by behavior or reputation, including marrying into White families until the mid-1800s (Davis 1991; Menke 1979). This intermingling was possible, in part, because the so-called one-drop rule— indicating that any known African ancestry meant someone was racially "Black"—had not yet become firmly entrenched. For example, the South Carolina judiciary in the 1850s refused to apply the one-drop rule to a free mixed-race person with "invisible but known one-sixteenth black ancestry" given that "acceptance by whites is more relevant than the proportions of white and black 'blood'" (Davis 1991, p.35). During this period, White elites had greater respect for and appreciation of free mixed-race individuals, who were viewed as more affluent, more cultured, and more similar to themselves (Frazier 1930; Williamson 1980).[3]

The formal institutional and bureaucratic assessments of race during the early nineteenth century also reflected this ambiguity through efforts to capture diversity within the African American population. Beginning in the 1830s and 1840s, the Census categorized people into one of three racial categories: "free Whites," "free coloreds," and "slaves" (Davenport 2018). The subsequent move away from categorizing individuals based on one's status as free or enslaved did not diminish the government's efforts to continue distinguishing mixed-race individuals. From 1850 through 1920, the category for mixed-race individuals ("mulatto") remained on the Census alongside the racial category "Black" (Allen, Telles, and Hunter 2000; Hickman 1997; Menke 1979). Beginning in 1890, recording finer-grained Black racial ancestry was viewed as important enough to warrant specific instructions to Census enumerators regarding how to distinguish between "Blacks," "mulattos," "quadroons," and "octoroons" (Davenport 2018; Saperstein and Gullickson 2013). Skin color thus served as the distinguishing feature among the separate tier of mixed-race individuals in the American racial hierarchy (Hochschild and Powell 2008; Ostfeld and Yadon 2022b).

In the early twentieth century, however, a shift occurred such that the "Black" racial category began to encompass both Black *and* mixed-race individuals. Among Whites, this change stemmed from a desire to keep a starker dividing line between themselves and racial out-groups following emancipation (Reece 2021; Womack 2017). The one-drop rule marked a clear boundary around categorical Blackness in America (Davis 1991; Williamson 1980; Menke 1979). This served to separate Whites from Blacks, but it also further enmeshed the status associations with light skin. Following this shift, the American legal apparatus constructed laws in the United States that made phenotype—that is, one's appearance—the central marker of race. Efforts were made to maintain this system by restricting opportunities for blurring racial phenotypic boundaries through interracial relationships and other means (Haney Lopez 1997).

Given these deep institutional roots in American society, it should come as no surprise that skin tone continues to be a meaningful marker of status, opportunity, and perceived stereotypes in society. As darkness of one's skin tone increases, so too does the likelihood that that person will be seen as more dangerous, incompetent, and unattractive (Maddox 2004; Maddox and Gray 2002). Put differently, although scholars often allude to "racialized stereotypes" with respect to categorical racial groups, those stereotypes are applied in a more continuous fashion based on the extent to which one is seen as being more prototypical of a racial group. While these perceptions extend across ethnoracial groups, power is not shared equally across various groups, which means that such perceptions have disparate *impacts*. One example of this is found in the classroom setting, where the combination of race, skin tone, and gender influences the likelihood that a student will be suspended from school (Blake et al. 2017; Hannon, DeFina, and Bruch 2013). Even after accounting for individual- and school-level characteristics associated with suspension rates, dark-complected African American girls are nearly twice as likely as their White peers to receive a suspension from school. In contrast, there is no similar relationship for lighter-skinned Black girls compared with White girls (Blake et al. 2017). This example more broadly highlights that White Americans—who are more likely to work as educators, bankers, doctors, and judges—have opportunities through their positions of power to perpetuate colorism and influence other's life trajectories based on skin tone.

Thus far, this discussion of skin tone's importance in society has centered perspectives of those in power. This is important in underscoring Whites' role in creating a system that has propped up racism and colorism as intertwined systems of oppression. Unsurprisingly, White people's efforts to sustain colorist systems and the societal value associated with Whiteness or lightness of skin tone have not gone unnoticed by sharp-eyed observers. In May 1962, Malcolm X spoke in Los Angeles at the funeral of Ronald Stokes, a Black man killed by members of the Los Angeles Police Department. During his speech Malcolm X asked the crowd of Black mourners: "Who taught you to hate the texture of your hair? Who taught you to hate the color of your skin? To such extent you bleach, to get like the White man. Who taught you to hate the shape of your nose? And the shape of your lips? Who taught you to hate yourself from the top of your head to the soles of your feet?"[4] Through this series of questions, Malcolm X points out that White people have associated more Afrocentric features, including dark skin, with badness and more Eurocentric features, including light skin, with goodness. Complementing Alice Walker's observations from the outset of this chapter, Malcolm X's statement illuminates colorism as not only an external impediment to Black communities, but also an agent in creating hierarchies within Black communities.

COLOR-BASED DIVISIONS AMONG AFRICAN AMERICANS

When society repeatedly emphasizes the value of a given attribute like one's complexion, it is not just the dominant group that internalizes these messages. The repeated associations between lightness and perceived value can lead to an internalization of these beliefs among Black people and other communities of color. While White people worked to stratify who gained access to valued opportunities and resources through phenotype, this system of stratification was also perpetuated within Black communities with phenotype as a dividing line. This internalization is consistent with theorizing that systems of oppression rest, in part, on consent from some marginalized individuals (Cohen 1999; Sidanius and Pratto 2001). Some subgroups are deemed to be "less worthy" of attention because they are perceived to draw out negative stereotypes of the group, for example. Even within a shared group, people can be marginalized by fellow in-group members. Consistent with this, political scientist Cathy Cohen notes that heterogeneity and cross-cutting cleavages have always been present in Black communities: "Whether in the writings of Du Bois, the economic and social plans of Washington, or the charity work of middle-class black women involved in the club movement, concerns over class, gender, and respectability have historically influenced which political issues and which segments of black communities were thought to be suitable for public ownership (James 1997; Gaines 1996; Higginbotham 1993; Washington 1995; Du Bois 1986)" (Cohen 1999, p. 14).

With respect to skin tone, the status and power differentials between those with lighter and darker skin have been clear to African Americans throughout history. Color-based class divides have roots going back to the institution of slavery and have contributed toward differing concerns and priorities among these groups. For example, lower-class Black people were concerned with jobs, wages, and housing, while upper-class Black people—who already had access to these privileges—were instead focused on improving the group's public image and removing barriers to career advancement (Shelby 2005; Tate

1998). Similar questions about the political solidarity among increasingly diverse African American communities continue in the present day (Dawson 1994; Reece 2021; Taylor 2023).

Efforts made by lighter-skinned African Americans to maintain their higher status throughout history should not be entirely surprising, then. One well-documented example of such efforts is the high rates of complexion homogamy, or intermarriage, among light-skinned Black people. Complexion homogamy was a means of protecting and growing one's own assets, resources, status, and legacy (Bodenhorn 2006; Bodenhorn and Ruebeck 2007; Monk 2014). Evidence suggests the powerful influence of these decisions on family wealth: "Mulatto homogamous households in the mid-nineteenth century had between 30 and 90 percent more wealth than households with at least one black spouse" (Bodenhorn 2006, p. 259).

The creation and maintenance of a number of elite social, religious, and educational organizations attempted to further signal and maintain status among "elite" African Americans (Frazier 1932; Menke 1979; Russell et al. 2013). Social organizations were created to cater to high-status Black people, which often relied upon lighter skin as a factor for inclusion. For example, light-skinned Black elites in Washington, DC, founded the Lotus Club in the mid-1800s to differentiate themselves from lower-class, darker-skinned Black people who were migrating to the city (Menke 1979). Decades later, the Jack and Jill of America was founded in 1938 by upper-middle-class Black mothers who wanted their children to experience the same benefits as upper-middle-class White children. The organization recruits members by invitation and is thought to disproportionately recruit lighter-skinned Black members (Graham 1999; Lacy 2007).

Some social, religious, and even educational organizations have more explicitly relied on phenotype-based tests for membership, which both reflected and perpetuated colorist notions. Among African Americans, for example, the creation of "blue vein societies" conditioned membership on one's skin being light enough to see veins underneath, while "comb tests" determined whether one's hair was smooth enough to run a comb through (Korgen 1998; Kuryla and Jaynes 2005). "Brown paper bag tests" similarly required one's skin to be lighter than the color of a brown paper bag to gain access. Indeed, this was rumored to be a key factor in evaluating applicants to many historically Black colleges and universities (HBCUs), such that HBCUs were more likely to admit Black people who passed the brown paper bag test (Kerr 2006; Broady, Todd, and Darity 2018). In other words, the same discriminatory tests used by Whites were adopted and extended as intra-racial metrics of "status" in certain Black communities. Even religious organizations were not exempt from instituting colorist practices. The Methodist Church split on the basis of skin color in the late 1800s—with dark-skinned African American parishioners remaining in the African Methodist Episcopal Church, while lighter-skinned parishioners moved to the Colored Methodist Episcopal Church (Russell et al. 1993). Lighter skin tone also opened doors to more esteemed positions within both Black institutions and White society, with more opportunities for building social, economic, and educational capital (Korgen 1998; Reuter 1918; Hunter 2002).

In short, then, while colorism may have originated among White people and systems, Black communities are not immune from internalizing and perpetuating colorist views.

SKIN COLOR OR MULTIRACIALISM?

The historical connection between African Americans' skin tone and mixed-race ancestry is an important element of this project. Looking back to the institution of slavery, lighter-skinned Black people received better treatment and more opportunities from Whites—*and* they were also more likely to have a White father. To what extent are we capturing multiracialism when discussing the influence of skin tone in the present day? Do lighter-skinned Black people have, for example, more wealth and better health outcomes than their darker-skinned Black counterparts not because of skin tone, but due to mixed-race parentage and access to resources through White family members?

While parentage or ancestry is certainly part of the story, it is not the full story. First, skin color variation is not necessarily indicative of multiracial ancestry. There is broad skin color variation found around the world. Many African communities are relatively lighter-skinned, in part because of geography, varying levels of ultraviolet radiation across regions, and migration flows throughout the continent (Jablonski and Chaplin 2000). Thus, it is possible to be a light-skinned Black person without having a White enslaver as an ancestor. Even among Black people with mixed-race ancestry, being multiracial does not always mean that one will have a light skin tone, just as having two Black parents does not mean one will always have a dark complexion (Tharps 2016). Within many families, siblings with the same biological parents differ in skin tone, sometimes dramatically.

Second, skin tone has been shown to have its own distinct associations and influences separate from those of multiracialism. Research shows that skin tone effects persist among African Americans who report having two Black parents (Monk 2018). Among children with both a Black mother and Black father, the lightness or darkness of the child's skin tone is powerfully associated with the likelihood of receiving school suspensions (Hannon, DeFina, and Bruch 2013). Thus, it is *skin tone* rather than biological relationship to a non-Black parent that drives many of the associations noted throughout the contemporary colorism literature. Even after accounting for parental socioeconomic status, darker skin is associated with African Americans' occupation, income, and educational attainment (Keith and Herring 1991). Similarly, among people within the same family, darker-skinned siblings have higher likelihoods of arrest and greater risk of cardiovascular hypertension (Kizer 2017; Laidley et al. 2019). Skin color, then, has additional and distinct effects with respect to lived experiences, wellness, and opportunities above and beyond effects driven by mixed-race parentage or multiracial identification.

Of course, this does not mean that multiracialism is not worthy of study; in fact, there is a growing body of important research in this area (Davenport 2018; Lemi 2020; Leslie and Sears 2022; Masuoka 2017). Instead, the central takeaway for this book is that while multiracialism and skin tone variation are related, they are not two sides of the same coin. Put differently, while part of the value placed on lighter skin tone in mainstream society is that lighter skin signals further proximity from Blackness, studying skin tone is not equivalent to studying multiracialism or mixed-race parentage. Scholars recognize that racial hierarchies function in nuanced and complex ways, and important complexity would be lost by focusing solely on ancestry while setting aside skin tone.

Foundational Examinations of Skin Tone and Politics

Despite the legacy of colorism in the United States and a broad body of evidence documenting its socioeconomic associations, substantially less work has explored the potential importance of African Americans' skin tone with respect to their political attitudes. One reason that this relationship has not been thoroughly explored is due to lack of measurement of skin tone alongside questions of politics. Without such a measure, scholars are unable to examine how skin tone's influence on one's daily life—such as those noted by Alice Walker at the outset of this chapter—may spill over into the political. Fortunately, though, three datasets collected between 1979 and 1994 included a measure of skin tone alongside some political items, providing a first opportunity to examine African Americans' skin tone and political attitudes.

In their groundbreaking work, political scientists Jennifer Hochschild and Vesla Weaver (2007) theorize that a "skin color paradox" exists in the United States. That is, despite color-based disparities in African Americans' experiences, there should not be detectable differences in political attitudes based on complexion. They argue this is "because most blacks see the fight against racial hierarchy as requiring their primary allegiance, they do not see or do not choose to express concern about the internal hierarchy of skin tone" (Hochschild and Weaver 2007, p. 643). Subsequently, Hochschild and Weaver explore how skin color relates to perceptions of discrimination and levels of both linked fate and racial group identity in two studies: the 1979-1980 National Survey of Black Americans (NSBA) and the 1992-1994 Multi-City Study of Urban Inequality (MCSUI), which surveyed individuals living in Detroit, Atlanta, Los Angeles, and Boston (Bobo et al. 1998; Jackson and Gurin 1987). These two surveys were cutting-edge for simply including a measure of skin tone. In both cases, skin tone was assessed by interviewer observation; skin color in the NSBA was rated using a five-point word scale from very dark to very light, and the MCSUI used a three-point measure from light to dark. Although Hochschild and Weaver find evidence that darker skin tone is correlated with lower socioeconomic status and a lower likelihood of holding political office, they find little association between respondents' skin tone and either levels of linked fate or perceptions of discrimination.

This pattern of attitudinal non-findings was also consistent with the one earlier study attempting to examine skin color and political attitudes. Political scientists Richard Seltzer and Robert C. Smith (1991) explored the relationship between interviewer-assessed skin color and political ideology, government spending, support for civil liberties, and confidence in American institutions using data from the 1982 General Social Survey (GSS). Like the NSBA and MCSUI, the 1982 GSS incorporated an interviewer-assessed measure of skin tone using a five-point word scale from very dark to very light, which Seltzer and Smith collapse to a three-point scale for their analyses. They, too, conclude that despite the importance of skin color stratification, skin color does not appear to be associated with "the attitudinal configuration of Afro-American society and politics" (Seltzer and Smith 1991, p. 285).

Across these first-wave skin tone and political attitudes studies, then, there did not appear to be any clear relationship between skin color and African Americans' political views. Were scholars therefore justified in concluding that no further attention should be paid to this topic?

There are three reasons why it is important to reexamine the skin color paradox. First, there have been significant advancements in measurement of skin tone since the last dataset from this first-wave of skin tone politics research was conducted (i.e., the 1992-94 MCSUI). The NSBA, MCSUI, and 1982 GSS data provided exciting opportunities to begin exploring a potential relationship between color and politics, but the purpose of all three studies was not explicitly about either color or political attitudes. As with any study, then, the goals of the study influence the questions included and the time invested in training interviewers. Indeed, the assessment of participants' skin tone was relatively coarse—i.e., using either three- or five-category scales with no visual anchor. Until more recent studies like the 2012 ANES, there was not documented evidence that interviewers were trained in how to use the skin color scales included within the surveys. Seltzer and Smith recognized these measurement challenges and noted at the outset of their article that "we therefore caution that the results should be viewed as suggestive rather than definitive" (1991, p. 280).

More recent innovations in skin tone measurement, however, have included the use of visual color palettes in an effort to help standardize assessments (Yadon and Ostfeld 2024). The inclusion of these visual color palettes, including in the 2012 American National Election Study (ANES) and the 2020 Collaborative Multiracial Post-Election Survey (CMPS), presented an opportunity for my coauthors and me to uncover evidence that African Americans' skin tone is, in fact, associated with political attitudes (Hutchings et al. 2016; Yadon 2020; 2022). Moreover, measurement practices have also shifted from a primary focus on interviewer assessments historically to also including self-assessments and even machine-ratings of skin tone, in some cases triangulating across measures to understand when these measures capture similar or distinct data (Gravlee and Dressler 2005; Ostfeld and Yadon 2022b). Overall, advancements in measurement present opportunities to reexamine the links between skin color and politics, and some of my prior work highlights a link between African Americans' skin tone and political views.

Second, the skin color paradox is worth reassessing because the first-wave surveys were limited not only by the measures of skin tone used, but also by a relatively small set of political items. The political topics examined by the first-wave researchers included propensity to hold elected office, levels of linked fate, perceptions of discrimination, ideology, government spending, civil liberties, and confidence in American institutions. Thus, the conclusion that skin tone has no association with political attitudes among African Americans is based on relatively limited evidence. It seems plausible that skin tone *could* be associated with political attitudes—particularly on issues where color-based disparities are especially pronounced, such as policies related to education, wealth redistribution, or criminal justice—but that scholars have not yet had a chance to assess due to data limitations. Here, too, my recent work provides some evidence that this is the case (Hutchings et al. 2016; Yadon 2022). Thus, having access to data with a broader set of political items would be beneficial toward understanding the contours of the skin color paradox.

Third, there have been significant changes to the American racial landscape in recent decades. As I discuss in more detail in the next section, multiple factors—including growing levels of immigration, the incorporation of sizable new ethnoracial groups into the American racial hierarchy, and the emergence of an official multiracial identification option—have all served to shift the racial hierarchy and increase heterogeneity both within and across categorical racial groups. Additionally, a heightened emphasis on being a colorblind society may lead to a somewhat lessened focus on categorical race in some areas while factors like skin color may paradoxically become more meaningful.

Undergirding these societal changes is the tightly intertwined nature of color and class over time as a necessary but insufficient condition to observe a link between skin color and politics. The broad evidence that one's socioeconomic class and resources are powerfully associated with political attitudes may mean that heightened color-based disparities may become more politically meaningful. In my work with Mara Ostfeld, we argue that this color-class connection should help to make skin tone more politically salient across ethnoracial groups in the United States. Among African Americans, we note that the profound impact of race and organizing efforts around the Black racial category may inhibit a strong tie between skin tone and political views compared with groups such as Latinos or Asian Americans. These dynamics may be changing, however, since "racial boundaries are blurring to an extent that may make skin color more meaningful now or in the coming years than it was only a few decades ago" (Ostfeld and Yadon 2022b, p. 72). To assess the relationship between skin tone and political attitudes in our study, we conducted a face-to-face survey in the Midwest that had four political attitudinal items selected with an eye toward examining potential links between skin tone and politics among Black, Latino, and White participants. While we did not find a consistent connection between African Americans' skin tone and these items in our survey, this should not be taken as the final word: "There is some reason to think that this result would be different in other contexts—for example, if we had asked a broader range of politically relevant items, or if we had conducted our face-to-face surveys outside of the Detroit and Chicago metro areas" (Ostfeld and Yadon 2022b, p. 170). Thus, some of the critiques of first-wave efforts to study African Americans' skin color and politics are applicable to my work with Ostfeld, too. In turn, a deeper examination of the link between African Americans' skin tone and politics is valuable toward painting a clearer picture of the skin color paradox.

Advancements in measurement of skin tone, the inclusion of a wider-range of political items, and other contextual shifts—for example, changes in the racial hierarchy—leave room for valuable further examination of the skin color paradox. While a handful of articles have taken up questions of African Americans' skin tone and political attitudes, there is only so much room for deep theoretical development within the space constraints of an academic paper. One goal of this book project, then, is to provide a stronger framework for thinking about colorism among African Americans in the United States. I began developing a general framework in my first book with Mara Ostfeld for when, where, and how skin color may be linked to political views across ethnoracial groups. This book complements and extends that framework by more deeply theorizing and empirically examining the political manifestations of colorism among African Americans specifically. This is especially valuable given the unique history of colorism and racial dynamics between Black and White Americans.

My argument regarding how skin color is likely to manifest politically has two components involving Black Americans' political attitudes and sense of color-based identity. First, because African Americans observe differential treatment and opportunities based on both race and skin color, I expect that these considerations will also influence their political views in some domains. This does not mean, however, that race is no longer relevant to Black people's political views, or that skin tone will always be politically meaningful. Skin color should be meaningful in domains where skin color disparities are especially pronounced—for example, related to jobs, income, or criminal justice. Darker-skinned African Americans may hold more liberal views on these color-relevant issues given a recognition that they are doubly marginalized based on both their race and skin tone. Throughout the remainder of this chapter, I elaborate on this theoretical background and framework.

Second, I argue that skin color will be taken up as a meaningful social identity in addition to race among many African Americans. Shifts to the racial landscape in recent decades—including growing levels of immigration and multiracialism, as well as increased heterogeneity within racial groups—provides the context in which skin tone may become a stronger form of intragroup identification. Other social psychological factors—including the high visibility, stickiness, external labeling, and similarity to group prototypes—also increase the likelihood that darker-skinned African Americans, in particular, will internalize color as a meaningful part of their identity. This color-based identity may be driving any relationship between skin color and political attitudes. While the colorism literature frequently examines connections between skin tone and various outcomes, my project not only links skin tone with political views but also proposes a mechanism that joins the two: skin tone identity. I develop the theoretical framework related to skin tone identity in chapter 5, drawing on the expansive body of work examining identity and politics (e.g., Abrajano and Alvarez 2010; Brown and Lemi 2021; Cohen 1999; Davenport 2018; Harris-Lacewell and Junn 2007; Masuoka and Junn 2013; McClain et al. 2009; Pérez 2021; Wong et al. 2011).

Reconsidering a Potential Link between Skin Color and Politics

The historically interwoven nature of skin color and racial categorization for African Americans has given way to expectations that race is the most relevant factor for understanding political attitudes and behavior. Indeed, African Americans' racial group identity has been strongly linked to the study of Black political behavior given that race serves as a principal status marker (Carter 2019; Gaines 1996; Shingles 1981; White and Laird 2020). Historically, Black people with a strong racial identity have higher rates of participation in politics (Bobo and Gilliam 1990; Miller et al. 1981; Olsen 1970; Verba and Nie 1972), as well as indicating greater support for policies and government interventions linked to the group (Bobo 2004; Dawson 1994). Group attachment and solidarity, then, are crucial to understanding Black politics.

But does race always supersede other intra-group variation? Everyone holds multiple identities that vary in meaning or salience across contexts. For example, the Black feminist perspective has long argued that Black women have a unique struggle within the American political system, given that the system was created by White men and that Black women are oppressed in terms of both their racial and gender identities (Combahee River Collective 1977). Exploration of intra-racial heterogeneity has occurred by examining race alongside ethnicity, gender, immigration status, class, religion, and sexual orientation, for example, and reveals multiple associations between these intersecting identities and one's political views and behavior (Austin 2018; Brown 2014; Brown and Lemi 2021; Cohen 1999; Crenshaw 1990; Dawson 1994, 2001; Greer 2013; Harris, Sinclair-Chapman, and McKenzie 2005; Harris-Lacewell and Junn 2007; hooks 2000; Simien 2012; Simien and Clawson 2004; Slaughter 2021; Slaughter and Brown 2022; Smith 2014; Stewart 2018; Williams 2021).

What about varied experiences based on skin color? This is, of course, a unique case in some regards given that skin tone has historically served as a marker of race rather than a distinct category like gender. Given skin tone's importance in the process of racialization and its status implications, it may develop as a complementary identity alongside one's racial identity. While skin tone diversity has been present and meaningful in the lives of Black people in the United States for hundreds of years, the significance of skin color may be becoming more pronounced due to multiple shifts in American society (Bonilla-Silva 2003; Monk 2014; Reece 2021). The racial landscape has changed since the 1970s, 1980s, and 1990s, when the datasets used by first-wave researchers found no association between African Americans' skin tone and a limited set of political views. I argue that there are three primary reasons to expect that skin tone may be associated with politics in our current political moment and is worthy of further examination.

THE PERNICIOUS CLASS-COLOR LINKAGE

First, the recurring connections between skin color, status, and ability over the course of several centuries has left a close imprint between not just race and class, but also color and class (Ostfeld and Yadon 2022b). Consequently, skin color and economic opportunity have remained closely intertwined, with each serving as an implicit signal of the other (Bailey, Saperstein, and Penner 2014; Goldsmith, Hamilton, and Darity 2007; Monk 2014; Reece 2018b; Schwartzman 2007; Telles 2004; Telles and Flores 2013). One way to understand the continued importance of this linkage between color and class is by examining how historical trends compare with evidence from the present day. Just as evidence dating back to the Civil War showed that lighter-skinned people had greater wealth and better health, similar patterns continue to persist today in these domains and more—from wages to unemployment to criminal justice to social interactions (Monk 2021).

This pernicious association between class and color suggests that skin color may, in turn, influence how one views the social and political world. Indeed, an expansive literature highlights the influence of resources and opportunities on political views across groups (e.g., Bartels 2013; Gelman et al. 2007; McCall and Manza 2011; McCarty, Poole, and Rosenthal 2006; Ogorzalek, Piston, and Puig 2019; Stonecash 2000). Political scientist Michael Dawson (1994) notes that after the civil rights movement some Black Americans shifted from viewing racial identity as the predominant influence on their lives and begin to view other factors, such as class, as more meaningful. Similarly, philosopher Tommie Shelby (2005) argues that racial solidarity, premised on the idea that any Black person will have more needs in common with other Black people than any other group, no longer holds in the post-civil rights era. Given the tie between color and class, skin tone stratification within the Black community could become more salient in the post–civil rights era. In contrast to the skin color paradox, then, the expectation that one's resources correspond to political views or political engagement might also apply with respect to skin tone.

Building from the sustained color-class connection in American society, I anticipate that there may be an association between African Americans' skin color and political views in domains where skin color disparities are especially pronounced—for example, those related to income, jobs, or policing. Thus, examining a broader set of items across multiple national surveys will help paint a clearer portrait of these color-based dynamics. While race continues to serve as a meaningful point of societal stratification and is associated with political views, skin tone can also be relevant for issues where colorism is especially salient—or, at least, salient to group members who are doubly penalized in mainstream society on the basis of both race and skin tone. In contrast, this may not be the case for political issues where color-based disparities are less pronounced. Thus, while the persistent color-class linkage lays a foundation for skin tone to become associated with political views, two additional factors—shifting demographics and being a "color-blind" society—create a pathway linking African Americans' skin tone and contemporary political attitudes.

SHIFTING DEMOGRAPHICS IN THE UNITED STATES

Significant sociodemographic shifts within the United States in the last several decades may increase the salience of skin color for African Americans' politics. These include growing levels of immigration, the incorporation of new and sizable ethnoracial groups into the United States such as Latinos and Asian Americans, and rapidly increasing levels of multiracial identification (Davenport 2018; Masuoka 2017; Monk 2021b; Reece 2021). These demographic shifts complicate the traditional boundaries between Blackness and Whiteness that have historically been placed at the center of American racial divisions (Davenport 2020). Not only have these sociodemographic shifts increased the number of categories included within the racial hierarchy, they have also contributed to a blurring of boundaries around many of these groups (Ostfeld and Yadon 2022b).

Census data help visualize these changes over time.[5] As shown in figure 2.1, significant shifts in racial self-identification have occurred in Census data since the 1950s. These self-identification shifts include the addition of the "other" racial category, which has grown from near zero to more than 8 percent of the population in only 30 years. An even more sizable shift has occurred among those identifying with multiple racial groups. Multiracial group identification composed over 10 percent of the US population in the 2020 Census, while just decades earlier it was not even a bureaucratically recognized option. The growth in Black-White multiracialism, specifically, has

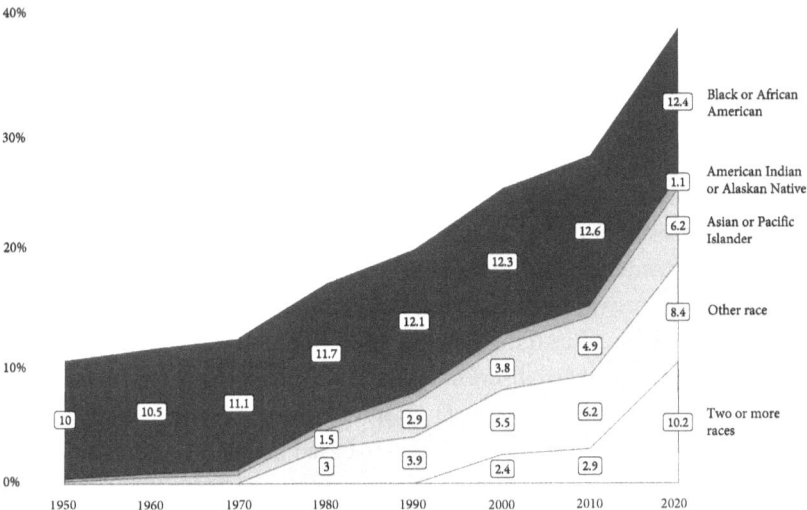

FIGURE 2.1. Growth and Change in the Non-White Population over Time
Source: US Census Bureau data, Racial/Ethnic Demographics of the United States from 1950 to 2020.
Note: Labels are provided for population sizes above 1%.

been even larger than the general patterns and is the fastest growing multiple-race subgroup (Davenport 2018). Thus, the formal identification options available to those in the United States and, in turn, the contours of racial categories have evolved in recent decades.

These shifts in understandings of the racial hierarchy allows other types of stratification to become more prominent, (Bonilla-Silva 2004b; Hochschild 2005; Hochschild, Weaver, and Burch 2012; Ostfeld and Yadon 2022b). The blurring of boundaries around groups and shifting understandings of racial hierarchy may make more prominent the variation in experiences among people *within* shared racial groups. As discussed further in the next section, these shifts to the racial hierarchy—including the addition of new groups in combination with increased heterogeneity within categorical groups—suggest that there may be incentives to differentiate oneself from the group. That is, there is a desire to fit into a group while also being perceived as distinctive in some way (Brewer 1991; Hornsey and Jetten 2004). In search of finding the balance between commonality with and distinction from their racial group, people may place a heightened importance on other defining features, which may be especially likely for attributes in which there is a perceived illegitimacy of status. Thus, attributes like skin color may take up greater importance among African Americans toward understanding where one fits within the group and the injustice of dark skin being regarded as the lowest rung of the racial hierarchy. Not only is this perception likely to give way to a heightened importance of skin tone as a meaningful attribute, these perceptions of injustice or illegitimacy are also a precursor to collective action (Ellemers 1993; Huddy 2001).

Of course, the importance of skin color does not mean that categorical race is *unimportant*. Race continues to be a potent force that informs one's lived experiences. Consistent with this, a body of evidence highlights substantial divides in public opinion between Black and White Americans (e.g., Kinder and Sanders 1996; Kinder and Winter 2001). Political scientist Davin Phoenix (2019, p. 43) summarizes this familiar trend as follows: "black people view spheres such as criminal justice, education and employment through the lens of systemic racial discrimination." In contrast to skin color, however, race is a more amorphous concept because it is neither visible nor directly measurable (Banton 2012). Growing color-based inequality and polarization may lead to a broader recognition of the multidimensional nature of racial experiences. To this point, Monk (2021b, p. 86) notes that "skin tone stratification appears to be quite pervasive in the United States, so much so that it seems quite fair to label it a pigmentocracy, despite the media's and academia's relative marginalization of skin tone stratification." If skin color has become more prominent to one's lived experiences, it should also become meaningfully associated with political views—even among African Americans who have historically had brighter racial boundaries and more political cohesion around race. In this case, it might be prominent in domains where color-based discrimination is more prevalent or well known. Moreover, it would suggest that doubly-marginalized individuals—that is, darker-skinned Black people—should be more likely to associate skin color with their political views. Put differently, if color-based heterogeneity becomes more apparent, people may view some issues through both a race- *and* color-based lens.

THE COLOR IN A COLOR-BLIND SOCIETY

The third factor relevant to the potential significance of skin tone for political views is evidence from recent decades showing a decline in reported levels of overt racial discrimination as well as a heightened emphasis on being a "color-blind" society (Bobo et al. 2012; Bonilla-Silva 2003; Monk 2014; Reece 2021). This emphasis on color-blindness is even seen among politicians, whose rhetoric has shifted to include more color-blind language (Gillion 2016). Paradoxically, this increasing emphasis on color-blindness might suggest that skin color could become *more important* over time. This is because biases related to color-based discrimination are not subject to the same processes that inform efforts toward minimizing some displays of race-based discrimination (Blair, Judd, and Chapleau 2004; Monk 2014; Weaver 2012). As summarized by political scientist Vesla Weaver (2012, p. 166), "Unconscious bias around skin color is not governed by conscious norms of equality, and therefore, not subject to control." While there are norms of political correctness surrounding race, skin tone largely lacks similar norms despite its powerful association with life outcomes (Blair et al. 2004; Monk 2021). Experimental evidence demonstrates that although people can suppress race-based stereotypes or discrimination, they are frequently incapable of doing so with respect to skin tone (Blair et al. 2002; Blair et al. 2004).

If efforts toward emphasizing color-blindness ultimately led to either stagnating or increasing levels of color-based biases in society, skin tone's importance should also become more noticeable to those who are marginalized. Consistent with theorizing about how racial ties may weaken (Dawson 1994; Reece 2021; Taylor 2023), then, some have argued that a widening divide between lighter- and darker-skinned Black Americans could further influence the reorganization of racial strata. For example, sociologist Robert Reece (2021) notes that like the entrenching of the one-drop rule, "A space may be opening between Blackness and Whiteness that light-skinned Black Americans can again begin to fill. By distancing themselves from Blackness they might open new opportunities for themselves" (p. 11). Consistent with this idea of in-group heterogeneity, evidence from the Pew Research Center highlights that 37 percent of African Americans agree that "Blacks today can no longer be thought of as a single race because the black community is so diverse" (Pew 2007). In the same survey, 53 percent of Black respondents report feeling that the "values held by middle class black people and the values held by poor black people" have become more different in the past ten years.

While there will undoubtedly continue to be shared experiences based on categorical race, other aspects of race—be it skin tone, gender, class, or other factors—are associated with different experiences. In turn, these distinctions may manifest with respect to heterogeneous political opinions. This does not mean that race is no longer important or that Black people believe racial discrimination is a problem of the past. Instead, the point is that multilayered identities influence treatment by institutions and people, and that some combinations of factors—such as race and skin tone—may be rising in importance. As noted in the seminal book *The American Voter*, whether or to what extent various groups or issues are viewed as political can fluctuate over time, with matters that affect one personally becoming more politicized (Campbell et al. 1960, pp. 30-31). If skin color disparities among African Americans are especially pronounced, skin color may become a meaningful political attribute in addition to racial identity.

All three of these factors, in combination, underscore the importance of reexamining the linkage between skin color and political views among African Americans. Indeed, a growing body of evidence suggests that skin color is linked with political views across groups in the United States, including Latinos and even Whites (Ostfeld and Yadon 2022a; Yadon and Ostfeld 2020; Yadon 2022). While these groups have distinct histories relating to race and skin color, the arguments put forth here and in recent research on other ethnoracial groups point to a potential for African Americans' skin color becoming more politicized over time. This nuance may help us better understand our current political climate.

Summary

Throughout this chapter, I have outlined why it is important to account for skin tone in scholarly theorizing and measurement. I make a two-fold argument regarding how skin color may be associated with public opinion among African Americans, which, as I return to in chapter 5, may also be the foundation for a color-based identity. Table 2.1 provides a brief overview of the central arguments from the theoretical framework presented here, which I will test in chapters 3 and 4. The table also foreshadows the argument and expectations related to skin tone identity that I theorize and test in chapters 5 and 6.

I note three primary reasons why skin color may be associated with African Americans' contemporary political attitudes. The first is that the nature of color and class have become tightly intertwined over time, with myriad evidence signaling that class and resources are powerfully associated with one's political attitudes. Second, the American racial hierarchy has shifted in several ways during recent decades, and heterogeneity has increased within categorical racial groups. This includes growing levels of immigration, the incorporation of sizable new ethnoracial groups into the American racial hierarchy, as well as the emergence of a prominent multiracial identification option. Third, a heightened emphasis on being a colorblind society may lead to reduced discussions of categorical race, while factors like skin color may paradoxically become more meaningful.

In combination, all these factors may make color increasingly salient in society and, in turn, for politics. Specifically, skin color should be associated with political issues where color-based discrimination is more pronounced, such as education, income, or policing. I expect that darker-skinned African

TABLE 2.1: The skin color politics theoretical framework and roadmap of the book

Chapters 3 and 4	Chapter 5	Chapter 6
Central Argument		
Skin color will be associated with political issues in instances where color-based discrimination is more pronounced, such as education, income, or policing-related issues.	Skin color will be a meaningful social identity to many African Americans.	Skin tone identity should be related to social and political views that explicitly invoke skin tone.
		Further, if skin tone identity works in a fashion similar to that of other identities such as race, class, or gender, then it should be possible not only to make skin color salient but also to influence subsequent political perceptions after asking people about their level of skin tone identity.
Testable Implications		
Darker-skinned African Americans should hold more liberal views on issues in which color-based disparities are especially pronounced given their doubly marginalized status in White society based on both race and skin tone.	Darker-skinned African Americans should hold a particularly strong skin tone identity given perceived similarity to group prototypes, proximity to racial borders, more consistent external labeling, and status differentials.	Darker-skinned African Americans who identify strongly with their skin tone identity should be highly supportive of actions to remedy colorism and color-based inequities.
		Lighter-skinned African Americans who identify strongly with their skin tone identity may or may not exhibit attitudes similar to their strongly identified dark-skinned counterparts given competing factors (i.e., their own color-based privilege vs. recognition of the harms of colorism to the progress of the racial group as a whole).

Americans will hold more liberal views on these issues given a recognition that they face a double disadvantage in White society based on the combination of race and skin tone. This chapter provides essential context for understanding colorism and African Americans' political views, which lays a groundwork for understanding the multidimensional nature of race.

3

Revisiting the Link between Skin Color and Politics: Combining Observational and Qualitative Data

> I think that people associate darker-skinned Black people with the people who are on welfare, the people who need affirmative action. You know, as jacked up as that is. I think that—But I also think that that's the image presented to them in the media all the time.
> 29-YEAR-OLD, brown-skinned woman interview participant

Over the course of 100 interviews with African Americans in the Midwest, I heard expressions of skin tone's importance in multiple domains. This ranged from day-to-day issues around perceived beauty, feelings of self-love or confidence, and dating experiences, to potential life-and-death interactions with police and the court system. Participants often referred to their interactions with White people and the opportunities afforded to Black people partly based on appearance. One interview participant was Nicky, a 20-year-old woman who identified as brown-skinned—that is, neither light- nor dark-skinned. She succinctly summarized themes expressed across many conversations:

> Yes, skin color is important. There's a lot of—if we're talking strictly just in the Black community—light skin privilege. It is up there, it is up there. The closer in proximity, whether you like it or not, to Whiteness, the more job opportunities you're going to have. The more people are gonna think you're beautiful. It's like, that's huge. And though people think it's getting better because maybe to them diversity for darker skin [people] has gone higher. It's like [sarcastic tone] 'Is it *actually* [getting better] though?' And at my job—Where I work, they were trying to increase the number of Black folks that were working here. And that's not in corporations, that's like in [retail] stores. . . . Who's all the Black people they hire? All light skins. All White-passing people. . . . I think no matter what, you're gonna be Black, but also [sigh] someone who's dark-skinned compared to someone who's light-skinned, that is never gonna be even. It's just never gonna add up no matter what. So like they'll still be oppressed, but it won't be on the same level.

The themes that Nicky touched on were repeated, extended, further complicated, but largely corroborated across interview participants—among men and women, older and younger individuals, and across participants' levels of formal education or income. Although not everyone I spoke to would likely agree with every statement made by Nicky, my synthesis of these conversations leads me to expect that very few, if any, would entirely reject her perspective. Given the recurring nature of these stories, then, the importance of skin tone is clear. The broad connections between skin color and a vast array of outcomes—both those for dating or employment mentioned above, as well as broader themes related to wealth and criminal justice demonstrated in the social science literature—suggest that skin color is highly politicized. Indeed, the link between darker skin and more unjust institutional outcomes is clear.

Yet, what do scholars know about the *political associations* of skin color among African Americans? Until recently, only two studies examined the link between skin color and political attitudes. Political scientists Jennifer Hochschild and Vesla Weaver examine the relationship between skin tone and a number of outcomes in their foundational 2007 article. They begin by examining the long-standing relationship between skin tone and socioeconomic status. Drawing on five datasets from 1961 to 1994, they show that lighter-skinned African Americans have consistently higher family incomes and more years of formal education than their darker-skinned counterparts. They next examine whether there is a correlation between African Americans' skin color and election to statewide or national political office. Here they find that "light-skinned blacks have always been considerably overrepresented and dark-skinned blacks dramatically underrepresented as elected officials" (Hochschild and Weaver 2007, p. 651). Finally, they note that one's political attitudes and behaviors are typically connected to socioeconomic standing. Colorism, then, should influence one's political attitudes and sense of linked fate with the racial group. Drawing from the 1979-1980 National Survey of Black Americans (NSBA) and the 1992-1994 Multi-City Study of Urban Inequality (MCSUI), which surveyed individuals living in Detroit, Atlanta, Los Angeles, and Boston (Bobo et al. 1998; Jackson and Gurin 1987), Hochschild and Weaver find little consistent evidence that interviewer-assessed skin tone is linked with political attitudes as they relate to perceptions of racial discrimination, linked fate, or racial identity. This pattern of non-findings was consistent with the conclusions drawn by political scientists Richard Seltzer and Robert C. Smith, who examined the relationship between interviewer-assessed skin color and political ideology, government spending, support for civil liberties, and confidence in American institutions using data from the 1982 General Social Survey (Seltzer and Smith 1991).

Hochschild and Weaver therefore proposed that a "skin color paradox" exists in American politics. That is, despite color-based disparities in experiences among African Americans, no differences in political attitudes based on color will be detectable given that the history of the one-drop rule—the notion that any Black racial ancestry, no matter how little, results in an individual being categorized as racially Black—leads to prioritizing efforts toward reducing racial discrimination over all else (Hochschild and Weaver 2007). The authors argue this is "because most blacks see the fight against racial hierarchy as requiring their primary allegiance, they do not see or do not choose to express concern about the internal hierarchy of skin tone" (p. 643). If this is true, there should not be a connection between skin color and political attitudes among African Americans.

Following the article's publication, scholars generally accepted the skin color paradox argument. Given the highly influential nature of Hochschild and Weaver's work, little attention was devoted to further investigation of the topic. Of course, a limited number of datasets measured race, skin tone, and political attitudes simultaneously, which made assessing these questions difficult in the first place. And the plausible nature of the skin color paradox argument provided few incentives for scholars to rush toward adding skin tone measures onto their surveys. Importantly, though, the existing scholarship from this first-wave of research did not account for the possibility that skin color may be associated with other political views that were not assessed in those studies—e.g., policy items, spending-related items, or broader sets of items focused on skin tone or colorism specifically. Furthermore, neither of the first-wave studies on skin color and politics could consider whether skin tone might be important to African Americans' sense of self apart from examining whether skin tone was associated with levels of racial group identity. Thus, the possibility that a meaningful sense of skin tone identity exists has not yet been examined. It is also possible that other changes might influence how scholars could understand potential relationships between skin color and politics for African Americans. For example, there have been significant advancements in measurement of skin tone over time beyond the relatively coarse three- and five-category word scales used in the 1979–1980 NSBA, 1982 GSS, and 1992–1994 MCSUI. As I discuss further in the next section, these advancements could be helpful towards unearthing nuanced yet meaningful color-based dynamics.

Other significant societal and sociodemographic changes have also occurred in the decades since the most recent dataset was analyzed by these first-wave skin color politics scholars. As discussed in chapter 2, there are three primary reasons to believe that the skin color paradox does not hold today. First, there has been a persistent association linking class and color through history. This suggests that skin color may, in turn, influence how one views the social and political world. A broad literature demonstrates that group resources are associated with political views and engagement, thereby suggesting that the connection between skin color and socioeconomic status may also be linked to politics (Ostfeld and Yadon 2022b). This line of reasoning indicates that skin color should be more politically meaningful in domains where skin color disparities are especially pronounced. That is, the salience of the issue may influence whether skin color is meaningfully associated with political views. This would mean that in domains where colorism is especially prominent and well-known—e.g., related to education, jobs, wealth, or policing—that skin color may be more strongly associated with political views. This persistent color-class linkage lays a foundation for skin tone to become associated with political views, but the other two factors—shifting demographics and being a "color-blind" society—should pave the way for a contemporary link between African Americans' skin tone and political attitudes.

Second, significant sociodemographic shifts in the last several decades—namely, growing levels of immigration; incorporation of new and sizable ethnoracial groups into the United States such as Latinos and Asian Americans; and increased levels of multiracial identification—have contributed to a reshaping of the American racial hierarchy (Davenport 2018; Masuoka 2017; Monk 2021; Reece 2021). These sociodemographic shifts have increased the number of categories included within the racial hierarchy and contributed to a blurring of boundaries around many of these groups (Monk 2021; Ostfeld and Yadon 2022b). A greater variance in experiences among members of a shared racial group owing to factors such as color has the potential to influence the salience of color on lived experiences and corresponding political views. The increasing salience of in-group heterogeneity may also serve to help individuals differentiate themselves from the group in an effort to find "optimal distinction" (Brewer 1991; Hornsey and Jetten 2004). Given the multilayered marginalization associated with having darker skin within any racial group and the easy accessibility of skin tone as a physical marker, skin tone is an attribute of particular importance in a shifting racial hierarchy. In turn, those doubly marginalized individuals—that is, darker-skinned Black people—should be especially likely to associate skin color with their views on relevant political issues. Put differently, if color-based heterogeneity becomes more apparent, one would expect that individuals who are doubly marginalized by race and color would view issues through both a race- *and* color-based lens.

Third, increasing emphasis on color-blindness in recent decades may suggest that skin color could become more important over time. This is because biases related to color-based discrimination are not subject to the same processes that inform efforts toward minimizing some displays of race-based discrimination (Blair, Judd, and Chapleau 2004; Monk 2014; Weaver 2012). Although people can suppress race-based stereotypes or discrimination, they are frequently incapable of doing so with respect to skin tone (Blair et al. 2002; Blair et al. 2004). If these efforts toward emphasizing color-blindness lead to either stagnating or increasing levels of color-based biases in society, skin tone's importance will become even more salient to those who are marginalized as a result.

The ability to broadly examine relationships between skin color and a variety of political views or issues highlights the extent to which the skin color paradox may or may not persist. Throughout this chapter, I turn to a combination of observational and qualitative data sources to examine where, when, and how skin color is associated with political views in the contemporary American racial landscape. Before turning to these analyses, though, I discuss the data sources that I will bring to bear on these questions and then turn to an examination of the link between skin color and politics.

Data and Measures

One reason that examining race and skin color is often more difficult than examining other combinations of characteristics—such as race, gender, or class—is due to measurement. The study of skin color requires great care given its historical usage by eugenicists to argue through pseudo-scientific means that physiological factors have inherent, "biologically based" meaning (Duster 2003; Ostfeld and Yadon 2022b). These efforts were self-serving to those professing these racist ideologies; it helped insulate them from facing the prejudicial nature of their own world views and, in turn, recognizing these prejudices as undergirding the systems that led to the disparate outcomes they observed across groups. Thus, studying attributes like skin tone requires caution given the history of nefarious pseudo-scientific practices to advance racist ideologies.

Importantly, however, this history does not mean that skin tone is inappropriate to study in and of itself, but that it requires great care in terms of both measurement and discussion. The combination of skin tone and race are enormously consequential with respect to lived experiences and opportunities in society. From health to wealth to educational attainment or criminal justice outcomes, people with darker skin—both within and across racial groups—face worse outcomes (Monk 2021). Thus, the study of skin tone alongside race requires a cautious and conscientious approach that does not harken back to eugenicist frameworks. Accordingly, measures of skin tone

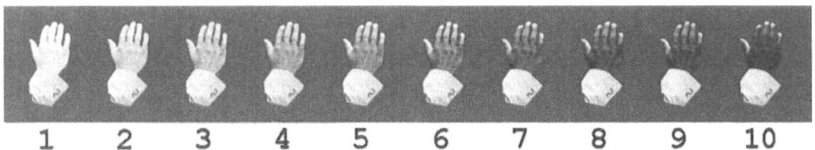
FIGURE 3.1. Massey-Martin Skin Tone Scale
Source: Douglas S. Massey and Jennifer A. Martin, *The NIS Skin Color Scale* 2003.

have become incorporated into a broader set of social scientific research in recent decades, but such measures have not traditionally been incorporated into political surveys. This inhibits scholars' ability to understand whether or how race and color are associated with political views. More specifically, only a few existing surveys have measures of skin color, political outcomes, and sufficiently large samples of non-White respondents to allow for subgroup analyses.[1]

The first opportunity for an extensive look into the relationship between race, skin tone, and politics is offered by the 2012 American National Election Study (ANES) Time Series data. The inclusion of the Massey-Martin (2003) skin tone scale to the 2012 ANES provided an opportunity to reconsider this relationship more deeply—both with a higher-quality skin color measure that relies on a visual scale, as well as a broader set of political items than other past surveys that included a measure of skin color. Not only did interviewers assess the skin color of every survey participant in the face-to-face portion of the 2012 ANES regardless of race, but the survey also had an oversample of self-identified monoracial Black participants in 2012 (n = 511). This presents an opportunity for a more comprehensive exploration of skin color politics than those in prior studies, one that I undertake later in this chapter.

To supplement the ANES data, I also acquired access to restricted data from the nationally representative 2001-2003 National Survey of American Life (NSAL). Not only did the NSAL include a large sample of both native- and foreign-born Black people, but it also measured self-assessed skin color and a small selection of political questions. For the purposes of this book, I focus on the subsample of approximately 1,540 native-born African Americans with recorded demographic data (e.g., age, gender, income, region, partisanship, and skin tone). Over 90 percent of these participants identify as having two Black biological parents. While the NSAL is more than a decade older than the rest of the data in this book, to my knowledge evidence from this study has not previously been published as it relates to political views. In turn, the NSAL data present an opportunity to complement prior published work by examining how skin color was linked with political views in the early 2000s.

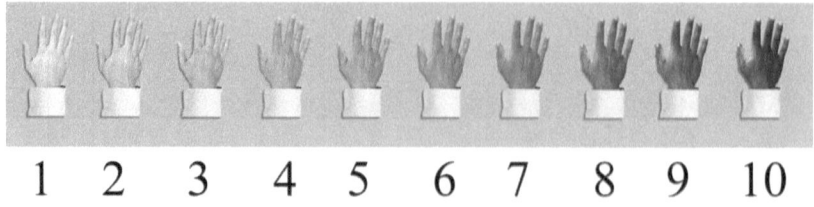

FIGURE 3.2. Yadon-Ostfeld Skin Color Scale
Source: Mara C. Ostfeld and Nicole D. Yadon. "The Yadon-Ostfeld Skin Color Scale," in *Skin Color, Power, and Politics in America* © 2022 Russell Sage Foundation, reprinted with permission.

The most recent survey evidence I draw from is the 2020 Collaborative Multiracial Post-Election Survey (CMPS). This national online survey was conducted between April and August 2021 with nearly 15,000 completed interviews across multiple ethnoracial groups, including over 3,900 US-born Black respondents. The CMPS includes the largest number of multiracial respondents of any data source in this book, with 23 percent of US-born Black respondents identifying with more than one race. The CMPS included the Yadon-Ostfeld Skin Color Scale, which is the first interval-level skin color scale that provides even spacing between skin tones of each hand on the scale. Participants self-identified their skin tone in the survey, as well as answering several questions regarding criminal justice-related experiences that I examine in chapter 4.

Finally, I turn to several original surveys to examine how self-identified skin color is associated with political views and skin tone identity. To this end, I ran four online surveys of African Americans between 2016 and 2019. The first was a 2016 MTurk study with 229 monoracial Black participants. The next was a 2016 YouGov study with 577 monoracial African American participants from their survey panel. The 2016 MTurk and 2016 YouGov studies used the Massey-Martin skin tone scale for participants to self-report their skin tone. A 2018 study was conducted via Lucid's opt-in survey panel and included 1,824 Black respondents, of which 92 percent identify as monoracial African American.[2] The 2019 study was conducted via NORC AmeriSpeak's nationally representative panel and included 1,041 monoracial Black participants. Like the CMPS, the 2018 Lucid and 2019 AmeriSpeak surveys included the Yadon-Ostfeld Skin Color Scale for self-identification of skin tone. Because all of these studies were developed with a central focus on skin tone, they include a broader array of political items related to skin tone than prior studies.

Throughout this book, I also analyze 100 in-depth qualitative interviews that I conducted along with a team of research assistants in the Columbus and Detroit metropolitan areas. A total of 67 interviews were conducted in southeastern Michigan from 2016 to 2017, with an additional 33 participants living in central Ohio who were interviewed virtually in 2021 due to the COVID-19 pandemic. There were a total of five interviewers—two in Michigan and three in Ohio. The interviewers self-identified as a light-skinned White woman (n = 43 interviews conducted), a light-skinned Black woman (n = 24), a dark-skinned Black woman (n = 13), a brown-skinned Black woman (n = 10), and a dark-skinned Black woman (n = 10).

The variation in the interviewers' race and skin tone was purposeful for allowing an examination of differences in conversational style and substance. Each interviewer has distinct experiences with the intersection of race, color, and power based on her own appearance and background, which are brought into each conversation implicitly (Brown 2012; Young 2004). The substance of the conversations revealed similar patterns in responses and views regarding skin tone's importance across interviewers. The style of the conversations, however, was distinct based on the race and skin tone of the interviewer. As the White interviewer, my racial outsider status required more effort toward building rapport and trust with the Black interview participants, but also allowed room for greater extrapolation because I was presumed to be unfamiliar with colorism. The Black interviewers' status as a racial insider meant that participants often signaled an expectation of mutual understanding, which sometimes inhibited in-depth responses. Importantly, however, Black interviewers' racial insider status did not translate to shared insider status in all domains—for example, based on gender, skin tone, or education. Indeed, Black interviewers reported feeling more instances of hesitation or reluctance from participants in answering some questions than the White interviewer, especially if there was a skin tone mismatch between the interviewer and interviewee.

More details about the interview dynamics, recruitment process, and sample demographics are included in the chapter 3 appendix. As a brief overview, participants were recruited through multiple means, including flyers posted in public venues (e.g., libraries, coffee shops), email listservs, church bulletins, and using a snowball sampling method. The aim was to recruit a diverse sample of people with respect to age, education, gender, and skin tone. Each interview progressed as follows: The conversation began with a discussion of the participant's reactions to a set of photographs of African Americans. Participants were prompted to discuss the key values and characteristics thought to be important to many Black people in their community. The conversation then shifted to an explicit focus on skin color—asking if the participants believed skin color to be important in society and if it operated differently by gender or age/generation; participants were then asked to share stories about themselves or others related to color-based discrimination. Finally, there was a discussion about potential policy or movement responses geared toward addressing colorism. At the conclusion of the study, participants answered a series of demographic questions and were asked to provide feedback to the interviewer about the interview experience. In this chapter and the next, I examine the substance of these conversations as they relate explicitly to politics—including nuanced understandings of historically racialized policies, views about policing, and movement organizing strategies.

Overall, the varied data sources, measures of skin color, and politically relevant questions examined across these datasets provide fertile ground for reassessing the link between skin color and political attitudes. Looking across these various sources—which include both national and nationally representative samples of African Americans—allows for a thorough examination of skin color, political preferences, and representation broadly. Descriptive statistics for these datasets are included in appendix table 3.1. These data sources serve as a promising opportunity for deeper examination of whether and how skin tone is associated with African Americans' political views.

Correlates of Skin Tone in the 2012 ANES

Before diving into the primary statistical analyses of interest, it is important to examine the contours of skin tone and its associations in the 2012 ANES. I concentrate on this sample for simplicity given that it is nationally representative, had an oversample of Black participants, and has historically been considered the gold-standard political survey in the United States. The 2012 ANES includes 511 non-Hispanic, monoracial Black respondents in its face-to-face survey.

Skin tone was assessed by interviewers who were trained to use the Massey-Martin skin tone scale, which ranged from 1 to 10, gradually increasing in darkness. The distribution of skin color is as follows: approximately 32 percent of African Americans were categorized between hands 1 and 5, 40 percent were categorized as hands 6 to 7, and the remaining 28 percent were categorized as hands 8 to 10. These three categories are roughly what can be understood as representing the terms light-skinned, medium- or brown-skinned, and dark-skinned. Of course, perceptions of what constitutes light versus medium complexions, or medium versus dark, vary to some extent. The classifications I laid out have the virtue of roughly mapping onto reasonable assessments of these three categories, as well as creating three groups with relatively equal numbers of participants in the 2012 ANES. For most of what follows in this chapter, I draw from the continuous measure of skin tone. In cases where more explicit categorical comparison is necessary, I use these cut-points given both their plausible mapping onto perceptions of light, medium, and dark color categories and for analytical reasons given the roughly equal number of participants across these categories. While it is challenging to say how the skin tone distribution in the 2012 ANES corresponds to the true distribution of skin color among African Americans, the data reveal a range of skin colors—using all 10 hands on the scale—represented among participants who racially identify solely as African American.

Now that we have a sense of the distribution of skin tone in this sample, we can examine the sociodemographic factors associated with African Americans' skin color. A body of literature demonstrates that skin tone is associated with a wide array of factors within racial groups, so it is valuable to see how these associations appear in the 2012 ANES. Indeed, there are several significant associations with interviewer-assessed skin tone in this survey: gender, income, homeownership, and living in the South. There is no association between skin tone and level of formal education, employment status, or marital status in the 2012 ANES (see table 3.1).

Consistent with prior research, women have, on average, slightly lighter complexions than their male counterparts (Jablonski and Chaplin 2000; Ostfeld and Yadon 2022b). Similarly, living closer to the equator—such as in the southern United States—is associated with having slightly darker skin (Jablonski and Chaplin 2000). Perhaps most relevant for the purposes of this book is that darker-skinned African Americans have lower family incomes. The average family income is $65,000-$69,999 among the lightest-skinned Black respondents compared to $45,000-$49,999 among those at the darkest end of the spectrum. Thus, there is an intra-racial, color-based difference in income of approximately $20,000 among monoracial African Americans in the 2012 ANES ($p < .01$). Darker-skinned Black people in the ANES are also 6 percentage points less likely to report that they are homeowners compared with their lighter-skinned counterparts ($p < .04$). While this is, of course, consistent with the broader body of literature related to colorism, it underscores the persistence of these intra-racial divides based on complexion.

Overall, these descriptive statistics demonstrate two key findings. First, there is noteworthy variation in skin tones represented in the African American subsample of the 2012 ANES. If there were little variation in the complexion of respondents, then it would be difficult to speak to any relationships between skin tone and political attitudes. Second, examining the correlates of skin tone serves to highlight that the general contours of how colorism operates continue to hold true in the present day, particularly when examined

TABLE 3.1: Skin tone correlates in the 2012 ANES

Female	−0.049**
	(0.024)
Age	−0.001
	(0.004)
Income	−0.133**
	(0.053)
Education	0.018
	(0.047)
Homeownership	−0.056**
	(0.027)
Unemployed	−0.038
	(0.027)
Married	−0.005
	(0.026)
South	0.077***
	(0.024)
Constant	0.646***
	(0.039)
Observations	1,992
R-squared	0.127
N_sub	458

Note: Standard errors in parentheses; *** $p < 0.01$, ** $p < 0.05$, * $p < 0.1$

for the first time using the gold-standard ANES political survey. In the next section, I shift to examining potential linkages between African Americans' complexion and political attitudes.

Policy Preferences

EXAMINING THE 2012 ANES

To begin my exploration of the skin color-to-politics link, I turn to the 2012 ANES data and then supplement these findings with the more limited set of political preference items in the NSAL data. The models presented throughout the book include a number of sociodemographic controls, including demographic characteristics, partisanship, ideology, and racial group attachment. The inclusion of these controls helps to establish whether skin tone's relationship with political views operates primarily through one's socioeconomic status or racial group attachment, or whether skin tone may be a distinct social identity within which political views vary. (I take up an examination of a potential skin tone identity more closely in chapters 5 and

6.) The analyses presented throughout this book rely on model estimations with extensive controls. Nevertheless, the general patterns persist regardless of how minimal or extensive the controls are; appendix table A3.3 includes three sets of model estimations to demonstrate that the results concerning skin tone's relationship with political views are consistent, regardless of how many controls are included in the models.[3] The relationship between skin tone and some of the socioeconomic variables—for example, income and homeownership—suggests that the models may provide a conservative test of skin tone's influence.

Recall that my theoretical expectations suggest that skin tone may be growing in importance given the shifting American racial landscape, thereby making skin tone and color-based discrimination more politically salient. Given the double-layered marginalization faced by individuals who are both African American and darker-skinned, we would expect that darker-skinned Black people would be more supportive of liberal policy preferences in domains where color-based inequities are especially well known and pronounced—for example, education, income, and criminal justice. Alternatively, if the skin color paradox persists, we should *not* find evidence of color-based stratification in political views among African Americans.

Contrary to the skin color paradox argument, my examinations of the 2012 ANES data reveals that skin color and policy preferences are meaningfully related in several domains (see figure 3.3; full models are presented in appendix table A3.2). Consistent with my theoretical expectations, color stratification in political views is most prominent in domains where colorism is highly salient. Specifically, darker-skinned Black people are significantly more supportive of policies implicating color-based inequities than their lighter-skinned counterparts. To help synthesize my analyses in this chapter, table 3.2 summarizes the relationship between skin tone and various political preferences.

What are some of the specific issues where color-based divides in opinion are present, and how large are the differences between lighter- and darker-skinned African Americans' views? If color-based disparities are noteworthy, then we should expect to see darker-skinned African Americans be more supportive than lighter-skinned African Americans of policies that could serve to reduce such disparities. For example, this might include the use of affirmative action policies that aim to assist underrepresented groups in gaining employment or admission to college. Indeed, those at the darkest end of the color spectrum are over 30 percentage points more supportive of affirmative action in the workplace than those at the lightest end ($p < .03$). Substantively this is equivalent to those at the lightest end of the scale slightly

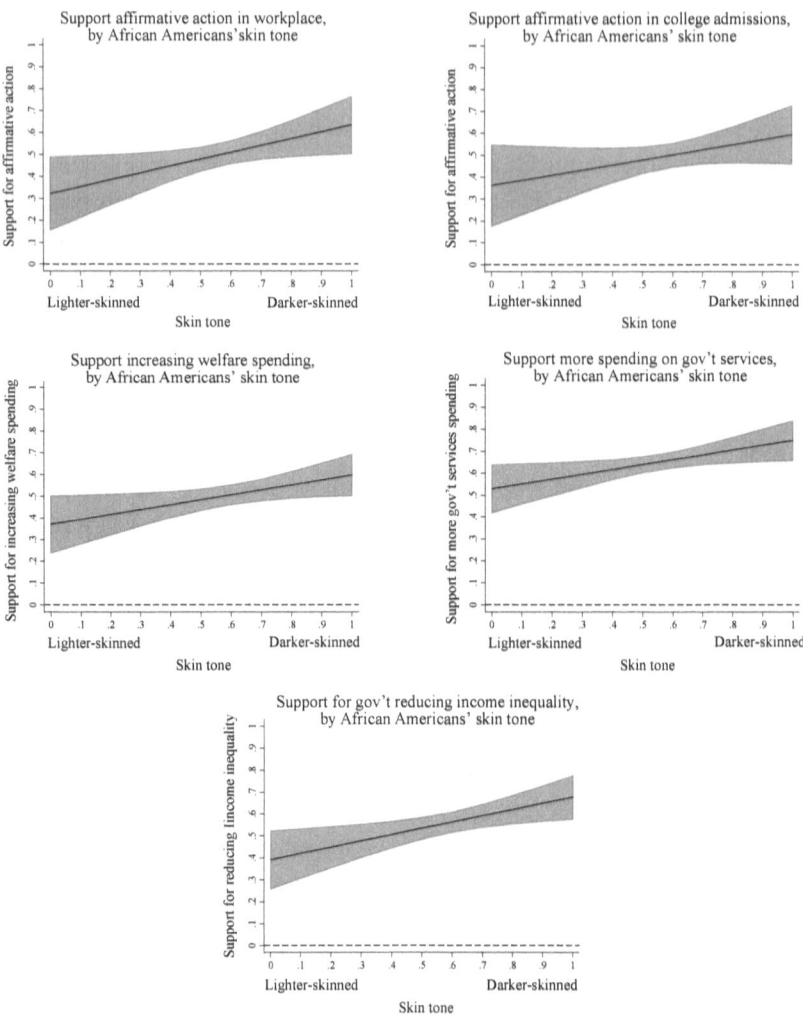

FIGURE 3.3. Association between Skin Color and Political Attitudes (2012 ANES)
Note: This model includes 95% confidence intervals and controls for gender, age, income, education, home ownership, employment status, partisanship, ideology, region, egalitarianism, interviewer's skin tone, linked fate, and racial group importance.

opposing affirmative action in the workplace while those at the darkest end of the scale slightly favoring the same policy. There is a similar pattern with respect to affirmative action in college admissions, though the relationship is weaker. Here, darker-skinned African Americans are 23 percentage points more supportive of affirmative action policies in college admissions, though this fails to meet traditional levels of statistical significance and thus provides less confidence in this relationship ($p < .07$ one-tailed). Those at the darkest

TABLE 3.2: Summary of associations between skin tone and political dependent variables

2001–2003 NSAL

	Affirmative action (work)	Government-guaranteed jobs	Rich pay higher taxes	Government help Black people	Racial identity strength
Skin tone	*	*			*
Skin tone	Linked fate *				

2012 ANES

	Affirmative action (work)	Affirmative action (college)	Welfare spending	Government should provide more services	Immigration levels
Skin tone	Immigrants take jobs *	Limit imports to protect US jobs	Feeling thermometer: Hispanics *	Feeling thermometer: Asians *	Support for death penalty
Skin tone	Approval of President [Obama]	Anger at President [Obama]	Approve of Obama's handling of health care law *	Favor 2010 health care law	Know someone who lost a job *
Skin tone	Support abortion rights	Support gun ownership	Favor marijuana legalization	Support increasing federal crime spending	Support increasing federal defense spending
Skin Tone	Feeling thermometer: military	Government assistance to Black people	Levels of political knowledge	Racial identity strength	Linked fate
Skin Tone					

Note: * = statistically significant at 90 percent level of confidence with one-tailed test end of the spectrum, on average, are slightly more likely to favor affirmative action in universities, while those at the lightest end of the spectrum are slightly more likely to oppose such policies. In short, darker-skinned Black people appear more supportive of affirmative action policies than their lighter-skinned counterparts.

There is also a meaningful relationship between skin color and views on welfare spending. Here, moving from the lightest to darkest end of the skin color spectrum is associated with being 23 percentage points more supportive of increasing welfare spending ($p < .03$). This is substantively equivalent to those at the lightest end of the skin color scale leaning toward believing that welfare spending should be decreased somewhat, while those at the darkest end of the scale lean toward believing that it should be increased somewhat.

We might also expect to see differences in support for government intervention in these domains. To this end, I examine attitudes on two related items: government-provided services and government efforts to reduce income inequality. Here, too, darker-skinned Black people are 22 percentage points more supportive of increasing government-provided services than their lighter-skinned counterparts ($p < .02$). Those at the lightest end of the spectrum feel that government services should be kept the same, while those at the darkest end feel that government services should be increased. Similarly, darker-skinned individuals are 29 percentage points more supportive of the government reducing income inequality ($p < .01$). Put differently, those at the lightest end of the scale lean toward somewhat opposing government action to reduce income inequality, whereas those at the darkest end of the scale are closer to agreeing somewhat that the government should take action to reduce income inequality.

In contrast to the skin color paradox, then, the evidence reveals noteworthy differences in political views based on skin tone. These relationships are consistent with theoretical expectations that color-based stratification in political views will be especially prominent in domains where colorism is more salient and has more detrimental effects on darker-skinned Black people. Indeed, darker-skinned Black Americans are consistently more liberal in their political views in these domains than their lighter-skinned counterparts. The doubly marginalized status of darker-skinned Black people leads them to be more supportive of these policies, while the relative privilege of lighter-skinned Black people in these areas corresponds to less support for such policies.

Darker-skinned individuals appear somewhat more conservative than their light-skinned counterparts in two issue areas of the 2012 ANES, however. The first is immigration. Consistent with the theoretical expectations

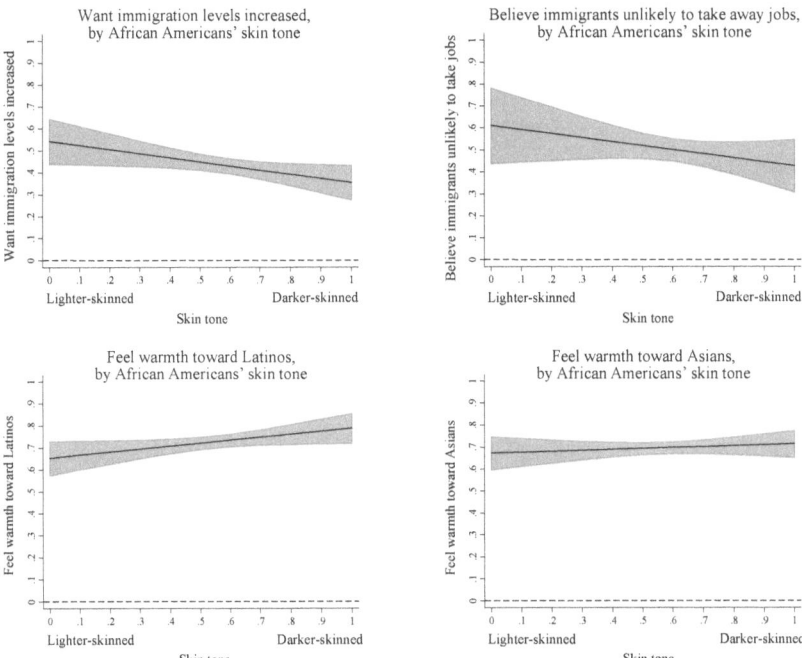

FIGURE 3.4. Association between Skin Color and Immigration-Related Attitudes (2012 ANES)
Note: These models include 95% confidence intervals and controls for gender, age, income, education, home ownership, employment status, partisanship, ideology, region, egalitarianism, interviewer's skin tone, linked fate, and racial group importance.

regarding colorism and employment opportunities being intricately linked, the more economically vulnerable position of darker-skinned African Americans may mean they are less supportive of efforts to increase the number of immigrants coming to the United States. This preference may be driven by concerns about the impact of immigration on their own employment prospects. On support for more immigration, as shown in figure 3.4, darker-skinned Black Americans are about 19 percentage points less supportive of increasing immigration levels than their lighter-skinned counterparts ($p < .03$).

This relationship seems to be driven by concerns about economic competition as opposed to animus toward immigrant groups such as Latinos. Darker-skinned Black respondents are about 18 percentage points more likely to believe immigrants take away Americans' jobs compared with their lighter-skinned counterparts ($p < .09$ one-tailed). Darker-skinned African Americans are also far more likely than their lighter-skinned counterparts to favor efforts to limit foreign trade in order to protect American jobs ($p < .02$). Do darker-skinned African Americans view immigrant groups like Asian Americans and Latinos more negatively, on average? If so, this would suggest that a distrust of immigrant groups is not specific to the employment realm. In contrast, no association or a positive association between skin tone and attitudes toward immigrant groups might signal a distinction between feelings toward these groups versus the economic implications of immigration. The data suggest that there is no difference in feelings of warmth toward Asians based on skin tone, but there is with respect to Latinos: darker-skinned African Americans rate Latinos 14 points more favorably as a group on the 101-point feeling thermometer compared with lighter-skinned African Americans ($p < .05$). In combination, this highlights that while darker-skinned Black people hold more favorable views of Latinos, fears surrounding economic competition may be informing their reluctance to support increased immigration levels.[4] This conclusion is consistent with arguments that Black people are often ambivalent toward immigration, in part because it serves as a reminder of their status in the racial hierarchy (Carter 2019; Greer 2013).

The second issue on which darker-skinned African Americans are more conservative than their lighter-skinned counterparts is with respect to the death penalty. Counter to my expectations, moving from the lightest to darkest end of the color spectrum is associated with a 31 percentage-point increase in support for the death penalty ($p < .06$). Unlike the other patterns demonstrated throughout this chapter, however, this finding is not robust; the effect weakens further both substantively and statistically when estimating the model with a simplified set of demographic controls, and it disappears entirely when examining skin tone groups rather than skin tone as a continuous variable. It is difficult to interrogate the relationship between skin tone and criminal justice attitudes further in the ANES because the only other item in this domain is about support for federal spending on police. Consequently, in the next chapter I draw from other data with more comprehensive batteries of items to thoroughly examine the relationship between skin tone and criminal justice-related attitudes.

Now that the broad patterns from the 2012 ANES linking skin tone to political attitudes are clear, it is worth reiterating that my argument is *not* that skin tone will surpass race in relative importance. American politics has historically centered on racial categorization as a key organizing feature. My argument is that skin color is a highly salient and meaningful attribute of race that can, in turn, influence not only one's experiences but also one's political views. Consistent with this, it is not the case that skin color should be associated with views on every political or racialized issue. There are several issues and policies—including presidential approval ratings, support for President Obama's signature health care law, abortion rights, gun rights, and foreign policy issues—for which there is *no association* between skin color and political attitudes, nor is there a theoretical reason to expect there to be (see table 3.2; appendix table A3.3). This highlights that skin tone is not relevant in every domain, but in certain domains and on specific issues, colorism is particularly salient. Put differently, the pattern of relationships found here are broadly consistent with the theoretical expectation that skin color can be associated with political views in areas where color-based disparities are prominent.

EXAMINING THE 2001–2003 NSAL

The double-digit differences in political views between lighter- and darker-skinned Black Americans observed in the 2012 ANES are substantively large and provide evidence of color-based political stratification. Across several domains—especially those where colorism is known to have its strongest effects—skin tone appears to be significantly related to political views among African Americans. This represents a departure from prior understandings of how race and skin color operate for African Americans in a political context, and refutes the notion of a skin color paradox.

To complement the patterns from the 2012 ANES, I next turn to the political items available in the 2001-2003 NSAL. The NSAL included five items related to government policies and interventions in its survey: support for affirmative action in the workplace, belief that the government should provide jobs for all job-seekers, belief that the wealthy should pay more taxes than the poor, support for reparations, and belief the government should make every effort to improve the position of Black people in the United States. Some of these items are more clearly associated with skin tone-based experiences—for example, potential employment challenges which could be ameliorated through affirmative action or government-guaranteed jobs—and so one would expect that opinions on these issues would be associated with complexion. Other issues are arguably less clearly linked, and so it is not obvious that a relationship should be present. Still, I examine each below.

Is there any association between self-assessed skin color and African Americans' political views on these items?[5] Consistent with the patterns found in the ANES, skin tone is associated with political views when there is a closer association between colorism and the policy at hand—for example, on support for affirmative action in the workplace and the government guaranteeing jobs (see appendix table A3.4). As shown in figure 3.5, African Americans with darker skin are 13 percentage points more likely to say they support affirmative action for Black people in hiring and job promotion

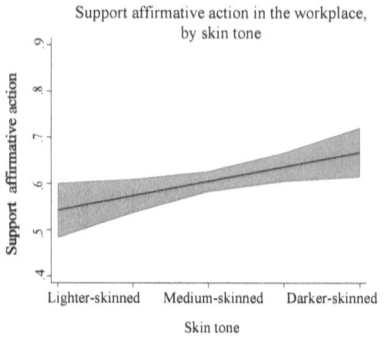 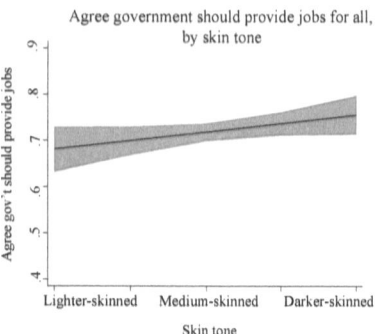

FIGURE 3.5. Support for Affirmative Action and Guaranteed Jobs by Skin Color (NSAL)
Note: These models include 95% confidence intervals and control for gender, party, age, income, education, linked fate, and racial group importance.

($p < .02$). Substantively, that means lighter-skinned African Americans are relatively neutral on whether Black people should be given special preferences in hiring and promotion, while darker-skinned African Americans agree somewhat that this should occur. Similarly, on the question about guaranteed jobs—which asks for agreement that "the government should provide a job for everyone who wants one"—darker-skinned Black people are about 7 percentage points more likely than their lighter-skinned counterparts to support this idea ($p < .07$). This finding is substantively equivalent to darker-skinned individuals falling between somewhat and strongly agreeing with this sentiment, while their lighter-skinned counterparts fall closer to somewhat agreeing that the government should provide jobs for all. Consistent with the findings in the 2012 ANES, then, this suggests that the different experiences faced by those with lighter or darker skin lead to different perspectives and priorities on employment-related issues.

There was no relationship between skin tone and attitudes toward the other three political items, however: taxing the wealthy, support for reparations, or government making efforts to improve the position of Black people in society. These three items are arguably not as closely or clearly tied to issues of colorism, with the potential exception of increasing taxes on the wealthy. Of course, one's own class status and corresponding views or comprehensive understandings of tax policies are not always clearly linked (Hochschild 1981; Kim, Pedersen, and Mutz 2016; Piston 2018). It is also possible that there is a ceiling effect given that support for each of these items is above 70 percent across the board, so it would be difficult to observe much higher support among darker-skinned African Americans. Overall, however, the NSAL data suggest that going back to the early 2000s there were some associations between skin tone and political attitudes in domains where color-based disparities are likely to be particularly salient.

Across both surveys, then, there is evidence that skin tone is related to certain political views dating back to the early 2000s and into the 2010s. In the NSAL, the political items associated with skin color involve employment and hiring opportunities. In combination with the even more sizable pattern of findings in the 2012 ANES data, this set of evidence highlights the impact of both race and color in influencing Black Americans' political views. Compared with the relatively limited explorations of skin color and politics in prior work, my examination underscores that skin color is important in contemporary American politics. Perhaps the extent of color-based stratification has grown enough in recent decades to spill over into perceptions of politics where it did not previously. Or perhaps color-based political stratification has always existed in some domains for African Americans, but prior surveys have not been able to adequately interrogate these questions.

Linked Fate and Racial Identity

One final domain likely to be of interest is whether skin tone is associated with racial group attachment for African Americans. There are competing arguments about whether and how skin tone might be associated with racial identity. On the one hand, a darker complexion is associated with being viewed as more prototypically African American (Maddox 2004). Some have even suggested the historical linkage between light skin and higher status in society may mean that people with lighter skin will "identify less strongly with black ethnicity and more with middle-class white culture and values" (Hughes and Hertel 1990, p. 1106). A clear counterargument to this point is the political cohesion based on African Americans' racial categorization that has taken shape since the solidification of the one-drop rule and the consistently high levels of racial identity within this group. Consistent with this, Hochschild and Weaver argue that "skin color is unrelated to racial identity because the latter is so widely shared [among African Americans], and it is unrelated to both the sense of linked fate and perceptions of discrimination because dark- and light-skinned blacks have been equally invested in fighting primary marginalization [based on race] and ignoring secondary marginalization [based on complexion]" (2007, p. 658). Here my view is similar to that of Hochschild and Weaver. I expect that although skin tone may be important and salient in contemporary politics, race continues to be so consequential and focal that it is not clear that there will be a strong connection between skin tone and levels of racial identity in our present political moment.

Evidence from prior explorations of this question has been mixed. A team of psychologists examined whether skin tone was differentially associated with perceived peer acceptance and self-esteem in two university settings: a predominantly Black university and a predominantly White university. They find evidence that darker-skinned African Americans report a stronger sense of racial identity than their lighter-skinned counterparts in both settings (Harvey et al. 2005). Prior work from a team of sociologists found a similar pattern linking darker skin with stronger racial identification, but these effects diminished after including socioeconomic control variables in their models (Hughes and Hertel 1990). Hochschild and Weaver also found mixed evidence. On the traditional linked-fate question regarding whether "what happens in general to black people in this country will have something to do with what happens in your life," *lighter-skinned* Black Americans were about 4 percentage points more likely to report agreeing strongly with this statement ($p < .05$). But regarding another survey item—whether one's "chances depend more on blacks as a group" rather than on what an individual does for herself—darker-skinned African Americans were almost 9 percentage points more likely to agree with this statement than their lighter-skinned counterparts ($p < .05$). Across four items related to racial identity, Hochschild and Weaver find that skin tone is only associated with one: darker-skinned Black Americans are 9 percentage points more likely to say they feel very close to "poor Black people" ($p < .05$). There is no similar relationship with respect to reported closeness to "middle-class" or "working-class Black people," however. Thus, the existing evidence regarding this idea of skin tone corresponding with racial group attachment does not provide a clear, consistent answer.

Is it the case that skin tone is associated with linked fate or the strength of one's racial identity in the 2012 ANES or the NSAL data? For the most part, no. Skin tone is associated with neither linked fate nor the strength of one's racial identity in the 2012 ANES data. African Americans of all skin tones report high levels of linked-fate and racial-identity strength. In the NSAL, however, there is evidence that darker-skinned Black people are 3 percentage points more likely to hold a stronger racial identity than their lighter-skinned counterparts, even when controlling for levels of linked fate ($p < .01$). While statistically significant, this effect is substantively small. There may also be a weak relationship between skin tone and linked fate, but it is not robust across varied model specifications and is substantively small at less than 2 percentage points. Despite a relationship between skin tone and political attitudes among African Americans in certain domains, then, there is not a clear relationship between skin tone and racial group attachment. Given the importance of color in society, a lingering question is whether a psychological attachment to one's *skin tone identity* exists. In chapter 5, I return to this question by examining skin tone identity and its association with racial identity.

Comparing Race- and Color-Based Stratification in Public Opinion

One may be left wondering how to make sense of stratification in political views among African Americans based on skin color, especially in comparison with long-standing *inter-racial* divides in public opinion between Black and White Americans. A broad literature going back decades has demonstrated expansive racial divides in public opinion (e.g., Jackman 1994; Kinder and Sanders 1996; Kluegel and Smith 1986; Schuman et al. 1997; Sigelman and Welch 1991). Consequently, I explore how the size of these color-based differences in political views among African Americans compares with the size of persistent race-based divides in public opinion.

To examine this, I present political attitudes broken down by the skin tone of African Americans alongside a well-known source of group heterogeneity among Whites: partisanship. Partisanship among Whites is associated with significant variation in political views and often in comparable domains where skin color is important. I am interested in adjudicating between two possibilities: Is it the case that despite opinion divides between lighter- and darker-skinned African Americans in some domains, both groups are still consistently more liberal in their views than White partisans? Or is it the case that the divides in opinion among African Americans based on skin tone mean that darker-skinned Black Americans stand apart as more liberal on some issues than both lighter-skinned Black people *and* White Democrats? Thus, I estimate the marginal effects of skin tone among Black people (in the top panel of figure 3.6) relative to the effect of partisanship among Whites (in the bottom panel).[6] This serves as a useful point of comparison such that we can see how attitudes compare both within and across racial groups using comparable model estimations. Recall that I do not expect skin color divides to *supersede* long-standing racial divides in public opinion, but I do expect to see meaningful variation in opinion based on skin tone in areas where colorism is more prominent.

Examining inter- and intra-racial group heterogeneity adds important nuance to traditional understandings of racial gaps in public opinion. There is frequently little difference in political views between lighter-skinned African Americans relative to White Democrats in domains where colorism is highly prominent. As shown in figure 3.6, lighter-skinned Black people's views are indistinguishable from those of White Democrats on attitudes toward welfare spending, affirmative action, support for the government reducing income

Support for Increasing Welfare Spending

Support for Increasing Spending on Government Services

Support for Government Action to Reduce Inequality

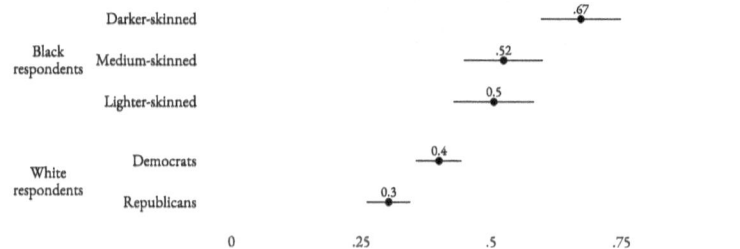

FIGURE 3.6. Comparing Policy Preferences of White Americans (by Partisanship) and Black Americans (by Skin Tone) in the 2012 ANES
Note: These figures display 95% confidence intervals. Models control for gender, age, income, education, home ownership, employment status, ideology, region, egalitarianism, and interviewer's skin tone. The models with African American participants also control for linked fate, racial group importance, and partisanship. The skin color measure is trichotomized.

inequality in society, and immigrants taking jobs from Americans ($p > .15$ for all). With respect to support for increasing spending on government services, however, light-skinned Black people are 10 percentage points more supportive of increasing spending than White Democrats ($p < .01$). In contrast, darker-skinned Black Americans are distinguishable from their lighter-skinned Black counterparts (as discussed throughout the last section), as well as dramatically distinct from White partisans in most cases. As noted earlier, there is an exception with respect to immigration. Darker-skinned

Support for Affirmative Action in the Workplace

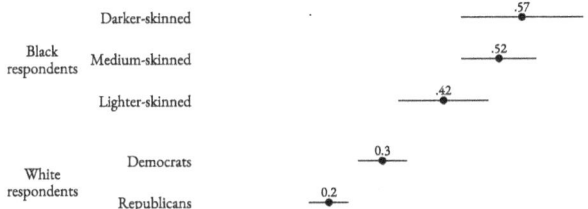

Support for Affirmative Action in College Admissions

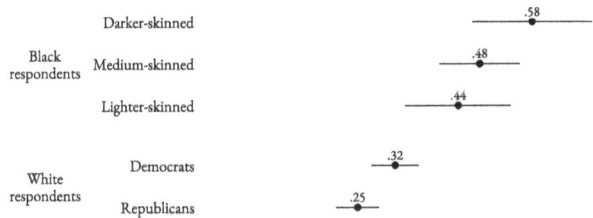

Support for Reducing Immigration Levels

Believe Immigrants Likely to Take Jobs

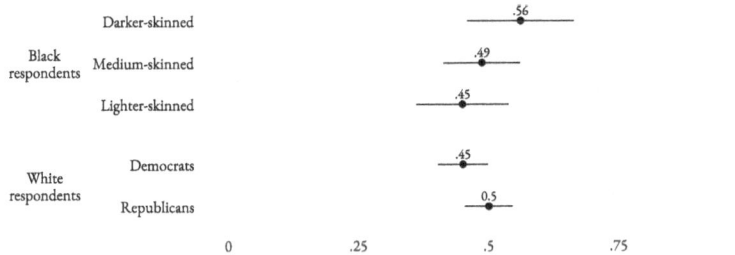

FIGURE 3.6. (*continued*)

Black Americans favor decreasing immigration, while lighter-skinned Black Americans are more open to keeping immigration levels the same. Darker-skinned Black people are also apprehensive that immigrants constitute a threat to American jobs. This suggests that concerns about economic competition vary across skin tone groups among African Americans, corroborating broader social scientific evidence of skin tone disparities in occupational opportunities, prestige, and pay (Goldsmith, Hamilton, and Darity 2007; Johnson, Farrell, and Stoloff 1998; Keith and Herring 1991).

Taken together, these findings emphasize the powerful relationship between skin color and political views. The skin tone divide is strong enough in some cases to mute the deep-seated racial divide in public opinion, with lighter-skinned Black people's policy preferences being comparable to those of White Democrats. Put differently, darker-skinned Black people hold substantively distinct—and typically more progressive policy positions—than both White Democrats and lighter-skinned Black people. All in all, this link between skin color and political views holds even after accounting for the socioeconomic factors that we know to be linked to skin color: education, income, homeownership, and employment status.

Perceptions of Skin Tone and Race-Based Policies

Thus far, the survey evidence from two nationally representative samples of African Americans highlights a meaningful association between skin color and politics. Across a number of items and domains—from government spending to education to income—I find a robust relationship between skin tone and political preferences. What the survey data cannot give us insight into, however, is *how* Black people talk about some of these policies and political issues in their own words. For this reason, I turn to my qualitative data from 100 interviews with African Americans in the metro-Columbus and metro-Detroit areas.

To what extent do Black Americans believe that skin color is associated with politics or policies? During the interviews, participants were prompted to discuss whether they felt that certain policies often discussed in racialized terms might also have underlying color- and/or gender-based connotations. Interview participants were asked what comes to mind for most people when they think of beneficiaries of racialized policies like welfare and affirmative action. In addition to tropes of the so-called welfare queen as a Black woman, many participants shared more nuanced perceptions of who is typically portrayed as benefiting from welfare programs (e.g., Gilens 1999; Philpot 2017; Winter 2008). Many participants felt that the typical welfare beneficiary is

TABLE 3.3: Number of interview participants linking race, color, and gender on two racialized policies

Group mentioned	Welfare	Affirmative action
Dark-Skinned Women	30	0
Light-Skinned Women	0	1
Dark-Skinned Men	0	4
Light-Skinned Men	0	2
Dark-Skinned People (no gender)	16	14
Light-Skinned People (no gender)	0	5
Black Women Generally (no skin tone)	9	0
Black Men Generally (no skin tone)	0	4
Black People Generally (no skin tone or gender)	11	19
Not asked / Didn't answer directly / Unsure	34	51
Total	**100**	**100**

portrayed not just as a Black woman, but a *dark-skinned* Black woman specifically (see table 3.3). Thus, participants consistently recognized that perceptions of race and applications of racialized stereotypes are not simply categorical but actually gradational in nature.

Among the 64 interviewees who shared a description of the specific mental image associated with a welfare beneficiary, over 70 percent (n = 46)—offered that darker-skinned Black people were portrayed as most likely to benefit from welfare policies. Of those 46 individuals who referenced dark-skinned people as the most frequently depicted image of a welfare beneficiary, more than 65 percent invoked darker-skinned Black women explicitly (n = 30). In fact, this was the most frequent response combining across skin tone and gender:

> Yeah there's literally people called "welfare queens." And in the media, it's been associated as poor, dark-skinned women with several kids who don't really do anything. Which speaks to a bunch of different stereotypes.—19-year-old, dark-skinned woman

> I think you always think of the Black mom in the projects. . . . You just see the person, just because they're on welfare, they're lazy and they're dark-skinned—or they're, they're not able to work. Where really that's not the case. Single mothers are the most resilient people on this planet.—20-year-old, dark-skinned man

> I think [for a welfare recipient] they think of a medium to dark complexion, overweight, Black woman with a whole bunch of kids. That's what I think when I think about welfare. I think when they think about affirmative action, they think about a dark complexion Black man who is undereducated.—39-year-old, brown-skinned man

> Look at the picture Reagan had of the criminal. He was a dark-skinned man. And then the whole welfare queen. . . . They think of a mammy with a bunch of kids.—50-year-old, light-skinned woman

The remaining participants made references to Black people generally, with no specific skin tone or gender provided, or to Black women with no reference to skin tone. As shown in table 3.3, it is noteworthy that no one referenced either Black men or light-skinned Black people as the stereotypical welfare beneficiary. Thus, understandings of racialized stereotypes such as the "welfare queen" appear to consistently be based on both race, complexion, and gender.

The mental image of affirmative action beneficiaries is murkier than it was in the case of welfare. This may not be surprising for two reasons: (1) greater media attention is paid to welfare, including portrayals or stereotypes of welfare beneficiaries, and (2) most of the interviews took place in Michigan, where race- and gender-based affirmative action in college admissions and public employment has been illegal since 2006 (Mears 2014). Additionally, the most common beneficiaries of affirmative action are actually White women,[7] which was noted by some interview participants.

Still, 49 of 100 interview participants reported having a mental image of the stereotypical beneficiaries of affirmative action. Of those who reported a mental image, just under 40 percent felt that the typical portrayal of affirmative action recipients invoked Black people generally, regardless of gender or skin tone (n = 19). Nearly 30 percent of participants invoked people who are darker-skinned and Black, regardless of gender, as the most likely perceived beneficiaries (n = 14). Perhaps unsurprisingly, there was a weaker gendered component associated with affirmative than welfare. Still, in a handful of cases, participants invoked light-skinned women (n = 1), light-skinned men (n = 2), or dark-skinned men (n = 4) as being perceived affirmative action recipients. None of the interview participants mentioned dark-skinned women as the prototype of affirmative action.

> When I think of affirmative action, I think of—This about to be very specific. But I think of like a young Black boy, probably dark-skinned, I think, coming from a poor, low-income background. He's probably coming from a place where he knew nothing, but to steal or like gangbang or whatever. . . . I hate that this is immediately what my mind thinks of. But I'm sure other people think of it, too.—18-year-old, light skinned gender non-binary interviewee

> I think when you think of someone that's either on welfare or benefiting because of affirmative action, the person you see in your mind is a darker-skinned Black person—or a poor dark-skinned Black person regardless of

which one you're thinking about.... I think they kind of tie into each other. When they think of someone on welfare, they think of a poor Black person. And when they think of someone who's benefiting from affirmative action, they think of that person's child from welfare that somehow just made it. And kind of—Yeah, that they're not deserving of either of the two [policies].— 26-year-old, light-skinned woman

Altogether, the interview conversations reflect an understanding of the intersecting nature of race, skin tone, and gender with respect to the portrayals of racialized policy beneficiaries. While the survey data earlier in this chapter demonstrated that policy preferences diverge between lighter- and darker-skinned Black Americans, the interview conversations provide insight into societal portrayals of *who benefits* from racialized policies. The latter point is important to investigate because even if policy preferences did not vary by skin tone, perceptions of who stands to benefit from racialized policies may still vary based on skin tone. This is important in considering how stereotypes are perpetuated, as well as potential downstream consequences of these stereotypes—which, as the qualitative data demonstrates, are aimed at darker-skinned Black people specifically—for opportunities and treatment in society. Thus, the qualitative evidence provides a complementary perspective to understanding color stratification and policies. The insights from the interviews reveal a political linkage between perceptions of skin tone and social positioning in society. This is an important finding with respect to understanding racialized policies, adding an even more layered view to traditional studies of racialized policies and the media, which often presume members of a shared racial group are uniformly—rather than gradationally—subject to stereotypes (e.g., Edsall and Edsall 1991; Gilens 1996, 1999).

Conclusion

This chapter has covered significant ground in reassessing the relationship between African Americans' skin color and political views from multiple angles. At each turn, I have found evidence of the ways in which skin color is intimately connected with public opinion. The qualitative evidence revealed that skin color and gender are tightly interwoven with perceptions of who is portrayed in society as the stereotypical recipient of racialized policies. The survey evidence underscored the existence of connections between skin tone and political views in domains where skin tone divides are especially pronounced—for example, related to jobs, income, and education. Given the independent effect of skin tone even when accounting for other socioeconomic factors and measures of racial identity, this suggests that skin tone may be taken up as a social identity that subsequently influences one's attitudes. I take up this examination of skin tone identity in chapter 5.

All in all, the evidence presented throughout this chapter paints a detailed portrait of how skin color is associated with African American public opinion in multiple ways. These patterns largely stand in contrast to the skin color paradox and signal the value in studying color stratification with respect to understanding policy preferences. The findings also suggest potential opportunities for mobilization around color-based issues, especially if colorism is more actively incorporated into mainstream media and political messaging. One domain that I theorize to be important but which was not closely examined in this chapter due to data limitations is policing and criminal justice. In the next chapter, I take a deeper dive into examining skin color's association with attitudes toward criminal justice—namely perceptions of policing, anti-police brutality movement organizing, and protest participation.

4

Examining the Connections between Skin Color, Perceptions of Policing, and Political Participation

> As far as law enforcement, I can touch on that. . . . If you're darker [skinned], I don't know, it's like they have more fear. I've heard cops say that before. I don't know if they'd be afraid that we'll want revenge—I don't know. They say we're violent.
> 34-YEAR-OLD, dark-skinned Black man

> Even if you look at just all the shootings that have happened, that's a very blatant and obvious statement to me that yes, they're treating them differently based on the color of their skin. . . . And even if you think about the color of the skin of people that have been shot, they're almost always on the darker spectrum of skin color.
> 26-YEAR-OLD, light-skinned Black woman

On a hot summer day in 2015, a group of teenagers were enjoying a birthday party at a community pool in McKinney, Texas. Although McKinney is a majority White city, many of the partygoers that day were African American. Unfortunately, the joy of youthful play and birthday celebrations took a sharp turn when police were called to investigate reports of "possible trespassing" at the pool (Shoichet et al. 2015). Upon their arrival, police officers began yelling at the group of mostly Black teenagers, and some people began recording videos of the interaction on their phones. The videos show officer Eric Casebolt handcuffing several darker-skinned Black boys while they sat on the grass. He then proceeded to throw a darker-skinned Black girl on the ground before pulling her hair and kneeling on her back. Video of this encounter quickly received national attention for the powerful visualization of a White male police officer using excessive force against a young Black girl (Cole-Frowe and Fausset 2015).

This incident fits within the larger history of police terrorizing Black people. Indeed, slave patrols were created in the southern United States as a precursor to modern-day policing. Slave patrols used aggressive tactics to instill fear in enslaved people, virtually all of whom were of African descent, with the goals of reducing incidents of runaways or attempted uprisings. These patrols were often appointed, managed, or otherwise sanctioned through state laws, county courts, and other local governmental bodies (Reichel 1988). Patrollers, who were mostly White men, were expected to pursue and find any enslaved people attempting to flee from captivity. State-sanctioned violence toward Black people in America, then, is intricately linked with the history of policing. Consistent with this history, a broad literature continues to demonstrate racial disparities in contemporary police contact, such that Black people have far more frequent and more negative interactions with police and the criminal justice system than their White counterparts (Burch 2013; Crabtree and Yadon 2024; Lerman and Weaver 2014; Nunnally 2012; Streeter 2019a, 2019b; Walker 2020; White 2019). Importantly, research has also demonstrated the power of protest in response to these instances of police brutality and injustice, as well as the corresponding political responses (Gause 2022b; Gillion 2013; 2020; Parker 2009; Prestage 1991; Towler and Parker 2018). Scholars have added valuable nuance to narratives about police targeting Black people through examining dimensions of class, gender, and ethnicity alongside race as well as political responses within these communities (Bonilla and Tillery 2020; Bunyasi and Smith 2019; Crabtree 2022; Lerman and Weaver 2014; Tillery 2019; Walker 2020; Woodly 2021).

One dimension that has received significantly less attention despite being especially relevant to the criminal justice domain is that of skin tone (Burch 2015; Eberhardt et al. 2006; Monk 2018).[1] Although it is discussed less frequently, skin color is a primary attribute which police can use to make biased decisions given the ease of assessing skin tone (Banton 2012; Lee 1993). Indeed, racialized stereotypes may be applied not just categorically but gradationally; that is, stereotypes are applied more strongly to Black people with more Afrocentric features, specifically darker skin, than those with less Afrocentric features (Dixon and Maddox 2005; Monk 2018). Recent evidence speaks to this point by highlighting that darker-skinned Black Americans are significantly more likely to be arrested or incarcerated, receive longer criminal sentences, and are more likely to receive the death penalty than their lighter-skinned Black counterparts (Burch 2015; Eberhardt et al. 2006; King and Johnson 2016; Kizer 2017; Monk 2018; White 2015). Importantly, these intra-group disparities based on skin tone among Black Americans are often of comparable magnitude to inter-group disparities between Black and White Americans (Monk 2018).

In the last chapter, I began testing the link between skin color and political attitudes for African Americans across a variety of domains. I found evidence of consistent associations between skin tone and political views, particularly in domains where colorism is well known such as issues related to jobs or income. Criminal justice is yet another arena where colorism is prominent, particularly given the history of state-sanctioned violence against Black people dating back to the institution of slavery (Reichel 1988). Despite the importance of race and skin tone in this domain, data limitations have hindered scholars' ability to examine potential connections between skin tone and criminal justice-related views. Indeed, few criminal justice-related items were included in the observational data I examined in the last chapter, so I turn to several new observational data sources for answers in this chapter. Consistent with my theoretical expectations, the domain of policing and criminal justice should be one where there are particularly strong associations with skin tone. This is expected, in part, given media associations linking darker skin with perceived criminality (Dixon and Maddox 2005), as well as the propensity to observe within one's own social circles that interaction with the police or courts may be varied based in part on one's complexion. Indeed, the enduring connection between darker skin and worse police treatment both historically and in the present day may, in turn, serve as a foundation for the formation of a skin tone identity. I explore whether a psychological attachment to one's skin tone identity develops in the next chapter.

Given the stronger application of racialized stereotypes to those with darker skin and more Afrocentric features, there is reason to believe that the combination of race, skin tone, and gender may influence one's perceptions and experiences. While police interactions are undeniably fraught for Black women, the associations between maleness and perceived strength, criminality, and aggression add further tension to police encounters for Black men. Stereotypes of Black men as menacing and intimidating are not new: "The brute image of Black men became significant moving into the early 20th century, when fear was reinforced with depictions of Black men as harmful. The film *Birth of a Nation*, made in 1915, shows Black men as savages trying to attack White women. . . . The result was Blackness becoming closely associated with criminalization" (Smiley and Fakunle 2016, p. 6). In the present day, these perspectives contribute to mass incarceration in the United States (Alexander 2020); Black men are the race-gender subgroup most likely by far to face incarceration, with estimates that 1 in 15 Black men over age 18 are incarcerated compared with 1 in 106 White men, 1 in 203 Black women, and 1 in 859 White women (Pew 2008).

Another factor that may contribute to the importance of gender in this domain is that narratives of Black men as victims of police brutality are often elevated over those of Black women. Heightened coverage of Black male victims of policy brutality both reflects their unique positioning on account of their race, skin tone, and gender, *and* also diminishes Black women's precarious experiences with policing. Social movement organizers have recently tried to counteract this pattern and highlight the paucity of media attention paid to Black women victims of police violence (Bonilla and Tillery 2020;

Lindsey 2015). The #SayHerName campaign, for example, sought to bring greater attention to Breonna Taylor's murder by police in 2020 just months prior to George Floyd's killing, which sparked national outrage and received more sustained media coverage. In combination, then, there is reason to believe that gender holds an additional layer of importance in the domain of policing and criminal justice. In contrast, it is less obvious what role gender might play in redistributive policy attitudes. Of course, future research would benefit from incorporating more theorizing and examinations of skin tone alongside gender across political contexts and issues.

This chapter takes a deeper examination of these dynamics using a mixed-methods approach. Although prior work has demonstrated associations between having a darker complexion and receiving worse outcomes in the carceral state, no prior research to my knowledge has examined Black people's perceptions of and responses to policing as potentially varying by one's skin tone. Thus, I seek to begin answering the following questions: Do African Americans perceive race *and* skin color as informing police interactions? Is there variation in opinion based on one's own skin color and gender? Do many Black people support the incorporation of skin tone into anti-brutality movement messaging, or as a separate political movement? Does participation in political protests or marches vary by skin tone? Building from the theoretical expectations laid out in chapter 2, I expect that African Americans—and particularly those with darker skin—will view skin color as especially informative for police interactions. If skin tone is viewed as meaningful to such interactions as well as more broadly in society, then skin tone may also be relevant for thinking about anti-brutality movement organizing or protest participation.

Skin Color and Views about Policing

To get a broader understanding of how color may stratify political views in the realm of criminal justice, I turn to a combination of survey data alongside my in-depth interviews. I examine both general perceptions of whether or how color is believed to matter as well as how self-identified skin color may be systematically associated with those views. In contrast, prior research has largely focused on bureaucratic data associating darker skin and worse criminal justice outcomes. Assessing Black people's perceptions of and responses to policing as potentially varying by one's skin tone adds depth and richness to understandings of Black people's experiences. This is especially true for group members who may face additional stigmatization in the criminal justice system based on being both African American and darker-skinned.

There may also be further variation based on one's gender given stereotypes linking dark-skinned men with being physically imposing or inducing fear (Dixon and Maddox 2005; Maddox and Gray 2002). Below, I first turn to my interviews and then discuss the survey sources and evidence.

Throughout 100 in-depth interviews, participants describe multiple socially and politically relevant domains where they felt skin tone was meaningful. Any mention of a given topic or issue as being associated with skin color throughout the conversation—for example, stereotypes, dating, job opportunities, interpersonal interactions—was coded and then a categorization scheme was developed to organize these individual mentions into broader, related domains. The most frequently mentioned institutional domain involved policing and criminality-associated stereotypes.[2] Specifically, participants often referenced stereotypes that linked darker skin to greater perceived aggression or physical strength. Consistent with prior work, then, the stronger application of racialized stereotypes to those with darker skin leads to a "double penalty" for darker-skinned Black Americans (Dixon and Maddox 2005; Hochschild and Weaver 2007; Maddox and Gray 2002).

Complementing the growing body of evidence demonstrating the importance of skin color in criminal justice outcomes, the interviews underscore that many Black people are well aware of the importance of skin color and gender in interactions with police. Twenty-six percent of the total mentions of domains where color mattered involve policing or criminality-related stereotypes, with almost 60 percent of interviewees referencing these topics (n = 59; appendix table A3.7). Interview participants mentioned an understanding that police treat darker-skinned Black people more harshly than those with light skin because darker skin is perceived as more threatening. Stereotypes regarding physical strength, aggression, or appearing suspicious are perceived to lead to worse outcomes at the hands of police.

> I used to have a roommate. . . . He was a lighter skin, you know . . . He looked very, very biracial. I'm going to say that. So we were driving to the Walmart, I guess that was a long time ago, and we got stopped by the police. And when we got stopped by the police, you know he just was bold, I guess I would say, very much. And he was talking to the officer some type of way. I was scared and, you know, we just got a ticket and that was it. . . . I wouldn't say that he thought it was 'cause of his skin color. But I saw that it may have been because of his skin color.—22-year-old, brown-skinned man

> I don't know what it is about a darker-skinned African American, [police officers] feel automatically like they have to defend themselves more around a darker skin than a lighter skin.—31-year-old, light-skinned woman

> [My cousin] has a DUI. He has like 3 of them. He got pulled over with a pistol. He's very light. [The police] didn't throw him down. They was so nice to him. They just talked to him calm and they only gave him 60 days. You know, people usually get 5 years. 60 [days] and then he'll be out. But I feel like if he were my complexion . . . it would have been different.—34-year-old, dark-skinned man

Participants noted not only the importance of skin tone, but the combination of skin tone *and* gender in understanding police encounters. As psychologists Keith Maddox and Stephanie Gray (2002, p. 258) summarize, "In popular media sources, [Black] men are often depicted as gang-related criminals, whereas [Black] women are depicted as welfare mothers. According to our data, those with lighter skin tone are less closely associated with those images." Importantly, this is not to say that Black women, or darker-skinned Black women specifically, do not have concerning interactions with police. Black women are significantly more likely than their White female counterparts to be incarcerated (Pew 2008; 2023). While police interactions are fraught for Black women, there is an additional layer of tension for Black men given associations between maleness and perceived strength, criminality, and aggression. Consistent with this pattern, my interview participants frequently referenced the intersection of skin tone and gender on experiences with, or concerns about, policing. Regardless of the participant's gender, discussions of the negative association between darker skin tones and police interactions were largely focused on men's experiences:

> I've been in a situation a couple of times where it's like the police will mess with one of my [darker-skinned] friends before they mess with me. They'll ask me a couple of questions, get a couple answers, and move on. But they'll fuck with them and get rowdy with them and try to make them pop. And you weren't just talking crazy to me and trying to make me get upset, but now you talking to him being all aggressive with him? . . . You looking at me like I'm innocent because I'm a brighter skin tone than him and he had to do it because he's darker.—23-year-old, light-skinned man

> Let's take into consideration a Black man with dark skin. . . . I think that there's been studies that have proven that the natural fear inclination for a police officer for a darker Black man is on a totally different level than it is for the light skin Black man. When they see a Black man, and they won't release these studies, but when they see a darker man, they fear.—29-year-old, brown-skinned woman

> Black folks know that the darker you are as a man, the more likely you're going to be perceived as a threat, you know. . . . Even O.J. [Simpson], they darkened

his picture, you know what I'm saying? Just to make him more menacing.—39-year-old, brown-skinned man

Because I've had many encounters with police based on the way I look. [laughs] Just by my pure appearance. Law enforcement happen to have a lot of angst and curiosity and just plain profiling approach when it comes to dealing with me. And I have evidence and track record throughout my whole life. And it's all based on the way I look. And I know that I'm not the only one, you know? . . . So I can tell you about an experience when I was younger. I would say like 15. I was coming from work. I basically got accosted by the police, basically from all different corners. There was a helicopter in the air. There was two, three cars surrounded me. Everybody had a shotgun, their guns pointed at me. And telling me I fit the description of some person that's in the neighborhood shooting a gun. And I just came from work, you know? Just about 15, just because I'm coming from work and I look Black.—39-year-old, dark-skinned man

The evidence thus far underscores that Black Americans recognize that a combination of race, skin tone, and gender influence police treatment. To further examine how African Americans perceive these skin color dynamics—as well as how one's own appearance may be associated with recognition of targeted policing practices—I next turn to evidence from two national surveys. Many of the questions included in these surveys were informed by the interview conversations. These original surveys of African Americans were conducted in 2018 via Lucid (n = 1,825 Black participants, 92 percent of whom identify as monoracial African Americans) and 2019 via NORC AmeriSpeak's nationally representative panel (n = 1,045 monoracially Black participants).[3] As shown in appendix table A3.1, the demographics of both samples are largely comparable to those from the nationally representative ANES. Recall from my discussion of data sources used throughout the book in chapter 3 that these studies both included the Yadon-Ostfeld Skin Color Scale for participants to self-identify their skin tone. In both surveys, I included a question related to *Perceived Colorism among Police*. This item asks how often one believes the following statement is true: "Black people with darker skin receive harsher treatment by police compared to those with lighter skin" (response options: always, most of the time, about half of the time, some of the time, never).

As shown in table 4.1,[4] the pattern of survey evidence supports the qualitative evidence: 85 percent of Black respondents in the 2018 survey said that darker-skinned Black people are treated worse by police *at least half the time* compared with lighter-skinned Black people. A smaller but still sizable number of Black respondents in the 2019 survey—60 percent—indicated that darker-skinned people receive worse treatment at least half the time. In

TABLE 4.1: Perceived relationship between darker skin tone and frequency of worse police treatment

	2018 Lucid (n = 1,824)	2019 AmeriSpeak (n = 1,041)
Always	30	10
Most of the time	41	2
About half of the time	14	21
Some of the time	1	31
Never	3	9
Total	**100**	**100**

Note: Numbers are percentages totaling to 100%

other words, most Black people believe that darker-skinned people habitually receive worse treatment by police than their lighter-skinned counterparts. Combining across all three data sources, then, there is strong evidence that most African Americans perceive skin color, in addition to race, as strongly informing treatment by police.

Given the link between skin tone and stratification in a number of areas, including perceived racial prototypicality, stereotyping, socioeconomic outcomes, and heterogeneity in experiences at the hands of police, skin color may be especially salient to the views of darker-skinned Black Americans themselves. Because both of my original surveys include large African American samples and a self-reported measure of skin color via the Yadon-Ostfeld Skin Color Scale, this presents an opportunity to explore color-based subgroup dynamics.

Is one's own skin tone associated with beliefs regarding police treatment? Indeed, there are sizable differences in *Perceived Colorism among Police* based on participants' self-identified skin tone. The models estimated using the 2018 survey highlight that even after controlling for factors like socioeconomic status and racial group identity importance,[5] those who self-identified at the darker end of the skin color scale are 10 percentage points more likely to believe that it is common that police treat darker-skinned people worse than lighter-skinned Black people ($p < .001$; figure 4.1). Here, 36 percent of dark-skinned respondents report that police *always* treat darker-skinned people worse; in contrast, about 24 percent of light-skinned respondents said the same. This pattern is also present in the 2019 AmeriSpeak survey: self-identified darker-skinned respondents are 9 percentage points more likely than their lighter-skinned counterparts to believe that darker-skinned people are treated worse by police ($p < .06$). In combination, then, the lived experiences associated with one's skin color are clearly linked to views of police interactions.

There is also evidence that the combination of skin tone and gender influences perceptions of police treatment. Interestingly, however, there is mixed evidence across the two surveys about whether skin tone is more important for dark-skinned men or women. In the 2018 survey, the effect appears to be largely driven by dark-skinned Black women, who are 15 percentage points more likely than women at the lightest end of the spectrum to agree that darker-skinned people are routinely treated worse by police ($p < .001$; figure 4.1). For Black men in this sample, there is no association between skin tone and belief regarding police treatment; on average, men lean toward feeling that darker-skinned people are treated worse by police most of the time, regardless of their own skin tone. In the 2019 survey, though, there is less variation in Black women's views based on skin tone but suggestive evidence that Black men's views vary with their skin tone. Here, men at the darkest end of the spectrum are approximately 12 percentage points more likely than those at the lightest end of the spectrum to feel that police treat darker-skinned people worse ($p < .06$ one-tailed). It would be valuable for future

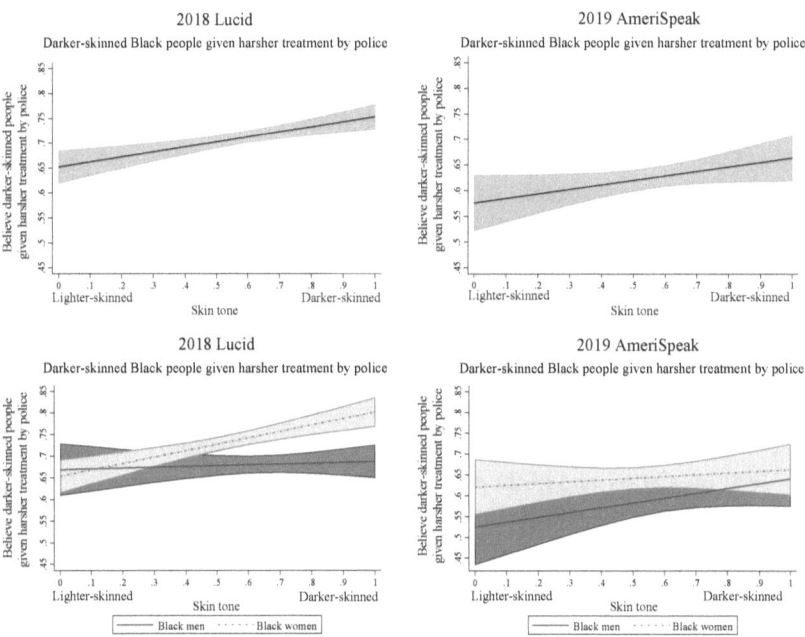

FIGURE 4.1. Belief That Police Treat Darker-Skinned People Worse
Note: OLS regression models in both datasets estimated with 95% confidence intervals and control for age, education, gender, income, region, partisanship, ideology, racial group importance, and survey design effects. Estimates from 2018 Lucid also control for Hispanic ethnicity, while estimates from 2019 AmeriSpeak also control for homeownership and unemployment.

research to continue interrogating the circumstances under which these varied color-gender differences in perceptions appear. Overall, the intersection of gender and darker skin appears meaningful with respect to perceptions of police treatment—in some cases for darker-skinned Black women and in other cases for darker-skinned Black men—whereas there is consistently little difference between the views of lighter-skinned Black men and women.

A final piece of survey evidence that is relevant to understanding this connection between race, skin tone, and perceptions of policing comes from the 2020 Collaborative Multiracial Post-Election Survey (CMPS). This national, online survey was conducted between April and August 2021 with nearly 15,000 completed interviews across ethnoracial groups, including 3,918 Black Americans born in the United States.[6] The 2020 CMPS included the Yadon-Ostfeld Skin Color Scale for participants to self-identify their skin tone, as well as a number of questions related to criminal justice-related experiences.

Consistent with prior work on skin tone, race, and policing, the CMPS data reveals that darker-skinned Black Americans are much more likely than their lighter-skinned counterparts to report personally being stopped by police, being charged or convicted of crimes, serving time in jail or prison, as well as having family or friends with similar experiences (see summary in table 4.2; full models in appendix table 4.1). While these items are related to criminal justice contacts and experiences, one CMPS item in particular is relevant to *perceptions* of police. This item asks participants whether they agree that "many officers see people like me as animals, thugs, and less than human." As shown in table 4.3, over 50 percent of Black participants agree with this statement that police view them as less than human. In contrast, only 13 percent of non-Hispanic Whites and just over 30 percent of Latinos in the 2020 CMPS hold similar views.

Do African Americans' views also vary based on skin tone? Moving from the lightest to darkest end of the Yadon-Ostfeld Skin Color Scale is associated with a 6 percentage-point increase in belief that police dehumanize people like the respondent ($p < .001$; figure 4.2). This is substantively equivalent to those at the darker end of the spectrum leaning toward agreeing that police view people like them as less than human, while those at the lightest end of the spectrum neither agree nor disagree with this sentiment. While this question does not explicitly invoke skin tone, it reveals that darker-skinned African Americans feel more dehumanized by police than their lighter-skinned counterparts.

Further examination reveals that it is Black men, specifically, who are driving this effect. As shown in the right panel of figure 4.2, darker-skinned Black men are 10 percentage points more likely than their light-skinned

TABLE 4.2: Summary of associations between darker skin and likelihood of criminal justice contact variables (2020 CMPS)

2020 CMPS				
	Stopped by police in car	Stopped by police on foot	Charged fine or fee for non-criminal infraction	Arrested or charged with crime
Skin tone	*	*	*	*
	Convicted of crime, even if not guilty	Charged a fine for criminal conviction	Been on probation or parole	Spent time in jail or prison
Skin tone	*	*	*	*
	Been the victim of a crime	Close friend/ family arrested or charged with crime	Close friend/ family convicted of a crime, even if not guilty	Close friend/ family spent time in jail, prison, probation, or parole
Skin tone	*	*	*	*

Note: * = statistically significant at 90 percent level of confidence with two-tailed test

TABLE 4.3: Distribution of responses to police dehumanization question (2020 CMPS)

"Many [police] officers see people like me as animals, thugs, and less than human"

	African Americans
	(n = 3,918)
Strongly agree	17
Agree	15
Somewhat agree	20
Neither agree nor disagree	26
Somewhat disagree	7
Disagree	7
Strongly disagree	8
Total	**100**

Note: Numbers are percentages totaling to 100%

male counterparts to report feeling that police view them as less than human ($p < .001$). On average, darker-skinned Black men are likely to agree that police dehumanize them, whereas light-skinned Black men lean toward neither agreeing nor disagreeing with this statement. Among Black women, there is no detectable effect of skin tone on feelings of dehumanization by police. Black women lean toward neither agreeing nor disagreeing that police dehumanize people like them. The importance of both skin tone and gender

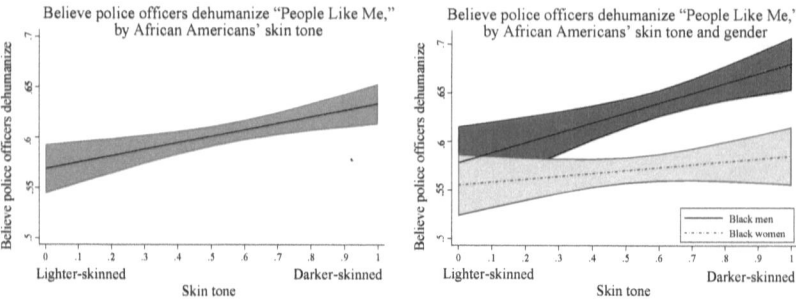

FIGURE 4.2. Belief That "Many [police] officers see people like me as animals, thugs, and less than human," by Skin Tone (2020 CMPS)

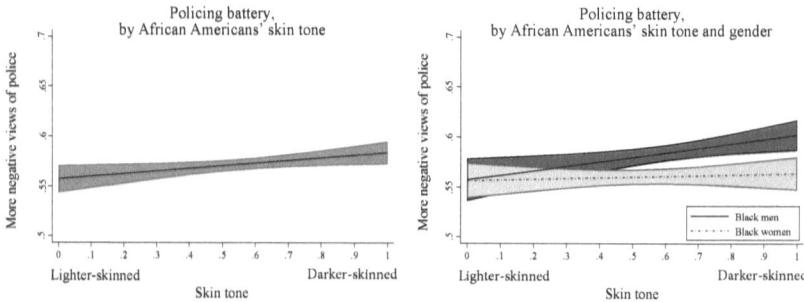

FIGURE 4.3. Index of Views toward Police (2020 CMPS)
Note: OLS regression models estimated with 95% confidence intervals and controls for gender, education, region, income, age, partisanship, ideology, homeownership, unemployment, racial group importance, and linked fate.

highlights the nuance associated with differing lived experiences based on multiple characteristics.

Next, I create a battery from multiple policing-related items included in the CMPS. These include a mixture of policy propositions—such as reducing police spending or removing police involvement from situations involving mental health issues—as well as attitudes about police; for example, whether police dehumanize people like the participant, whether police can be trusted, and whether police are able to do whatever they want (see appendix table 4.2 for a full list of the variables and question wording included in this scale). When looking at the overarching trends in views toward police, do similar patterns hold to what was observed on the dehumanization item specifically? Yes: I find that darker-skinned African Americans—and darker-skinned Black men in particular—hold more negative views of police than their lighter-skinned and female counterparts (see figure 4.3). African

Americans at the darkest end of the spectrum hold 3 percentage points more negative views of police in the aggregate compared with those at the lightest end of the spectrum ($p < .02$). This effect is even larger—at nearly 5 percentage points—when looking at darker-skinned men relative to lighter-skinned men ($p < .01$).

In combination, the qualitative and quantitative evidence underscores that African Americans are deeply aware of how both race and skin tone influence perceived police brutality. In addition to a general belief by Black participants that darker-skinned people receive worse police treatment, self-identified darker-skinned respondents are even more likely to believe this to be true. This further underscores the relationship between skin color and political views in domains where skin color is especially salient, complementing the findings from chapter 3. It suggests that mainstream discussions of the role of race in policing miss important subgroup nuances. The relationships examined here also serve the important role of confirming that subjective perceptions of police treatment among Black Americans are consistent with the objective reality demonstrated across prior studies that rely primarily on administrative data. All in all, these intertwined perceptions of skin tone and policing may lay a foundation for a potential skin tone identity to take shape, as I will examine in chapter 5.

Views of Movement Organizing around Colorism

Thus far, qualitative and survey evidence has demonstrated that skin tone is associated with how police are perceived to interact with Black people. Consistent with administrative evidence in prior research, Black people generally—and especially those with darker complexions—perceive that darker skin is associated with worse treatment at the hands of police. This association between skin color and views of policing suggests that skin color may also be associated with views of movement organizing in response to police brutality. Indeed, the Black Lives Matter (BLM) movement has crafted a multidimensional framework for understanding racialized experiences with police brutality. As political scientists Tabitha Bonilla and Alvin Tillery (2020, p. 2) summarize: "the most visible Black Lives Matter activists quickly coalesced around the view that intersectionality is the 'master frame' of the movement (Chatelain and Asoka 2015; Garza, Tometti, and Cullors 2014)." This has included drawing more attention to the marginalization of women and LGBT individuals, for example, through hashtags like #SayHerName and #BlackTransLivesMatter (Garza 2014; Tillery 2019). This strategy "opens our collective eyes to multiple dimensions of state and state-sanctioned anti-Black violence" (Lindsey 2015, p. 235). Serving as a contrast to prior movement-organizing tactics during the civil rights movement, these efforts suggest a belief that highlighting the nuances of racialized experiences with police are crucial toward raising awareness of the problems being faced and potential solutions (Lindsey 2015; Rickford 2016; Tillery 2019).

Given that high-profile BLM organizers intentionally incorporate the multidimensional experiences of Black individuals, one could imagine their messaging extending to include skin tone as another meaningful axis of marginalization. Complexion may be especially relevant in the digital age, when photos or video footage of police encounters are often recorded and widely circulated (Bonilla and Rosa 2015; Simonson et al. 2024; Torres 2019; Torres and Pugh 2024; Walsh and O'Connor 2019). With movement organizers recognizing and discussing gender and sexual orientation, is there public support for adding skin color to the conversation as well? Alternatively, do people prefer that the movement remain focused on race broadly, without highlighting subgroup disparities such as those based on skin color or gender? To answer these questions, I turn back to my interviews before examining complementary survey evidence.

Interview participants held an overwhelmingly positive view toward BLM, with nearly 75 percent of interviewees expressing support for the movement (n = 73). Given the BLM organizers' efforts to incorporate a more intersectional framework into the movement, I asked interview participants whether they felt that BLM should discuss subgroup disparities such as those based on skin tone.[7] This question came after hearing information about evidence of color-based disparities with respect to criminal sentencing, death penalty convictions, and other non-criminal justice domains.

The overwhelming response among interview participants was that race should remain the primary focus of BLM and that other characteristics—like skin color or gender—should not be used as part of the movement's messaging. Put differently, despite a majority of interviewees believing that police treat dark-skinned Black Americans worse, almost none felt that skin color should be incorporated into conversations about police brutality and responses by BLM. Feelings that BLM discussing subgroup disparities would serve as a distraction were almost universal—with nearly 90 percent of interviewees asked this question expressing this sentiment (n = 61):

> In a way, by only focusing on dark-skinned Black men, it takes away from lighter-skinned Black men still experiencing police brutality. Or just like Black women in general, who also experience a large amount of police brutality.—19-year-old, dark-skinned woman

If we focus on the complexities of gender and color, we lose—It causes more room for dissension in the movement between ranks and people, already more than what there was. So you sort of take it. Not take it, but you have to go with the bigger issues.—27-year-old, brown-skinned woman

I think that implicitly colorism probably does play a huge part in the movement. But I don't know how explicit those concerns are. I think we within the community know and recognize that. Who's being arrested, who's being beat up, who's being victimized in these situations. And we do notice their skin color. But I don't know—Like I said earlier, I don't know if it would be the wisest thing to say "Let's protect our dark-skin to medium-brown-skin African American brothers and sisters."—50-year-old, light-skinned woman

Running counter to BLM organizers' goals of intersectional messaging, then, most interview participants prefer that BLM maintain a focus on the broader racial group. These patterns complement recent work demonstrating challenges associated with the use of other subgroup messaging (Bonilla and Tillery 2020; Bunyasi and Smith 2019). While many interview participants recognized that the stereotypes associated with darker skin cause more challenges in police interactions, particularly among Black men, it did not translate into support for BLM taking up this issue. Thus, although participants across both sets of interviews recognized that darker-skinned people were often the victims of police brutality, many were also hesitant to believe that BLM should focus on subgroup disparities such as skin tone or gender. This sentiment is consistent with political scientist Cathy Cohen's (1999) seminal work highlighting that Black political actors embrace consensus issues (e.g., racial disparities) rather than cross-cutting issues that draw from multiple subgroup identities (e.g., color-based disparities among Black people, or Black women's issues) in an effort to prioritize perceived unity of the group.

Of course, this does not necessarily preclude a general openness to recognizing skin tone disparities or having a movement to respond to such disparities. It may simply mean that people do not believe that BLM is the appropriate venue for doing so. Accordingly, a separate question was asked regarding whether participants would support a movement related specifically to addressing color-based disparities in society. This question came shortly after participants were provided with some information about evidence of color-based disparities across social and economic domains, and was asked immediately prior to discussions of BLM.

Is there support for a separate movement focused on increasing awareness of or addressing color-based inequities? Here, there were clear distinctions between the two sets of interviews. This may be due, in part, to the timing, which seemed to influence perceptions of the power of social movements among interviewees: the first set of interviews occurred in 2016-2017, whereas the second set occurred in 2021, following the sustained summer 2020 protests. In the 2016-2017 interviews, about 30 percent of interview participants expressed support for the idea of a movement explicitly focusing on skin tone (n = 21). The remainder suggested that this was a bad idea because either it would be divisive within the African American racial group or was unnecessary.

> Well, I mean, we already have a bit of the Black Lives Matter movement dealing with [colorism], and that doesn't exactly discriminate between light skin and dark skin. And it has both sides coming together to, you know, fight for the injustices against Black people as a whole. So I think that's something. But I don't know if another movement exactly needs to start.—22-year-old, brown-skinned man

> That's scary. [INT: Scary?] It is because what I've seen so far with younger people is that they think it means not embracing the darkness but hating the light. Resenting—Instead of saying "Let's all join together," they say "Leave those people out. We're gonna embrace ourselves." And I don't like that.—50-year-old, light-skinned woman

> I do think that's needed. Because I know in my generation [colorism is still] there. I hear the kids talk about it. And I've thought to myself "That issue is still not addressed." We never really confronted it. The Black community never really confronted it.—59-year-old, brown-skinned woman

In the 2021 interviews, however, there was greater support for this idea. Nearly 80 percent of these interview participants said they would support a movement aimed at addressing colorism (n = 26). Importantly, though, while many people indicated an openness to a color-based movement, most opposed the idea of this movement being *political*. Rather, they emphasized the importance of a socially focused initiative to educate people about the history and continuing harms of colorism, as well as to open dialogues among African Americans about colorism:

> Yeah, I feel it's more a societal thing. It's like a social movement would be like more appropriate, 'cause I feel like it would be harder to . . . do a political movement. 'Cause—I don't know. I feel like it's already hard for like general, like racism to be recognized in Congress and stuff.—19-year-old, dark-skinned woman

> Yeah, I think that there should be [a color-based movement]. And that just goes back to—Like I said before, of loving yourself and having self-love. I think that, again, historically colorism was designed even during slavery to separate

us and to make us feel less than if you're a house-slave or a field-slave. . . . I think that that if there's gonna be a movement, it needs to be reminiscent of a psychological "Black Is Beautiful" movement, you know? It's that, you know, "love yourself and you're beautiful whoever you are." And I think if we can get past that, like I said we can get to the more impactful policies such as housing, health care, inequality, and classism.—20-year-old, dark-skinned man

I definitely think so. I think it's important people to be able to name things, you know? Like point to examples and experiences and like acknowledge that this is happening. . . . I think there would be some resistance, maybe more [among] light-skinned people, probably not among darker. They'd be probably like "We've been telling you this forever."—30-year-old, brown-skinned woman

I have to think about that [pause]. . . . My inclination is no. . . . You're either Black [laughs]—You know, regardless of how Black, you're Black.—55-year-old, brown-skinned man

Across all of these conversations, then, there is little support for either a color-based political movement or for the incorporation of intersectional frames within BLM to recognize colorism. This hesitancy to address colorism explicitly within a political movement like BLM fits with understandings of the challenges of addressing cross-cutting issues within any group (Cohen 1999; hooks 2000). Much of this hesitation stems from concerns that any such conversation will divide the group and weaken the movement's effectiveness. Do these patterns suggest a hesitancy to talk about skin tone, in part, because it has the potential to divide the group hold true in a national sample? To assess this, I turn to the *Skin Tone Distracts from Race* item in the 2019 AmeriSpeak survey. This item asks Black participants how often they feel this statement is true: "Talking about skin tone is just a way to divide Black people and keep us from talking about the bigger issue of race" (response options: always, most of the time, about half of the time, some of the time, never).

As shown in table 4.4, there is a general agreement that skin color can distract from broader issues of race. Here, 53 percent of Black respondents say skin tone is a distraction from race "most of the time" or "always." This finding underscores heterogeneity in perceptions that discussing skin color disparities may inhibit progress on resolving racial disparities. Despite a broad recognition that darker-skinned Black people face harsher treatment at the hands of police, respondents feel that discussing color-based disparities can distract from resolving racial disparities.

Like the earlier findings on *Perceived Colorism among Police*, one's self-identified skin color also informs one's views on this question. Consistent

TABLE 4.4: Perception that discussing skin tone distracts from discussing bigger issue of race

	2019 AmeriSpeak (%; n = 1,041)
Always	28
Most of the time	25
About half of the time	17
Some of the time	20
Never	10
Total	**100**

Note: Numbers are percentages totaling to 100%

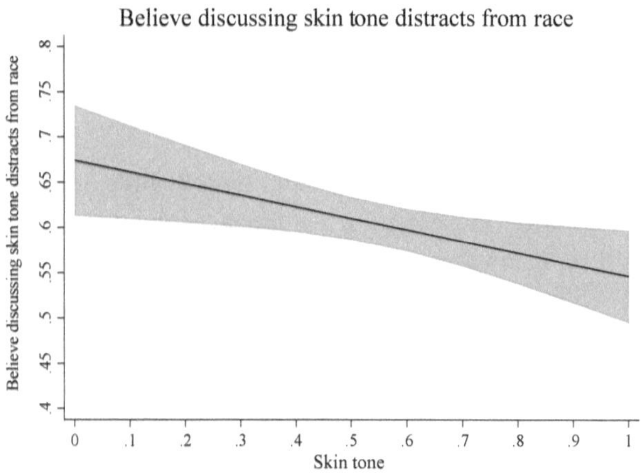

FIGURE 4.4. Belief That Discussing Skin Tone Distracts from Bigger Issue of Race, by Skin Tone (2019 AmeriSpeak)
Note: OLS regression model estimated with 95% confidence intervals and controls for gender, education, region, income, age, partisanship, ideology, homeownership, unemployment, racial group importance, and survey design effects.

with my theoretical framework, self-identified darker-skinned participants are 13 percentage points less likely than their lighter-skinned counterparts to believe that talking about skin color is a distraction from race ($p < 0.01$; figure 4.4). This is substantively equivalent to self-identified light-skinned Black people saying that skin tone distracts from race "most of the time" while dark-skinned Black people say this is the case only "half of the time." While many respondents exhibit a hesitancy to incorporate discussions of color alongside race, self-identified darker-skinned individuals are more open to discussing both axes of marginalization.

In sum, African Americans widely believe that police use skin color as a marker by which to gauge their interactions with Black people. Yet most interview participants oppose having BLM explicitly incorporate discussions of colorism into their messaging and do not favor the idea of a separate political movement focused on addressing colorism. While general reluctance exists across the board, darker-skinned Black Americans express greater openness to recognizing the importance of color alongside race. This hesitancy suggests mixed evidence for the continued relevance of the skin color paradox in political organizing. On one hand, color is viewed as strongly tied to the institutional domain of policing, and as demonstrated throughout chapter 3, closely associated with political attitudes in domains where color-based inequities are well known. This serves as a necessary foundation for potential political organizing responses. Yet, on the other hand, many African Americans prefer messaging tactics for BLM to focus only on racial disparities as opposed to acknowledging subgroup disparities based on color or gender; nor is there general enthusiasm for a color-based political movement. Is it possible that political mobilization can still occur based on skin tone even without skin tone being explicitly cued by organizers? I examine this next.

Skin Color and Protest Mobilization

I close this chapter with an examination of whether darker-skinned African Americans are more likely to participate in political protests. Given that skin color is associated with various attitudes, including those around criminal justice and experiences with police, it is plausible that skin tone could also be associated with one's willingness to head to the streets in protest. A broad literature demonstrates that group attachment and group threat can lead to protest mobilization (Ellemers et al. 1988; Ellemers, Van Knippenberg, and Wilke 1990; Tajfel and Turner 1986). And the effects of protest activities can have significant influence not only on the public's attitudes, but also on legislative responsiveness in the wake of protest (Gause 2022b; Gillion 2013; Lee 2002).

In the specific case of skin tone and political mobilization, the link between darker skin and more negative perceptions of police could serve as precursors to darker-skinned individuals being more likely to mobilize against police brutality because they perceive their group as unduly targeted by police. That is, the heightened salience of police brutality to darker-skinned African Americans may be associated with an increased motivation to express their discontentment on the issue during anti-brutality movements. Even though there may not be enthusiasm for political movements addressing colorism

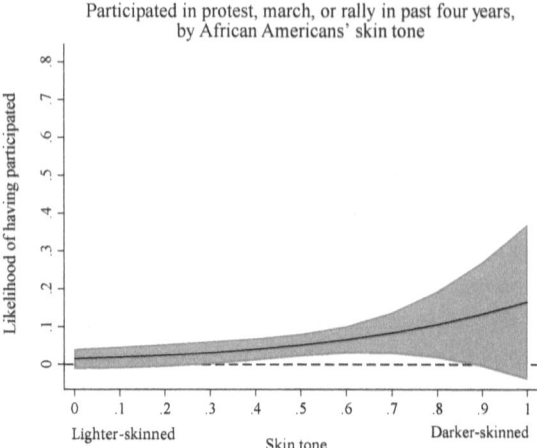

FIGURE 4.5. Likelihood of Having Participated in a Protest, March, Rally, or Demonstration in the Last Four Years, by Skin Tone (2012 ANES)
Note: Logistic regression model estimated with 95% confidence intervals and controls for gender, age, income, education, employment status, partisanship, ideology, region, homeownership, egalitarianism, linked fate, racial group importance, and interviewer's skin tone.

explicitly, this does not necessarily preclude an association between race, skin tone, and protest behavior.

To test whether there is a relationship between skin tone and political mobilization, I turn to two previously examined surveys: the 2012 ANES and the 2020 CMPS. The 2012 ANES does not contain many political participation items, but it does include an item related to participation in a protest or march within the past four years. While participation rates are relatively low—with only 6 percent of African Americans indicating they have protested in the last four years—there is still some suggestive evidence that darker-skinned African Americans are more likely to report participating in protests than their lighter-skinned Black counterparts ($p < .10$). As shown in figure 4.5, those at the darkest end of the color spectrum are nearly 10 times more likely than those at the lightest end of the spectrum to report participating in a protest in the last four years.

I next turn to the 2020 CMPS to examine whether there is a similar pattern of protest participation by skin tone. Because the CMPS was conducted in the spring and summer of 2021, it follows a crucial period of political upheaval and protest activity in the United States, the likes of which have not been seen since the civil rights era (Chudy and Jefferson 2021). The CMPS item asks respondents whether they have participated in a protest, march, rally, or demonstration since January 2020. The baseline levels of reported participation remain relatively low—though much higher than previous periods in a smaller timespan—with about 15 percent of African Americans reporting that they either believed or were certain that they had participated in some protest activity during this period.

Is there an association between skin tone and propensity to report participating in a protest in the 2020 CMPS? The data reveal a similar pattern of results to the 2012 ANES: darker-skinned Black Americans, on average, appear more likely to report participating in protests than their lighter-skinned counterparts. As shown in the left panel of figure 4.6, African Americans who self-identified at the darkest end of the Yadon-Ostfeld Skin Color Scale were about 4 percentage points more likely than those at the lightest end of the spectrum to report participating in protest activities since January 2020 ($p < .08$). Substantively this is equivalent to darker-skinned African Americans being nearly 1.5 times as likely as their lighter-skinned counterparts to report participating in protest activities.[8]

Because the CMPS includes such a large sample and the survey was completed after the summer 2020 protests, this provides a valuable opportunity to examine whether there are differences in protest activity among African Americans based on a combination of skin tone and gender. If it is the case that darker-skinned Black men are specifically targeted by police, are they also the gender-color subgroup most likely to report protesting? Interestingly, there are no color-based differences in reported participation in the CMPS among either Black men or women. In both cases, darker-skinned people appear somewhat more likely to participate in protests, but these differences are not statistically significant when broken down by gender. On average, Black

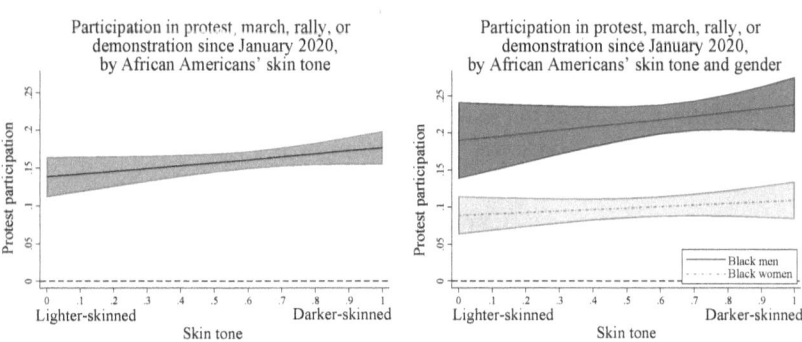

FIGURE 4.6. Likelihood of Having Participated in a Protest, March, Rally, or Demonstration since January 2020, by Skin Tone (2020 CMPS)

Note: Logistic regression model estimated with 95% confidence intervals and controls for gender, education, region, income, age, partisanship, ideology, homeownership, unemployment, racial group importance, and linked fate.

men are more likely than Black women to report participating in protests since January 2020, however ($p < .01$). It is possible that these gender imbalances may reflect expressive responding by men about the issue of police brutality. However, there is some evidence from other recent work that men are more likely to have protested than women (Gause and Arora, n.d.). Regardless, these differences in protest participation in the CMPS are not substantively large, but they suggest that darker-skinned Black people—and men in particular—may have felt especially frustrated by police violence and were more likely to take to the streets.

In combination, this evidence suggests that darker-skinned African Americans appear more likely to report participating in political protest activities. Despite the relatively low level of enthusiasm for incorporating skin tone into either existing or new political movements uncovered in the last section, skin tone appears to be associated with protest behavior in the 2010s and early 2020s. Even as protest activity increased relative to prior years, especially during summer 2020, there is some evidence that darker-skinned African Americans were still more likely to protest to express their voices. Given a recognition that both race and skin tone influence one's treatment in society, this suggests that skin tone is a politically potent undercurrent for political behavior. Moreover, it highlights that a color-based identity may exist among African Americans and this identity may be undergirding the political associations of skin tone.

Conclusion

The evidence throughout this and the prior chapter underscores that African Americans' skin color is associated with political views across multiple domains and also with a propensity to participate in political protests. While color-based discrimination across a range of institutions and institutional actors seems clear from the existing social scientific literature, this chapter makes an important and novel contribution by examining how *perceptions* of skin color and color-based treatment are associated with African Americans' views of police brutality, potential movement organizing, and participation in political protests. The domain of policing is a particularly important one given the fraught history connecting state-sanctioned violence against Black people through slave patrols across the South and associations between darker skin and heightened fear or intimidation (Dixon and Maddox 2005; Maddox and Gray 2002; Reichel 1988). In turn, policing and criminal justice issues may be associated with African Americans' political views, as well as serving as a foundation for development of a skin tone identity.

The qualitative and quantitative evidence both revealed that it is broadly recognized that police treat darker-skinned Black people worse than their lighter-skinned Black counterparts. Above and beyond these general perceptions, self-identified darker-skinned Black people are consistently more likely to believe this to be the case. There was also complexity regarding the connection between skin tone and gender, with dark-skinned men being most likely to report that police mistreat dark-skinned people in some cases while dark-skinned women are more likely to do so in other cases. There were no differences observed between lighter-skinned men and women in their perceptions, however. Future work would do well to continue teasing apart the intersections of race, skin tone, and gender on these issues. With respect to political participation, darker-skinned Black Americans appear more likely to participate in political protests, marches, and rallies across two surveys from 2012 and 2020. This suggests that observed differences in treatment based on skin tone serve to mobilize darker-skinned African Americans absent any explicit color-based messaging campaigns. Such protest activities can influence legislators' impressions of their constituents' salient concerns and issue priorities (Gause 2022a; 2022b).

These patterns raise interesting questions about Black political solidarity. Philosopher Tommie Shelby makes an argument consistent with the skin color paradox by contending that "what holds blacks together as a unified people with shared political interests is the fact of their racial subordination and their collective resolve to triumph over it" (2005, p. 56). In contrast to this view, the patterns presented throughout chapters 3 and 4 highlight widely recognized and sizable color-based variation in experiences and perceptions. While there continues to be a sense of subordination based on race among Black people, Black people *also* recognize that darker-skinned people are treated worse at the hands of police and more broadly in society. Thus, there is an acknowledgment that subordination based on skin tone intersects with racial subordination to powerfully shape lived experiences.

More consistent with the skin color paradox, however, is the hesitancy I found with openly discussing skin tone disparities through political movements such as BLM. This finding complements a growing set of literature highlighting a hesitancy among many African Americans to discuss subgroup disparities in anti–police brutality movement messaging (Bonilla and Tillery 2020; Bunyasi and Smith 2019). This seems to suggest that the skin color paradox persists with respect to political movement organizing around subgroup disparities such as skin tone or gender. Like other examinations of subgroup variation among African Americans such as political scientist Michael Dawson's examination of class (Dawson 1994), I find that despite attitude variation based on skin tone there remains a prioritization of the overarching racial group with respect to movement organizing tactics. Of course, this stands in contrast to BLM organizers' desire to avoid marginalization of certain subgroups by incorporating intersectional frames. It also presents challenges for naming and combatting colorism alongside racism while also increasing movement support. Efforts to prioritize the racial group as a whole without emphasizing disparate subgroup impacts—such as those based on skin tone—contribute to the persistence of marginalization of these subgroups (Cohen 1999).

Overall, the evidence reveals that skin tone holds a significant relationship with political views, experiences with police, and protest participation, even after accounting for sociodemographic factors like income, education, and racial group attachment in the statistical models. The independent effect of skin tone above and beyond these socioeconomic factors suggests that something else may be at work here beyond one's lightness or darkness alone. That is, perhaps it is not only skin color as an attribute doing this work, but one's attachment to a skin tone group—that is, one's *skin tone identity*. Indeed, it seems plausible that a color-based identity could develop in response to the historical emphasis placed on skin tone, perhaps particularly through enduring challenges associated with race, skin tone, and treatment by police. Although skin tone identity has not been previously assessed, I conceptualize and measure it in the next chapter.

5

Skin Tone Identity:
A Theoretical Framework and Measurement

> I think that the same way that privilege operates for a lot of different social identities, skin color privilege operates. I don't think it's any mistake that I've made it to where I am based on my skin color.
> 26-YEAR-OLD, light-skinned woman interview participant

"You said *more positive* treatment because of my skin color?" asked Eric, a 21-year-old, dark-skinned male interview participant. During the course of each conversation, participants were asked to share stories related to experiences with colorism that they'd heard through family, friends, or experienced first-hand. This included a prompt for negative color-based experiences, after which Eric quickly came up with a story drawn from an experience his friend had with respect to dating. That story complemented his earlier references to historical manifestations of colorism and his discussion of present-day instances of colorism in the media. An additional prompt then asked about examples of positive treatment based on skin tone. Eric made a skeptical face and took a long pause following this question, something he had not done previously in the conversation. He continued:

> Honestly, it's really difficult to think of positive times. But if I would have to like, I guess, try to think, conjure up one, it would have to be—No, I can't even think, I can't even think of one.... I used to be so insecure about how dark my skin tone is.... Over these past couple of years of being in college, being surrounded by darker-skinned Black folk, brown-skinned Black folk who loved themselves and who won't settle for less when it comes to, I guess, partners or people who love them for themselves. And, just seeing that, I guess that has encouraged me to find that love for myself.

Consistent with broader themes from these interviews, Eric expressed a recognition of color-based stratification that he'd witnessed, learned about, or experienced personally through the course of his life, underscoring the importance of skin tone in multiple aspects of his life and especially on his journey of self-acceptance.

Recognizing the broad impact of skin tone complements the evidence from the last two empirical chapters demonstrating a meaningful association between African Americans' skin tone and political views. In combination with the growing body of colorism research across the social sciences, then, this pattern of findings underscores the range of perceptions and outcomes associated with the lightness or darkness of one's skin color. A growing literature has amassed meaningful evidence linking skin tone with various outcomes, including economic outcomes, criminal justice experiences, health outcomes, and more. And as I showed in the last two chapters, skin tone is linked with political views in many of these same domains. So how is it that skin color comes to be meaningfully linked with the political views of African Americans? I posit that skin tone is not just a characteristic or attribute but a meaningful social identity that can influence one's views.

Recall from chapter 2 that institutions throughout history have placed a great deal of emphasis on skin color. This includes organizations using the paper bag test as a metric prior to admission, as well as bureaucratically by Census enumerators to assess one's racial categorization and through shifting legal definitions of Whiteness and non-Whiteness hinging on one's skin tone (Davenport 2018; Haney Lopez 1997; Russell, Wilson, and Hall 1993). In turn, skin tone was taken up as a meaningful symbol of status and influenced access to certain Black social organizations, but also interpersonal interactions up to and including dating and marriage possibilities (Bodenhorn 2006; Reece 2018a). Given this background, it seems plausible that African Americans' skin tone could be internalized as meaningful to one's sense of self. Of course, identities are understood to be multifaceted and heavily influenced by interpersonal experiences (Burke 1980; Davenport 2016; Foote 1951; Stryker 1968; 1980; Stryker and Serpe 1982). This suggests that a color-based identity will not be evenly distributed across the skin tone spectrum. A darker complexion is more closely associated with prototypes of Blackness, which, in turn, suggests that racialized stereotypes will be applied more rigidly to African Americans with darker complexions than to those with lighter complexions. For darker-skinned African Americans, the combination of clear categorization within the Black racial group, stronger application of racialized stereotypes, and the color-based status associations all increase the likelihood that this group will develop a psychological attachment to a skin tone identity.

Throughout the remainder of this chapter, I develop a theoretical framework suggesting that skin tone may be a social identity and begin assessing the underpinnings of a potential skin color identity. Turning to a combination of interview and open-ended survey items, I explore how people recognize and understand skin color groups, as well as some ways that people appear to signal their attachment to these groups. Subsequently, I develop survey questions to measure skin tone identity importance. Drawing from multiple large national samples of African Americans, I consistently find that more than 50 percent of Black people report their skin color as important to their sense of self. This is especially true for darker-skinned African Americans. I also assess whether measuring skin tone identity is just another way of measuring racial identity or self-reported skin tone, demonstrating that this is not the case. Thus, skin tone identity appears to be a distinct construct and a complementary social identity to racial identity. In the final portion of the chapter, I examine what sociodemographic factors are associated with the propensity to report holding a stronger skin tone identity. This lays a foundation for examining the potential links between skin tone identity and political views in chapter 6.

Skin Tone as an Identity

Given skin color's importance in society, I argue that it may not only influence one's lived experiences and political views, but also one's sense of identity. The combination of race and skin tone has operated as a means through which societal stratification and gatekeeping occurred for African Americans in the United States. This stratification dates to the institution of slavery, but also extends into the present day in terms of disparate levels of wealth, health, and criminal justice contacts, among others (Monk 2021). Skin tone, then, operates as a form of bodily social capital in American society such that complexion serves "as embodied markers or cues of social categories and perceived social status" (Monk 2018, p. 5). This line of thinking is consistent with observed efforts toward social closure throughout history, including color-based homogamy in marriages—i.e., lighter-skinned Black people marrying other lighter-skinned Black people—and formation of elite African American social groups based on skin tone. Recall from chapter 2 that various roots within the Roots of Race conceptualization developed in my prior work are meaningful identities, including identification with one's categorical racial group, political groups, or religious groups (Ostfeld and Yadon 2022). I extend the argument in this project by positing that skin color, too, is a meaningful sociopolitical identity.

Every person holds a combination of identities. Indeed, "when attributes are visible, membership in the categories based on them will also be visible" (Chandra 2006, p. 417). It is also the case that the relevance or importance of a given identity is dynamic over time and across situations (Citrin and Sears 2009; Garcia-Bedolla 2007; Garcia-Rios, Pedraza, and Wilcox-Archuleta 2019;

Montoya et al. 2021; Robinson 2023; Turner et al. 1987). As noted by sociologist Mary Waters, "racial and ethnic identities are not zero-sum entities; it is possible to hold several at any one time, and they are very clearly situational. In one situation a person can feel very American, at another time Irish, and at yet another time white" (Waters 1999, p. 47). This pattern is especially apparent in literature about how racial identity operates in distinct ways alongside ethnicity, gender, immigration status, class, and/or sexual orientation, for example (Brown 2014b; Brown and Lemi 2021; Cohen 1999; Crenshaw 1990; Dawson 1994; Gay 2004; Greer 2013; hooks 2000; Simien and Clawson 2004; Smith 2014). This background underscores that a color-based identity need not necessarily compete with or supersede one's racial identity. Instead, it is possible that both can be meaningful to a person's sense of self, with varied importance or salience over time or across contexts.

The value associated with any given identity is also dynamic. In the case of skin tone, the lightness and darkness of complexion can be viewed differently depending on the social setting or people involved. It is not the case that darker skin is *always* associated with worse social outcomes or uniformly negative assessments while lighter skin is *always* associated with better social outcomes and uniformly positive assessments. For example, a dark complexion may be valued negatively by White hiring managers or in predominantly White school settings. In other contexts, though, darker skin holds positive value; for example, darker skin is associated in some cases with perceptions of being more racially "authentic" among African Americans. In terms of dating, darker-skinned Black men may benefit from perceptions of being physically stronger or more loyal (Hunter 2005; Monk 2015). It is also not purely an intra-racial versus inter-racial dividing line that determines what value is placed on skin tone. In some majority Black contexts, darker skin can be viewed negatively—for example, with respect to being considered for inclusion in an elite social group like the Jack and Jill, or being subjected in the past to a brown paper bag test for admission to HBCUs like Howard University or Spelman College—while in other contexts, lighter-skinned Black people may be viewed with suspicion or feel a sense of not truly belonging to the racial group because their appearance differs from the group prototype (Graham 1999; Hunter 2005; Russell, Wilson, and Hall 2013).

Thus, the value assigned to skin tone can vary based on context and group composition. As sociologist Ellis Monk summarizes, "As a variant of subjective social status, self-rated skin color measures individuals' dynamic and relational sense of status in the social circles and contexts they live out their lives" (2015, p. 434). Consistent with my perspective, then, this suggests that while assessments of skin tone may vary to some extent by context—for example, someone identifying as the lightest person in their family, but also as one of the darker-skinned kids in school—one's self-reported skin tone and skin tone identity provide valuable insight into how people see themselves as fitting into the world. The colorism literature demonstrates that Black people have developed cognitive constructs associated with skin tone. And, as I demonstrate later in this chapter, these constructs also correspond to a sense of emotional attachment to color-based groups. Capturing how people understand their self-assessed skin tone or their level of skin tone identity in their local environment sheds light on how people also perceive their broader views and experiences.

Complementing prior work arguing for the importance of investigating the diverse experiences of people within shared racial categories based on factors such as gender or immigration status, I argue that the combination of race and skin tone is worthy of closer attention. Complicating traditional discussions of categorical racial groups, adding skin tone to the conversation highlights that race or racialized attributes are often viewed and experienced in a gradational fashion. Given the association of darker skin with closer proximity to Blackness and lighter skin with closer proximity to Whiteness, even those within the same categorical racial group ("Black") but at opposite ends of the color spectrum will have very different lived experiences. A great deal of attention has been paid to skin tone differences throughout our country's history, and colorism has been absorbed into the national psyche. In turn, I expect that this foundation and the value repeatedly associated with skin tone may result in the development of a *color-based identity* among African Americans.

Given the use of skin tone as a marker of race, I posit that its prominent historical importance and difficulty to change (i.e., "stickiness") lead to skin tone's development as a meaningful identity in its own right. For darker-skinned African Americans, in particular, a combination of factors—including the salience of color as an attribute, clear categorization within the Black racial group, stronger application of racialized stereotypes, and the more stigmatized status associated with darker skin—should lead to a heightened attachment to a color-based identity relative to those with lighter skin. In other words, if racialized treatment occurs in a gradational fashion based on a combination of categorical race and one's complexion, those at the darker end of the spectrum may face additional marginalization in mainstream society relative to those at the lighter end of the spectrum. In turn, those darker-skinned individuals who perceive and experience this stigmatization based on skin tone are likely to develop a strong sense of attachment not only to their racial group but also to their skin tone group. By contrast, African Americans with a lighter complexion face stigmatization based on their categorical race in mainstream society, but not with respect to their skin tone. Consequently, a color-based identity is less likely to be salient to them. In short, while Black people of all complexions face discrimination based on race, those with dark skin often face an *additional* layer of discrimination based on skin tone that may develop into a stronger sense of skin tone identity.

Two elements must be present for a color-based identity to not only exist but also be politically meaningful. The first is a recognition of identification with color-based groups. While this is a necessary foundation for any identity, the literature demonstrates that simple group membership or identification is insufficient to produce an identity-to-politics link (Lee 2007; McClain et al. 2009). The second component that is necessary to create this link is a sense of recognition that one's identity can be politicized—that is, the group identity is both relevant and meaningful for politics. This politicization can occur in multiple ways, including elite communication, intergroup conflict, the allocation of resources to groups, and protest or organizational efforts (Mora 2014; Valenzuela and Michelson 2016; Zepeda-Millán and Wallace 2013). Below, I outline how both of these components map onto skin color as a potential identity. This is important in laying a foundation for how a color-based identity might be politically meaningful. Just as I expected darker skin to be associated with more liberal views on political issues where colorism is more salient, I expect that a color-based identity should be especially meaningful to darker-skinned African Americans—and that this group should be most concerned about colorism and most supportive of anti-colorist policies.

GROUP MEMBERSHIP AND IDENTIFICATION: SKIN COLOR AS A CASE

Social psychologist Henri Tajfel defined a social identity as "the individual's knowledge that he belongs to certain social groups together with some emotional and value significance to him of this group membership" (Tajfel 1972, p.272). Importantly, group identifications provide a mental structure for individuals to navigate and participate in the social and political world. Two theories at the foundation of understanding group identities and intergroup relations are social identity theory and social categorization theory (Tajfel 1974; 1981; Tajfel and Turner 1979; 1986). The hierarchical nature of groups and the relative security of a group's position are important elements leading to the expression of a social group identity (Tajfel and Turner 1979; Terry and Hogg 1996). A need for positive self-regard or enhanced self-esteem is thought to motivate a desire to view one's in-group positively. Thus, when an individual feels a group they belong to is distinct from and better than other out-groups, their self-image as a group member is enhanced (Abrams and Hogg 1988; Tajfel and Turner 1986). Similarly, social categorization theory argues that people have a hard-wired tendency to draw on perceived group norms when classifying themselves. This means that group prototypes attempt to minimize in-group differences while maximizing intergroup differences (Terry and Hogg 1996).

This desire to maintain a positive image is true even among stigmatized groups. Members of marginalized groups must develop strategies to deal with threats to their social identity and the group's status (Jefferson 2023; Major and O'Brien 2005; Pérez and Vicuna 2023). Navigating the stigmatization of one's social identity groups is especially important given the differential power, privilege, and opportunity across groups. For example, political scientist Cathy Cohen (1999) theorizes the existence of "secondary marginalization," through which the needs of certain Black subgroups are not prioritized by Black elites. This is, in part, based on concerns that the (perceived) embarrassing "secrets" of the group being brought to light publicly would make it harder for other group members to be fully incorporated into the mainstream or upper echelons of society. This argument underscores the understanding that a group's status within the racial hierarchy is influenced by perceptions of its most stigmatized members. In turn, some members of stigmatized groups can serve to reinforce the existing hierarchy by engaging in secondary marginalization of their own group members. Political scientist Hakeem Jefferson (2023, p. 6) astutely notes that "these Black Americans believe that if group members behave better and carry themselves better, society will treat Black people better."

But, what constitutes an identity? The literature highlights that identities have two primary components: one *cognitive* and the other *affective* (Cameron 2004; Citrin and Sears 2009; Klandermans et al. 2002; Tajfel 1981). The cognitive component of a social identity requires self-categorization into the group: recognition that Groups A and B exist and that a person fits into a given group (Klandermans et al. 2002). While a given group may be recognized, it does not necessarily mean that one associates closely with said group. Thus, the second component—the affective dimension—is typically regarded as the most meaningful indicator of group attachment (Citrin and Sears 2009; Klandermans et al. 2002). It defines the psychological impact of group membership, concern about the well-being of the group, and even the ways in which perceptions of the group impact perceptions of the self. Research across identities reveals that stronger group identification is frequently associated with greater political cohesion. This includes a greater likelihood of internalizing normative group beliefs, adopting policy positions that benefit the group, and even protest behavior (Conover and Feldman 1984; Klandermans et al. 2002; McClain et al. 2009; Sears et al. 2003; Simon et al. 1998; Tate 1994). Thus, this affective component serves as a foundation for the politicization of group identities.

If skin color is a social identity, it would need to exhibit both a cognitive and affective component. Skin tone is certainly a meaningful marker within the African American community with research dating back to the 1940s finding a common set of names and stereotypic attributes to describe varying colors and color-based groups within the Black community. The names themselves reveal the more negative connotations associated with darker skin (*rusty black, burnt, blue-black, charcoal*) as compared with descriptors of lighter-skinned Black people (*bright, light, high yellow, fair*; Parrish 1946; Wilder 2010, 2015; Wilder and Cain 2011). The color names and associated stereotypes have remained consistent over time; for example, with stereotypical portrayals of lighter-skinned Black people as more attractive, more intelligent, more trustworthy, and more capable (Hunter 2005; Wilder 2010; 2015).

The consistency of color-based stereotypes and status connotations over time could also heighten any group-based attachment. This could manifest either in taking pride in positive assessments or twisting negative stereotypes to be more positive, as expected by social identity theory. For example, darker skin can be empowering in some contexts; it is often viewed as more prototypical for African Americans and can be associated with greater racial authenticity within Black communities (Harvey et al. 2005; Maddox and Gray 2002; Greer 2013; Gilroy 1993; Maddox 2004). This authenticity can serve as a form of empowerment, allowing darker-skinned Black people to be viewed as speaking with more authority on certain issues or taking on leadership positions working on behalf of the racial group (Hogg 2001; Hunter 2007; Medow and Zander 1965). Darker skin may serve as a point of pride through which Black people can embrace not only their race but also an ideological commitment to the racial group and a distancing from Whiteness. Some evidence suggests that darker-skinned people may have a stronger sense of racial identity, although this has not been consistent across studies (Harvey et al. 2005; Hughes and Hertel 1990; but see chapter 3 as well as Hochschild and Weaver 2007; Hutchings et al. 2016). In combination with the status connotations and application of racialized stereotypes varying on the basis of both race and color, a color-based identity may be especially salient to darker-skinned African Americans.

Recall that affective attachment is also necessary for politicization of a color-based identity. In addition to evidence of consistent color-based categorization and attributes among African Americans, there is good reason to believe this affective component also exists. Of course there have been historical efforts to carve out differential access to organizations and opportunities based on skin tone—be they religious, social, or educational in nature (see chapter 2 as well as Gatewood 1990; Monk 2021). This includes evidence of high rates of intermarriage among light-skinned African Americans historically, which is viewed as consistent with broader tendencies for marriages to occur among people of similar social, economic, or educational backgrounds in an effort to enhance one's legacy and status (Bodenhorn 2006). These sustained efforts to differentiate by skin tone point not only to status and value associations, but to the development of potential emotional attachment as well.

Colorism research also highlights the onslaught of messages linking Whiteness and/or lightness as the alleged "ideal" of beauty, purity, and intelligence (Glenn 2009; Hall 1995; Hunter 2002, 2021). These messages are internalized through some combination of interpersonal interactions, as well as engagement with various media sources beginning in childhood and continuing through early adulthood (Burnett and Sisson 1995; Clark and Clark 1940; Glenn 2009; Harvey et al. 2005; Harvey, Tennial, and Hudson Banks 2017; Hess and Torney 1967; Robinson and Ward 1995; Russell, Wilson, and Hall 2013; Sears 1983; Spencer 1982). Given the highly visible and easily accessible nature of skin tone, various media and pop culture sources—from music to movies to social media to advertisements—highlight, implicitly and explicitly, the value placed on lighter skin (Boepple and Thompson 2016; Glenn 2009). This even includes the use of hashtags like #TeamLightSkin and #TeamDarkSkin on social media to denote color-based groups (Williams 2016). These types of labels signal identification with color-based groups, attribution of group labels to others, and discussion of issues related to skin tone more broadly.

In sum, a combination of historical associations, efforts toward social closure, media cues, and interpersonal interactions points to fertile ground for skin color to become a meaningful social identity. As with other group identities, there is likely variation in how important or unimportant a color-based identity is across individuals. I explore these expectations further in the next section.

NUANCES OF A POLITICIZED COLOR-BASED IDENTITY AMONG AFRICAN AMERICANS

Theorizing about the layered manifestations of marginalization across identity groups—including race and gender—suggests that combinations of identities contribute to different perceptions, lived experiences, and relative identity importance (e.g., Cohen 1999; Collins 1989; Crenshaw 1990; hooks 2000). Just as racial identification is typically less salient for dominant groups in society than minoritized groups (Gurin 1985; Wong and Cho 2005), a color-based identity should work in a similar fashion. The strength of one's color-based identity should be influenced by one's own skin tone. Just as Black Americans are more likely to hold a stronger racial identity than Whites given the power and status differentials, on average, darker-skinned Black people should be more likely to embrace a color-based identity than their lighter-skinned Black counterparts. Specifically, the combination of clear categorization within the Black racial group, stronger application of racialized stereotypes given their darker complexion, and the status associations of complexion all increase the likelihood that darker-skinned Black Americans will internalize color as a meaningful part of their identity (Barth 1981; Turner et al. 1987; Huddy 2001).

Building from self-categorization theory, stronger identities are developed among group members who are more similar to the prototype (Hogg 1996, 2001b; Huddy 2001a; Lakoff 2008; Turner et al. 1987). Consistent with this, darker skin is among the constellation of features viewed as more prototypically African American (Gilroy 1993; Greer 2013; Harvey et al. 2005; Maddox and Gray 2002). Given the association between darker skin and greater perceived racial authenticity (Anderson and Cromwell 1977; Brunsma and Rockquemore 2001; Hunter 2005; 2007), skin color may be especially salient for darker-skinned Black Americans. A color-based identity, then, may also be internalized as more meaningful to this group.

Proximity from a racial border and external labeling are also likely to influence identity formation. As political scientist Leonie Huddy notes: "If group membership is obvious to others, it will be more difficult for a group member to avoid being labeled as such. . . . Less permeable group boundaries and a higher incidence of external labeling should increase the likelihood that a group member will internalize group identity" (2001a, p. 140). Consistent with this perspective, lighter-skinned Black people are likely to have more permeable boundaries around their racial identification, particularly in a shifting racial landscape. In turn, this provides more potential opportunities for light-skinned people to shift how they identify—or portray their identities—across contexts. In contrast, those with darker skin have greater proximity from a racial border and thus less permeable boundaries; they will consistently be labeled as African American. Where group boundaries are relatively impermeable, lower-status group members often redefine status by identifying more strongly with the stigmatized group to offset the effects of social exclusion (Ellemers et al. 1988; Ellemers, Van Knippenberg, and Wilke 1990). This, too, suggests that skin tone identity should be especially meaningful to darker-skinned Black people.

Importantly, people have a desire to find balance between fitting into a group and being perceived as individually distinctive (Brewer 1991; Hornsey and Jetten 2004). Optimal distinctiveness theory contends that "social identity derives from a fundamental tension between human needs for validation and similarity to others (on the one hand) and a countervailing need for uniqueness and individuation (on the other)" (Brewer 1991, p. 477). This can result in people exhibiting views or behaviors that seek to find a happy medium between full assimilation to the group and complete distinctiveness from the group—that is, achieving an optimal distinction. People can, for example, identify with subgroups within a given group, identify with a group perceived as not being part of the mainstream, or hold a perception that their group is especially unique (Hornsey and Jetten 2004). With respect to racial groups, of course, there are important attributes that intersect with race and influence one's experiences, including gender, class, religion, and skin color. As described by sociologist Tressie McMillan Cottom (2019, p.51): "I am dark, physically and culturally. My complexion is not close to whiteness and my family roots reflect the economic realities of generations of dark-complexioned black people. We are rural, even when we move to cities. Our mobility is modest. Our out-marriage rates to nonblack men are negligible. Our social networks do not connect to elite black social institutions. When we move around in the world, we brush up against the criminal justice system." Thus, skin tone may serve as a defining attribute that influences how people think of themselves and, in turn, increases the likelihood that skin tone will be a meaningful subgroup identity that serves as a point of distinction from the larger group.

As noted earlier in the chapter, context should be highly important for determining when skin tone identity may be more or less meaningful. If a Black person is in the presence of an entirely White group, for example, their racial identity is likely to be more salient. Still, the intersection of race and color may also influence to some extent how comfortable or uncomfortable they feel (Bailenson et al. 2008; Blair et al. 2002; Blair, Judd, and Chapleau 2004; Eberhardt et al. 2004, 2006; Goff et al. 2008; Harvey et al. 2005). In a setting among other African Americans, attributes besides race are likely to be more salient. For example, in a university with mostly Black students, darker skin is associated with more positive value in the forms of greater peer acceptance and higher self-esteem (Harvey et al. 2005). In some contexts, then, darker skin may serve as a source of "optimal distinction" by signaling greater racial authenticity and pride.

If there is recognition that the combination of race *and* skin tone influences one's experiences—such that perceptions or stereotypes are applied in a more continuous rather than categorical fashion based on the extent to which one is seen as being more prototypical of a racial group—then both identities may be brought to mind with respect to certain social and political views. I expect that darker-skinned Black Americans should adopt a stronger attachment, on average, to a color-based identity than those with lighter skin. Consistent with my theorizing and evidence from earlier in the book that darker-skinned African Americans observe that their group faces additional marginalization in society and consequently hold more liberal issue positions than their lighter-skinned counterparts, the application of a color-based identity should be similarly apparent in domains where color-based disparities are especially pronounced—for example, issues involving education, income, or criminal justice. If this is true, then skin tone identity may serve as the conduit through which skin tone is associated with varied political views among African Americans. Darker-skinned people with a stronger color-based identity should be especially concerned about colorism and most supportive of anti-colorist policies.

To be clear, my argument is *not* that skin tone identity will supersede racial identity in importance, but that it may serve as an additional identity that is salient under certain circumstances. It is worth underscoring that Black people of all skin tones face racial discrimination. Black people with darker skin also bear the additional burden of color-based discrimination in a society that emphasizes the value placed on lightness of skin tone. As a result, lighter-skinned individuals should have a different relationship with skin tone identity than those with darker skin. While lighter-skinned Black Americans receive some advantages in White society relative to their darker-skinned counterparts, they can be met with skepticism within the Black community about their degree of belonging or authenticity (Hunter 2005, 2007). One way in which this may be combatted is by attempts to signal their "Blackness" to others in the racial group (Brown and Lemi 2021; Brunsma and Rockquemore 2001; Hunter 2005; 2007), which may happen through expressions of their social or political views.

Consequently, there are two potential ways a color-based identity might operate among lighter-skinned Black individuals. When receiving information about color-based disparities, one possibility is that people with lighter skin could either move to being more protective of their privileged status based on skin tone. For example, if light-skinned African Americans feel that their status is threatened—such as by a shift from focusing on racial discrimination to addressing color-based discrimination—then their skin color may become more salient and meaningful. As expected in the broader identity literature, this status threat may result in more negativity toward dark-skinned African Americans and views that more negative outcomes for darker-skinned people are due more to personal shortcomings than to structural explanations (Ellemers 1993; Mummendey and Schreiber 1983; Tajfel and Turner 1979; 1986). In turn, this may result in decreased support for policies aimed at reducing color-based inequities.

Conversely, the interconnected nature of race and skin color could work in ways distinct from other overlapping identities. Lighter-skinned people may recognize that discrimination against darker-skinned African Americans serves to harm and disadvantage the racial group. In this case, when reminded of the pernicious effects of colorism, light-skinned Black people may go against their own potential color-based self-interest to advance the racial group's interest. This may be especially important toward signaling attachment to the racial group, given concerns or stereotypes about lighter-skinned people as less racially authentic (Harvey et al. 2005; Hunter 2005; 2007). Although advocating on behalf of resolving color-based disparities that disproportionately impact their darker-skinned Black counterparts would threaten their privileged status based on skin tone, they may feel that such efforts will benefit the entire racial group.

In brief, I expect that skin tone identity will be meaningful to many African Americans. For darker-skinned African Americans, the salience of color as an attribute, the more stigmatized status associated with darker skin in many contexts, and less flexible labeling options should lead to a heightened attachment to a color-based identity. This should, in turn, lead to political associations with skin tone such that darker-skinned people are more supportive of policies and issues where colorism is especially salient. In contrast, lighter-skinned African Americans may also take up a color-based identity, but the directionality and impacts of this identity are less clear. I consequently propose competing expectations about whether light-skinned Black people will seek to maintain their color-based privilege or to support efforts toward racial advancement by allying with darker-skinned identifiers. As introduced in chapter 2, the central arguments and testable implications of this book are reiterated in table 5.1. The full table is included for ease of reference, with the key portions related to skin tone identity covered in this chapter and chapter 6. In the next section, I begin to examine whether skin tone meets the cognitive and affective criteria necessary for identity formation.

TABLE 5.1: The skin color politics theoretical framework and roadmap of the book

Chapters 3 and 4	Chapter 5	Chapter 6
Central argument		
Skin color will be associated with political issues in instances where color-based discrimination is more pronounced, such as education, income, or policing-related issues.	Skin color will be a meaningful social identity to many African Americans.	Skin tone identity should be related to social and political views that explicitly invoke skin tone.
		Further, if skin tone identity works in a fashion similar to that of other identities such as race, class, or gender, then it should be possible not only to make skin color salient but also to influence subsequent political perceptions after asking people about their level of skin tone identity.
Testable implications		
Darker-skinned African Americans should hold more liberal views on issues in which color-based disparities are especially pronounced given their doubly marginalized status in White society based on both race and skin tone.	Darker-skinned African Americans should hold a particularly strong skin tone identity given perceived similarity to group prototypes, proximity to racial borders, more consistent external labeling, and status differentials.	Darker-skinned African Americans who identify strongly with their skin tone identity should be highly supportive of actions to remedy colorism and color-based inequities.
		Lighter-skinned African Americans who identify strongly with their skin tone identity may or may not exhibit attitudes similar to their strongly identified dark-skinned counterparts given competing factors (i.e., their own color-based privilege vs. recognition of the harms of colorism to the progress of the racial group as a whole).

Assessing the Foundations for a Potential Skin Tone Identity

Multiple factors likely contribute to the development of a durable skin tone identity, including media cues and societal cues frequently associating lighter skin with higher perceived value or status. In turn, this should be reflected in the ways that people talk about skin color in their own lives. Consequently, my interview data should help illuminate whether skin tone is taken up as an identity through participants' discussions of skin color. I explore discussions related to the socialization processes, shared language, and inherent status dimensions associated with color. I find that there is not only a recognition among Black people that different skin color categories exist, each with different experiences, but also a recognition that one belongs to a given color-based group. In combination, this evidence satisfies the two dimensions that can serve as the bedrock for the formation of a skin tone identity: the cognitive and the affective. After demonstrating consistent patterns of recognition of skin color groups and attributes associated with each group, I then explore in the second half of this section whether there is any preliminary evidence of an attachment to skin color groups.

The Cognitive Component of Skin Tone Identity

During the interviews, participants commonly provided insight into the socialization processes surrounding skin color. That is, participants frequently shared detailed stories and examples of how skin tone was discussed, avoided, derided, or praised in their social circles. Participants recalled memories from childhood and their teenage years that continued to stick with them many years or decades later. One component of this socialization process is navigating one's own color and treatment within families. This is, of course, complicated by the fact that there is often much color diversity within both extended and nuclear families. This can be seen by the repeated highlighting of skin tone across participant's distinct narratives that involved family:

> My nephew, his father was jet black . . .
> So also, by having a very fair mother . . .
> Even now, with me dating [my dark-skinned boyfriend], my grandma was like . . .
> And so in that context, my sister and I—my sister's a little lighter than me . . .
> The two darker kids in her family, my grandmother told me . . .
> A lot of people did [express color-based stereotypes], from sisters and brothers and cousins . . .

The diversity in appearance within families can lead to nuanced observations both implicitly and explicitly related to language and treatment, which children observe and internalize. Many interview participants reflected on a struggle as adolescents between accepting who they are and wanting to be lighter, given societal associations between lightness and positive attributes. Participants easily recalled stories surrounding their own socialization of skin color, as well as stories from their family and friends. Many people told stories about sisters of different shades arguing about differential treatment based on color, or of certain family members teasing or criticizing other family members based on skin tone. As one light-skinned male participant summarized: "It wasn't like one time, it was constant jokes about me being a 'pretty boy.'"

Perhaps unsurprisingly, then, several interview participants also broached the topic of skin bleaching. While the skin bleaching industry is a global phenomenon, recent estimates suggest that in the United States alone over $2 billion dollars a year are spent on bleaching products (Hall 2021). Consistent with this, some interview participants described considerations about and even attempts at bleaching their skin while growing up: "I saw how the light-skinned crowd was treated [so well], so it led me to wrestle with bleaching my skin." Others noted hearing or participating in conversations about skin bleaching—for example, recognizing that one's darker-skinned mother used skin bleaching products, despite it never being explicitly discussed. Importantly, however, these stories were not limited to those of an older generation, but even among adolescents in recent years:

> My sister and my younger brother are darker than me, but my mom is like brown. Like not light skin, but she's like brown-skin. My sister is—She has very dark skin. And she . . . was bullied so much for having super dark skin. . . . I remember people used to call her "midnight" and just really awful names. Which naturally made her not feel comfortable in her skin color. I remember for a while in high school that she would buy bleaching creams to lighten her skin. . . . But she took it to such an intense level. Her skin tone changed so, so dramatically until it totally started messing with her skin. But you can tell that White people and other Black people saying that your skin color's ugly and that you're ugly because your skin is dark really messed with how she perceived herself and what she felt like the ideal beauty standard was.—20-year-old, dark-skinned woman

> But as a teacher, I had students, Black students, who were always trying to bleach their skin. And things like that. And so I know that it's something that worries the dark-skinned children. How people can make fun of them, and things like that. . . . And so, unfortunately, I do think that the skin tone of African Americans does still—is still important and still has a bearing on people's self-esteem and their identity, who they are, and their opportunities and choices.—36-year-old, light-skinned woman

In addition, parents discussed their attempts to build up their darker-skinned children's confidence knowing the negative treatment they will more regularly face in society. This can present unique challenges, however, when the parents themselves are not dark-skinned. As one light-skinned father summarized: "My oldest daughter is dark-skinned, and she tries, and we try, but I can tell there's a void missing in her because there's no one dark-skinned around."

In discussing their teenage years, participants report the influence of the media and pressure to "fit in" as extending the discussion of skin color away from the family alone and to a broader social realm—with classmates and peers commenting and teasing one another based on color, as well as forays into dating and sexual relationships tied up with colorism. For example, with respect to what types of friends you should have, one brown-skinned (that is, neither light- nor dark-skinned) participant noted, "Some girls are like 'you have to be team light-skin,' or 'team brown-skin,' or 'team dark-skin' [to be friends]." And, skin color often plays an important role in making relationship decisions as adolescents begin to navigate the dating realm:

> [Growing up] there was a dark-skinned girl who I was attracted to, but she was dark-skinned . . . When the lights was off, she was everything to me. But, I also had another girl that was brown-skinned, light-skinned, who I had on my shoulder. Around me with my friends, wherever I would go. I had her in public, because, you know, she was light-skinned. And that was perceived as— Basically, the light-skinned girls are the girls you wife, marry, and treat with respect and honor, and the dark-skinned girls are the ones you sleep with, and creep with, but don't get into a committed relationship with.—30-year-old, brown-skinned man

> I don't know if you've ever tried to date on a dating site, but back in the day— Like, I mean, no one wants to date Black girls. And the more pointier your nose was, the more square your jaw was, the lighter you were, the longer your hair, the more wavy or whatever your hair was, the more attractive you were. I haven't, you know, I haven't dated for a while, but I just know that when, yeah, when I was dating, it was impossible. But Black women deserve love too. So it's just like, you know, if no one thinks you're cute, then how can you make a family? You know what I mean? Like it's, you know—Yeah, it affects us. And I just honestly—I don't know how far we've come.—39-year-old, dark-skinned woman

> I find that I speak more with my children about it. And it's naming it. If there's an elephant in the room, it's in the room. . . . It's when [my] grandmother said "Don't bring anything home darker than the paper bag," you don't do that. And that was a literal statement.—50-year-old, dark-skinned woman

As adults, participants reflected on their experiences surrounding skin tone in their childhood and adolescence with more insight. For example, many people acknowledge they wanted to be lighter when they were young without being able to articulate why. Many participants felt that they have a better sense of the historical context and media influences, and that they are more accepting of their natural skin tone as adults because they can better contextualize the link between skin color, status, and societal perceptions.

Participants also commonly referred to the role of the media in perpetuating race- and color-based stereotypes. Participants recognized that the combination of race and color operates in a continuous rather than categorical way to influence representations of beauty, fame, and even criminality. For example, they referred to television shows or movies that feature mainly lighter-skinned Black actors, as well as music videos that feature light-skinned women while making references to beauty. It was especially common for people to refer to the news as perpetuating negative stereotypes not only about Black people, but specifically about dark-skinned Black people—for example, in the realm of crime or receiving welfare benefits (Dixon and Maddox 2005). Younger participants also attribute the perpetuation of color-based stereotypes to social media, including YouTube videos:

> I heard a debate on CNN about music videos, that they're tending to use more lighter-skinned or quote-unquote "exotic looking" Black women, as opposed to using darker-skinned Black women because the lighter-skinned women appeal to the mass media. Sometimes things go from being a stereotype to being a fact. When you can put up statistics that show that—Just like, this picture in general, only people who are in elected officials' positions—Even our President, he wasn't a dark-skinned Black man. He wasn't a brown-skinned Black guy. He was a light-skinned Black guy. And even when you show elected officials and they're of lighter skin, those start to become—Stereotypes become facts. And I think that's more of a fact that people are more comfortable with people who are lighter because they seem less threatening or dominating personality, or they feel less of a threat or more assimilated to them.—32-year-old, brown-skinned woman

> My introduction into social media was very much so surrounded by that whole concept of light skin versus dark skin. At that time, it was more specific for men because it was more used as like a masculine versus a feminine type of thing. Or like not being masculine enough type thing. . . . I mean colorism has been here forever, but like I don't know if it's something—Maybe it's just because it's during my lifetime that it just feels like it's more prominent. But I don't remember much of a time where there wasn't a consistent, like, separation of light-skinned Black people, dark-skinned Black people. And one, it's confusing, it's divisive, it is violent.—38-year-old, dark-skinned man

These comments suggest that signals are not only sent to Black adolescents emphasizing that lighter skin is more valuable, but that they also influence Whites' perceptions of Black people based on skin tone—that is, associating more negative attributes with Black people seen as more prototypical, especially having darker skin.

> Among kids, there's a lot of colorism I experienced. And, yeah—And I think even outside of the Black community, I feel like White people and non-Black people, they perceive dark-skinned Black people and light-skinned Black people in different ways. [INT: In what ways?] I don't know. I feel like [pause]—I feel like personally, for me, people seem [to think] I'm intimidating. I don't know, if that's like me personally or because I'm dark-skinned. And I never feel like I had a lot of light-skinned friends who—It's much easier for White people to, I don't know, approach them and embrace them and that kind of thing. . . . [When] I'm at school, if I take the train, I don't know, I feel like a lot of people don't like to sit near me. Like if there's an open seat nearby, instead of sitting down they stand up. . . . It doesn't really affect me that much. I feel like I've grown used to it. It's like I don't really know anything else.—19-year-old, dark-skinned woman

These patterns throughout the conversations are consistent with research demonstrating the different lived experiences associated with complexion, as well as indicating that the media and social media play a key role in influencing both color- and race-based stereotypes, perceptions, and conversations about colorism. Given perceptions of the more continuous nature of racialized experiences or stereotypes based on a combination of race and skin tone, this suggests that there may be heightened concern about the well-being of one's skin tone group among darker-skinned people since they are more heavily policed, monitored, and discriminated against in society.

The contextual nature of the value associated with skin tone also came through in these conversations. Specifically, the interviews reveal a tension between negative stereotypes about dark skin and notions that darker skin symbolizes racial authenticity for African Americans. Participants frequently express competing sentiments related to darker-skinned members of their racial group as being the pinnacle of Blackness and simultaneously the most disdained in society:

> Somehow even though dark skin is derided within the Black community, I also think it's upheld as the ultimate form of Blackness. So for people that are like super down, super Afrocentric, I feel like your dark skin is a really great asset. It's not necessary, but it's kind of one of those things that people would

never question. . . . People believe that they're fighting and trying to do what's best for all Black people [because they're dark-skinned].—26-year-old, light-skinned woman

I've seen darker-skinned women have more interest for maybe like a Caucasian male, right? Because she's like the epitome of Blackness.—27-year-old, brown-skinned woman

But just the role in general society, the darker you are, more of the fear factor. And whatever stereotype people have about Black people, the darker you are, the more likely those might be attributed to you in society.—47-year-old, dark-skinned man

This paradox between darker skin being associated most strongly with negative racial stereotypes but also with racial authenticity or legitimacy, may be of differing importance for Black men and women across contexts. For example, given participants' repeated references to dark skin as cuing fear or aggression, the combination of race, color, and gender among Black men may be especially salient in police interactions or other criminal justice contexts. This is, of course, consistent with the patterns uncovered in chapter 4.

Overall, then, there appears to be a clear understanding of how skin tone is associated with the media, interpersonal relationships, and even family dynamics. This suggests that color-based stereotypes continue to be alive and well, just as research has documented for nearly a century (Parrish 1946; Wilder 2010). This is important given that consistent understandings of stereotypes based on color signal further evidence of the cognitive foundation of identity importance. To further assess this point, I turn to my in-depth interviews, as well as open-ended survey items regarding skin tone from my February 2016 MTurk survey (n = 229 Black participants, 97 percent of whom identify as monoracial African American). In this survey, I asked two open-ended items related to skin tone and stereotypes in which participants reported what comes to mind when they think about light-skinned and dark-skinned Black people.

Both data sources highlight that color-based stereotypes remain prominent today. As expected from the broader colorism literature, more negative attributes were consistently ascribed to darker-skinned Black people, whereas more positive attributes were ascribed to lighter-skinned Black people (e.g., Parrish 1946; Myrdal 1996 [1944]; Hunter 2002). For example, participants in both interviews and open-ended survey data regularly noted that lighter skin is associated with the following: being attractive, entitled, "soft," someone who is "not down for the cause," and feeling superior to darker-skinned Black people. Alternatively, the majority of responses related to darker skin tone invoked a distinct set of characteristics—for example, suffering more hardships, being more athletic, violent, criminal, being "hard to deal with," having a "bad attitude," being less intelligent, and experiencing a "harder time with law enforcement." Importantly, there is some suggestion that participants think in group-based categories through their in- and out-group language:

> I think people are afraid of **them** [dark-skinned Black people] because of the stereotypes from movies and tv shows.—light-skinned male MTurk Respondent

> A lot of people I hang around with are dark skin. So, it's like—When situations come in effect, people look at **them** more so as the stern, standoff-ish type of person. Where it's like, **they** might not even be like that. **They** might be friendlier, more welcoming, and warm than I am. But because **they** come in the room with me and they look at me and I'm light skin and they look at **them** like "Oh **they** dark skin," they automatically feel like Oh **they're** going to be more of a threat to them than I am. So yeah, I feel like, shit, all my friends get felt like that.—23-year-old, light-skinned man

> I have a few light skin friends and just seeing how it's easier for **them** to get jobs and how people interact with **them** is different from how people interact with me.—24-year-old, dark-skinned woman

> I remember first coming down here for school and I would see flyers that would literally have, you know, "light-skinned versus dark-skinned party." And I'm just like, what is that? Like where, where did that come from? . . . Like, the people that I'm around have experienced some sort of it at one point. So **we're** a little bit more sensitive when **we** hear it.—38-year-old, dark-skinned man

The Affective Component of Skin Tone Identity

The previous section presented evidence that participants have well-formed views about skin color groups. Of course, these patterns are consistent with the extant literature on colorism. Given a combination of factors—that is, a shared history based on skin tone, references to the history of colorism, and the reliance on group-based language—the deeply rooted nature of skin tone divisions in society are well known and continue to be relevant in society. Given these consistent patterns of recognition of skin color groups and corresponding associations with each group, I next explore whether there is preliminary evidence of an *attachment* to skin color groups. If skin tone is a meaningful social identity as I theorize, then we should see some evidence that people feel an affinity toward the color-based group with which they identify.

Consistent with this expectation, a theme that emerged from both data sources involves the potential signaling of attachment to color-based groups through language. There was some evidence of this in the final set of quotes in the prior section, but this pattern was found consistently throughout participants' responses. Specifically, in-group ("we") and out-group ("they") terms were commonly used to discuss skin color. This use of group-based language may not only signal self-identification with a given group but also some feelings of attachment to that group. This came through in many responses to the open-ended MTurk survey items in particular:

> I think **they** [light-skinned Black people] are same as me[,] the color is not important. I think **we** [dark-skinned Black people] are similar[,] the color is not important.—dark-skinned MTurk Respondent

> When I think of darker skinned individuals I think of people who hate themselves because of skin color. **We** are not proud to be who **we** are because of the melanin in our skins. **We** are thought to be ugly, dumb and under achievers.—dark-skinned MTurk Respondent

> [With respect to light-skinned Black people] I think of people who are isolated from the black community because **they** don't think **we** are black enough. However at the same time **we** are still discriminated against by white people. In the end **we** feel as if **we** don't belong anywhere.—light-skinned MTurk Respondent

Although the content of the responses varies, there is a consistent signaling of either being an in-group or out-group member. Many participants noted that skin color was divisive to the Black community or discussed its influence on their lives. Others opted not to write detailed answers, but no respondent wrote that they did not understand the question.[1] In fact, the MTurk participants wrote fairly detailed responses despite a general incentive to finish surveys as quickly as possible.[2]

My in-depth interviews reveal a similar pattern with respect to in- and out-group language. Here, too, participants use "we" and "they" terminology in the conversations to signal which color-based groups they align with.

> So in college most of my friends are Black and like **we're** both—**We're** all like pretty dark.... Our school's pretty predominantly White and so, I don't know, I just feel like [if we] traveled in a big group together and **we're** being loud, there's a lot of reactions from White people, non-Black people. And they have kind of like—a like—kind of like a preconceived notion that **we're**, I don't know, like disturbing the peace or something. **We're** just the same—like doing the same thing that everyone else is doing.—19-year-old, dark-skinned woman

> I'm not trying to sound messed up, but a lot of light-skinned people I meet, **they** think **they're** White. So I feel like it's a complex. The lighter you are—It's

a complex, I don't know how to explain it, but a lot of lighter-skinned people, **they** feel like **they're** White. **They** feel like **they're** better than you. **They** feel like, you know, **they're** on that pedestal. But I'm like "You're African American, just like me." It's weird. It's really hard to explain but I do notice that lighter-skinned people do feel more privilege. And feel like **they** have a little more leeway in life than other African Americans, and darker-skinned African Americans [especially].—28-year-old, brown-skinned man

As soon as the conquer and divide thing [happened during slavery], **they** [darker-skinned people] feel like **we** [lighter-skinned people] have it better than them. And **we** do to some degree, you know? **We** have built-in privileges because of our complexion. It's obvious **we** have some kind of European ancestry [laughs], you know?—48-year-old, light-skinned man

In sum, there is good reason to believe that skin tone may be taken up as a distinct social identity among African Americans. Consistent with the cognitive and affective expectations underlying any form of identity, my qualitative evidence underscores the recognition of color-based groups and an awareness of different color-based stereotypes. This appears to take shape over one's entire life, beginning with socialization processes occurring in the home and at school, through broader social networks (and more recently social media), and through media cues or advertising that signals the value associated with lighter skin. Consistent with prior literature, then, this examination provides further evidence that people hold shared understandings of color-based groups and self-categorize into these groups. Moving one step further, there is also some preliminary evidence of identification with these color-based groups by using in- and out-group language. Given this foundation, I more rigorously examine this potential attachment to skin tone identity groups in the next section.

Measuring Skin Tone Identity

While the cognitive and affective components of social identity are broadly agreed upon, there is less agreement on the appropriate *measures* for assessing identification. Some scholars have relied on questions regarding group closeness (Wong and Cho 2005) while others have used "feeling thermometers" to assess warmth or coolness toward different groups (Conover 1988; Winter 2008). Other measures tap into the notion of identity centrality as a way of assessing affective attachment to various groups (Citrin et al. 2001; Hooper 1976; Huddy and Khatib 2007; Jardina 2019; Junn and Masuoka 2008; Winter 1996). Consistent with this, I adopt a measure of identity centrality that has commonly been used in assessing partisan and other identities. This question simply asks how important it is for one to identify with a specific group.

This measure has several advantages. First, because participants are asked about groups they have self-identified with earlier on the survey—often race or partisanship—it takes into account the identity component of self-categorization. Through its brief question wording, it also assesses the centrality or importance of a given identity by directly asking how meaningful a given social group is to their sense of self. Finally, from a practical perspective, it is relatively easy to include on surveys because it is only a single measure. While this identity centrality measure has frequently been used with respect to ethnoracial groups, it has not previously been used or adapted to assess skin tone identity importance. Consequently, my measure of skin tone identity asks the following: "How important is your skin tone to your identity?" (response options: not at all important, a little important, moderately important, very important, or extremely important). This question was asked immediately following participants' self-assessment of their skin tone to ensure participants understood that the question referred to one's complexion. Throughout this chapter, I assess the centrality or importance of skin tone identification using this primary measure.

What patterns of identity importance are revealed using this skin tone identity measure? I examine five datasets with national samples of African Americans: 2016 MTurk, 2016 YouGov, 2018 Lucid, 2019 AmeriSpeak, and 2020 CMPS samples.[3] Across all five surveys—of varying size and levels of representativeness—I find comparable patterns indicating that (1) skin color identity is important to a majority of African Americans and (2) this identity is especially important to darker-skinned African Americans.

In each of the five surveys, over 50 percent of Black respondents said that their skin tone is important to their sense of identity. In the 2016 MTurk sample, over half of the sample reported their skin color is important to their identity to some extent. Nearly 30 percent of participants said their skin tone identity was either "very" or "extremely important" to them, and 23 percent said it was moderately important. Similarly, in the 2016 YouGov survey, 51 percent of Black participants reported that their skin tone was at least moderately important to them. More dramatically, in the 2018 Lucid survey 72 percent of Black respondents indicated their skin tone was important to their sense of identity. In the 2019 AmeriSpeak and 2020 CMPS samples, 55 percent and 57 percent of Black respondents, respectively, indicated that their skin tone was at least moderately important to their identity. Thus, across each of these samples and surveys, there is a similar pattern of responses to this skin tone identity question indicating that one's skin tone is viewed as being meaningful to the identities of many African Americans.

Second, there is evidence across all five surveys of differences in the *strength* of identification by self-reported skin tone. In every case, darker-skinned Black people are much more likely than their lighter-skinned counterparts to indicate that their skin tone is important to their sense of self. To begin, I turn to some bivariate analyses in figure 5.1 to get a sense of the relationship between skin tone and skin tone identity. In the MTurk data, participants who report being at the darkest end of the skin color spectrum are 47 percentage points more likely to report their skin tone as important to their identity than those at the opposite end of the spectrum ($p < .001$). This pattern is even more dramatic in the YouGov sample, where skin tone is 59 percentage points more important to Black people at the darkest end of the spectrum relative to those at the lightest end ($p < .001$). Substantively, this is equivalent to those at the lightest end of the spectrum reporting their skin tone is "not at all important" to their identity, while those at the darkest end of the spectrum are closer to feeling that it is "very important." In the Lucid and AmeriSpeak surveys, there is a difference of 29 and 32 percentage points, respectively, in reported skin tone identity importance between those with the lightest and darkest complexions ($p < .001$; $p < .001$). Substantively, the average skin tone importance for lighter-skinned individuals in the AmeriSpeak survey is around 0.3 on the 0 to 1 scale, or "a little important," compared with approximately 0.55 for darker-skinned participants ("moderately important"). The 2020 CMPS reveals a similar pattern, with a 29 percentage-point gap in skin tone identity importance between Black respondents at opposite ends of the color spectrum ($p < .001$). In the CMPS, the average skin tone importance for people near the lighter end of the Yadon-Ostfeld scale is around 0.33 (on the 0 to 1 scale) compared with an average closer to 0.56 for darker-skinned participants. Thus, across multiple national samples of African Americans, skin tone is seen as important to a large share of the racial group—and especially important to those with darker skin tones.

To complement this identity centrality measure, I also developed a second measure of skin tone identity drawing from the psychological concept of introjection. Introjection explores "the degree to which the group is experienced as an integral and inseparable part of the self" (Rosenberg 1979, p. 179). While this measure has frequently been used to ask about attachment to racial groups, I adapted this item for skin tone groups instead: "If someone said something bad about [light/medium/dark]-skinned people, how likely is it that you would feel almost as if they said something bad about you?" Here,

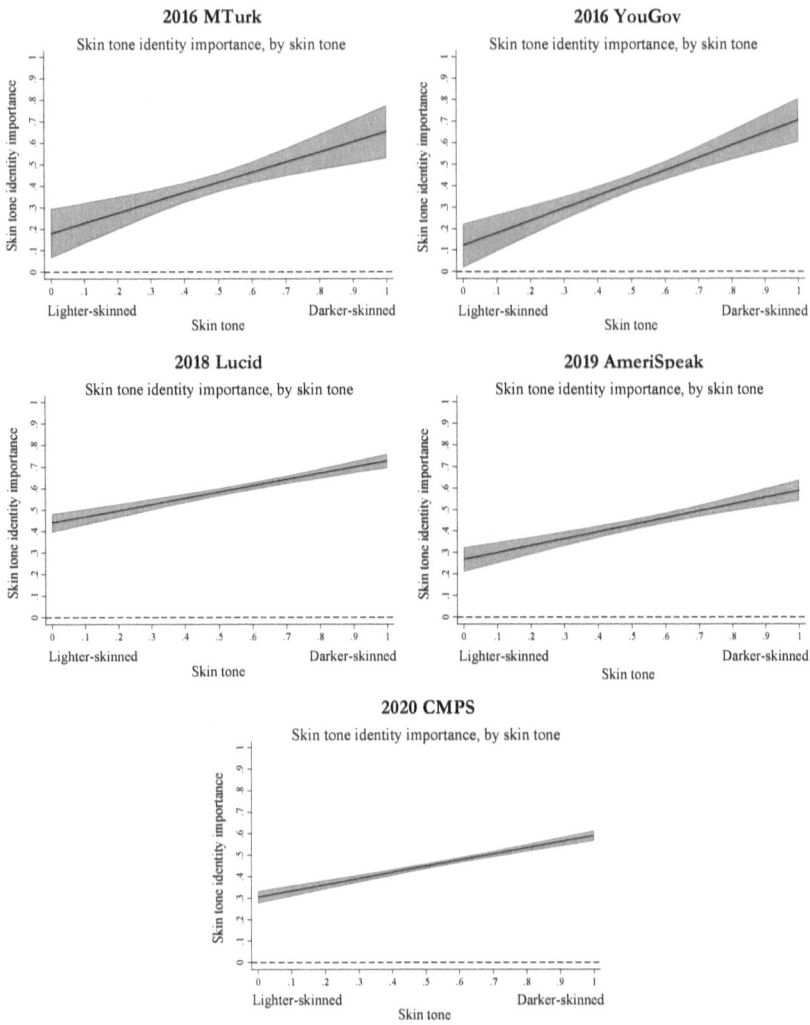

FIGURE 5.1. Skin Tone Identity Importance by Skin Tone (Bivariate)
Note: Predicted probabilities are derived from bivariate OLS regression model estimations with 95% confidence intervals.

which skin color group label is included in the question wording depends on participants' self-reported skin color or with which skin color group they had previously identified.

This skin color introjection measure was included in three of the five surveys (see figure 5.2). There is consistent evidence that a large share of African Americans say that a slight against their color group would feel personal. Again, this is especially strong among darker-skinned participants. In the YouGov sample, 57 percent of Black participants reported that if someone

SKIN TONE IDENTITY

said something bad about people of their complexion, it was likely they would feel as if that person said something bad about them personally. Participants at the darkest end of the color spectrum were 44 percentage points more likely to agree with that statement than those at the lightest end ($p < .001$). In the AmeriSpeak sample, I find comparable results: 56 percent of participants said that if someone spoke poorly about their skin tone group it was likely to feel like a personal affront. Moreover, a difference of 36 percentage points emerges between those at opposite ends of the color spectrum with respect to how personal a comment about the group would feel ($p < .001$).[4] This is substantively equivalent to those at the lightest end of the spectrum saying it would be "slightly likely" to feel personal if someone insulted their skin tone group, whereas those at the darkest end of the spectrum fall between saying it would be "moderately" or "very likely" to feel this way, on average. Finally, the 2020 CMPS reveals a similar pattern: about 66 percent of Black participants indicated that it was likely to feel personal if someone insulted their skin tone group. Here, too, darker-skinned participants are about 27 percentage points

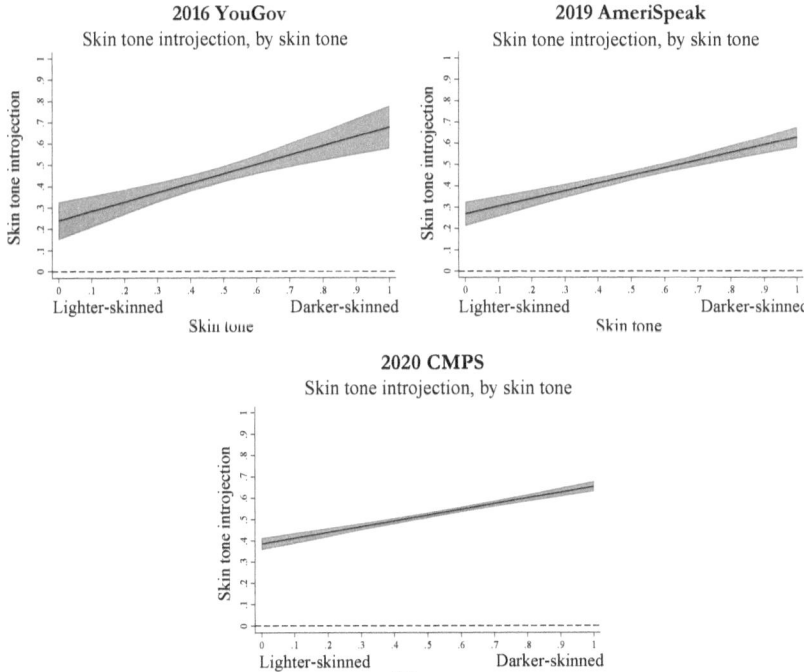

FIGURE 5.2. Skin Tone Introjection Measure by Skin Tone (Bivariate)
Note: Predicted probabilities are derived from bivariate OLS regression model estimations with 95% confidence intervals.

more likely than their lighter-skinned counterparts, on average, to indicate that such a comment would feel personal ($p < .001$).

Taken together, both measures of skin tone identity demonstrate that skin tone is meaningful to sense of self among a considerable portion of the African American community. Across multiple surveys and two distinct measures, a majority of Black people consistently reported their skin tone as important to them. Thus, skin tone appears to play a powerful role in the self-perceptions of many Black people. It also suggests that, like other social identities, skin tone identification may have important implications for how Black people think about and respond to their social and political environments, including the patterns found in chapters 3 and 4 related to skin tone and political views.

Importantly, if skin tone is its own social identity, it cannot be interchangeable with either racial identity or with self-assessments of skin tone. Looking at the distributions of skin tone identity and racial identity across the samples highlights that these are not the same construct. Consistent with the dominant focus on racial identity and race-based appeals in the United States, a much higher proportion of African Americans report that their race is important to their identity than those who say the same about skin tone across samples. For example, in the CMPS, 47 percent of US-born Black respondents indicated that their race is "extremely important" to them, compared with only 20 percent of Black respondents who said the same about their skin tone (see table 5.2). This pattern is repeated across all of my surveys. Additionally, the correlation and Cronbach's alpha—that is, a measure of how closely related items are—between skin tone identity and racial identity are modest across all four samples ($r = 0.39$ & $\alpha = 0.55$ MTurk; $r = 0.24$ & $\alpha = 0.38$ YouGov; $r = 0.44$ & $\alpha = 0.61$ AmeriSpeak; $r = 0.35$ & $\alpha = 0.49$ CMPS). The associations between the skin tone introjection item and racial importance item are even weaker ($r = 0.23$ & $\alpha = 0.38$ YouGov; $r = 0.27$ & $\alpha = 0.42$ AmeriSpeak; $r = 0.28$ & $\alpha = 0.40$ CMPS). Reporting attachment to one's skin tone group, then, is not simply another way of indicating one's racial group attachment.

Is saying your skin tone is important to your identity the same as self-reporting having darker skin? Recall that I consistently find that darker-skinned Black people are more likely to report a stronger skin tone identity. Does this mean that skin tone identity is another way of capturing self-assessed skin tone? Reassuringly, the correlations and Cronbach's alpha here are also relatively weak ($r = 0.27$ & $\alpha = 0.37$ MTurk; $r = 0.32$ & $\alpha = 0.41$ YouGov; $r = 0.20$ & $\alpha = 0.31$ AmeriSpeak; $r = 0.19$ & $\alpha = 0.36$ CMPS). In combination, then, these findings should increase confidence that questions about skin tone identity are tapping into something different from questions about either racial identity or one's location on the skin tone scale.

TABLE 5.2: Distribution of skin tone identity and racial identity (2020 CMPS)

	Racial identity					
Skin tone identity	Not at all important	Slightly important	Moderately important	Very important	Extremely important	Total
Not at all important	**226**	80	170	247	517	1,239
Slightly important	15	**73**	98	99	95	380
Moderately important	19	42	**298**	228	225	812
Very important	10	16	81	**262**	324	693
Extremely important	11	9	25	75	**674**	794
Total	280	219	672	911	1,835	3,918

For the next set of analyses, I turn to multivariate models that include a series of statistical controls accounting for sociodemographic and political characteristics in the three nationally representative survey datasets: YouGov, AmeriSpeak, and CMPS. These models include gender, education, income, region, age, party identification, ideology, and two standard measures of racial group attachment: racial identity importance and linked fate. This multivariate examination is valuable for providing further insight into whether skin tone identity is just another way of measuring racial identity. If this is the case, then the effect of skin tone identity should fall away in these multivariate models. Conversely, if skin tone identity is capturing something in addition to racial identity, then the association between skin tone and skin tone identity importance should remain.

After holding these other background characteristics constant, there continues to be a sizable relationship between self-assessed skin tone and skin tone identity importance across surveys. Darker-skinned Black people have a stronger skin tone identity, on average, than their lighter-skinned Black counterparts even after accounting for various demographic, socioeconomic, and identity strength measures. The YouGov sample reveals the starkest differences in identity importance by skin tone. Here, the difference in skin color identity importance among those with the lightest skin relative to the darkest skin is a shift from 14 percentage points to 69 percentage points on the primary identity item—a difference of 55 percentage points ($p < .001$; top panel figure 5.3). In both the AmeriSpeak and CMPS data, there is an approximately 20 percentage point gap in identity importance between those at the lightest and darkest ends of the self-reported skin color scale in this multivariate context ($p < .001$; $p < .001$). In the AmeriSpeak sample, moving from lightest to darkest skin shifts from 32 to 52 percentage points on the noted importance of the skin tone identity item. In the CMPS data, this shift is from 37 to 56 percentage points. Substantively, these are equivalent to a one-category response shift, moving

Skin Tone Identity Measure

Skin Tone Introjection Measure

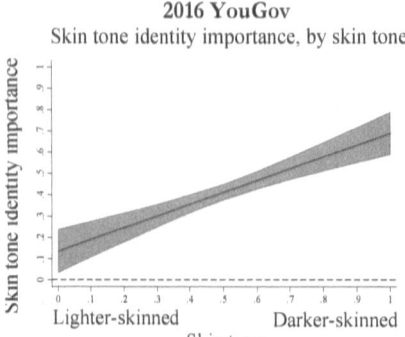

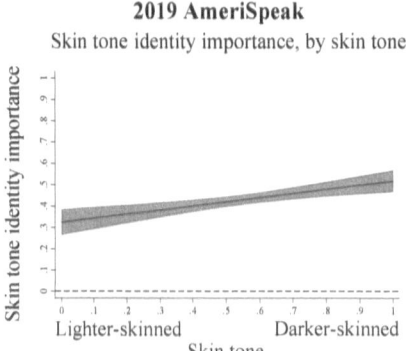
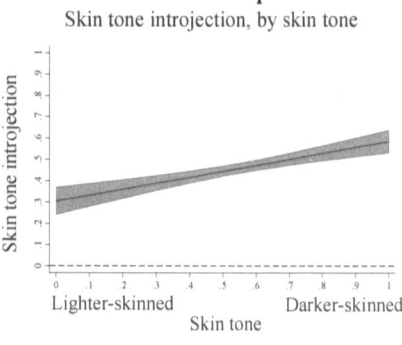

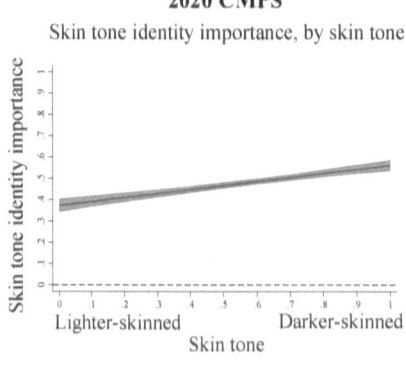
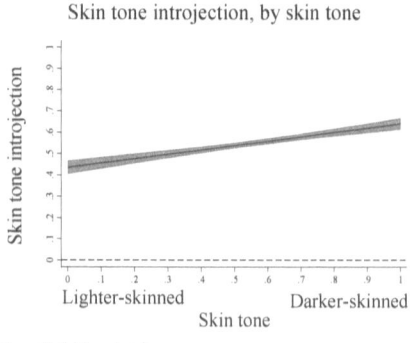

FIGURE 5.3. Skin Tone Identity Importance by Skin Tone (Multivariate)
Note: Predicted probabilities are derived from multivariate model estimations with 95% confidence intervals. Models control for gender, education, region, income, age, partisanship, ideology, racial identity importance, linked fate (except in the AmeriSpeak sample), and question ordering effects (in YouGov and AmeriSpeak).

from skin tone identity being reported closer to "a little important" to one's identity for those with lighter skin to firmly being "moderately important" for those with darker skin. Similar patterns are found across surveys with respect to the introjection measure as well, with sizable differences between those with lighter and darker skin even when controlling for myriad socioeconomic and racial group attachment items (see bottom panel of figure 5.3).

Overall, the evidence thus far reveals three key findings: (1) skin tone identity is meaningful to a majority of African Americans; (2) skin tone identity is especially meaningful to darker-skinned Black people; and (3) assessing skin tone identity is not just another way of measuring either racial identity or self-identified skin tone. These patterns hold across multiple national surveys and remain even after taking into account a number of other sociodemographic and political factors, including levels of racial group importance and linked fate. Given the importance of skin tone in the racialization process and the societal importance of color, there is evidence that a separate color-based identity develops alongside one's racial identity. Consistent with theorizing that racialized stereotypes and racialized perceptions occur in a more gradational than categorical fashion, this color-based identity is more meaningful to darker-skinned African Americans.

Correlates of Skin Tone Identity

Now that we have a sense of how skin tone identity is measured, its distribution across surveys, and how it varies across the skin color spectrum, we can dig deeper into understanding what factors influence reported strength of skin tone identification. Put differently, what demographic, socioeconomic, and/or political factors are associated with strength of identification with one's skin tone group? To answer these questions, I turn back to the three highest-quality, nationally representative samples—YouGov, AmeriSpeak, and CMPS—and estimate OLS regression models where skin tone identity is the dependent variable.

The two primary correlates of skin tone identity are (1) having darker skin and (2) reporting a stronger racial identity (figure 5.4). Consistent with the patterns from the previous section, self-identifying as darker on the Massey-Martin scale in the YouGov survey or the Yadon-Ostfeld Skin Color Scale in the AmeriSpeak or CMPS survey is associated with a greater likelihood of reporting a stronger skin tone identity across all three samples ($p < .001$; $p < .001$; $p < .001$). Further, those who report their race as important range from being 26 percentage points (in the YouGov sample) to 52 percentage points (in the AmeriSpeak sample) more likely to report skin tone as important to their identity ($p < .001$; $p < .001$; $p < .001$). Consistent with my theorizing about the gradational nature of racialized perceptions, this suggests that race and color identities work in conjunction—with people being likely to identify strongly with one also identifying strongly with the other. While both self-reported skin tone and levels of racial identity have big effects on skin tone identity, the effect of self-reported skin tone is over twice as large as the effect of racial identity in the YouGov data. In contrast, the AmeriSpeak and CMPS data suggest that stronger racial identity is the most important correlate of skin tone identity. Although some might expect that strongly identifying with the racial group would be associated with a tendency to minimize a potential skin color identity, this is not what the evidence suggests. In fact, it is those who identify strongly with the racial group who are also more likely to take up a stronger skin tone identity as well. This suggests that these two identities can, in fact, be complementary to one another.

A third factor that is consistently associated with propensity to report a stronger skin color identity is age. In all three samples, older age is associated with a lower likelihood of holding skin tone as a meaningful identity (figure 5.5). In the AmeriSpeak data, moving from the youngest to the oldest participant is equivalent to a 16 percentage-point decrease in likelihood of reporting their skin tone is important to their identity ($p < .002$). More dramatically, in the YouGov and CMPS data, older age is associated with a 30 and 32 percentage point lower likelihood of saying skin tone is important ($p < .001$; $p < .001$). This pattern suggests an interesting cultural or generational shift among African Americans with respect to understanding race or processes of racialization more broadly. African Americans growing up before or during the civil rights era may have been more centrally focused on addressing racism, consistent with the skin color paradox argument (Hochschild and Weaver 2007). However, shifts to the racial hierarchy in recent decades—including growing multiracialism and incorporation of sizable new ethnoracial groups—may have changed either salience of skin tone or increased the willingness of younger African Americans to discuss or identify with their skin tone. This pattern was also consistent with comments from younger Black people during the in-depth interviews expressing perceptions that their generation is more open to acknowledging or addressing colorism than older generations.

> I think this generation just thinks really deeply into certain topics, and they wanna get to the bottom of why things are the way they are. And I think this is a really like, this is a problem-solving generation. So if there's a problem where lighter-skinned Black people, you know, are seen as better than dark-skinned

Black people, they look at that and they wanna fix that. And they wanna educate people about that and why that happens. And they wanna help people kind of—They wanna help people notice that bias and strip it away. So I think, yeah, I think this generation is a really active generation in making life better for everybody.—18-year-old, light-skinned non-binary interview participant

I feel like I've seen more positive movement towards, you know, more progressive thinking [among younger generations of African Americans]. . . . I feel like we would definitely be more sensitive to [colorism], you know? Kind of the experiencing, like, acknowledging the different things that people go through based off of whatever their differences may be. Whereas, you know, 35, 50-whatever [year-olds], I feel like that's more kinda—I feel like that's still not as progressive, you know. That's not as progressive a group. Even though they are Black people, obviously, they care about Black people. . . . I'm not really sure if they're really caring about what colorism really is. Or if they're reinforcing it, and they really don't care that they're doing it, you know what I mean?—19-year-old, dark-skinned man

In contrast to suggestions that skin tone's relevance is decreasing among African Americans in the post–civil rights era (Gullickson 2005), my evidence highlights that skin tone identity among younger individuals is actually stronger than among older African Americans. In turn, skin tone and skin tone identity may be an issue of increasing political importance in the years ahead.

Apart from those three consistent correlates across all three surveys, a few other factors have less consistent associations with skin tone identity across samples. These include linked fate, income, education, and partisanship. While there is no association between linked fate and skin tone identity in the YouGov sample (and the question was not included in the AmeriSpeak survey), the CMPS data suggest that African Americans higher on linked fate are less likely to identify with their skin tone group ($p < .02$).[5] Interestingly, then, linked fate appears to work in the opposite direction of how racial identity and skin tone identity operate. This is consistent with work indicating that linked fate and racial group importance are not interchangeable measures, but tap into different facets of racial identity (Hutchings and Jefferson 2014). This negative association in the CMPS between linked fate and skin tone identity suggests that those who strongly feel that what happens to other Black people has an impact on what happens in their own life may believe that identifying with one's complexion is a "distraction" from problems of the racial group, consistent with the skin color paradox argument. It would be worthwhile for future studies to consider further exploring and unpacking this dynamic.

With respect to other correlates, there are no income associations with skin tone identity in the YouGov sample. Yet the AmeriSpeak and CMPS

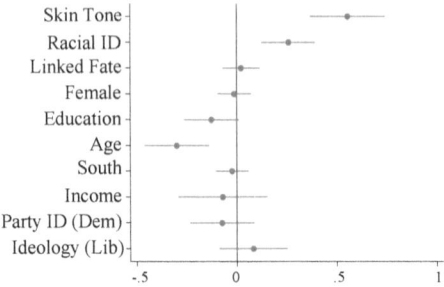

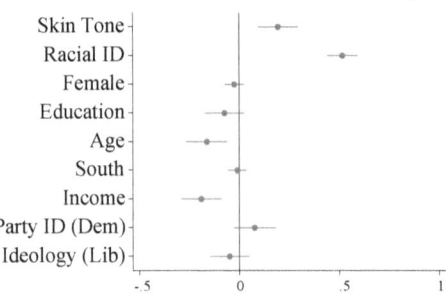

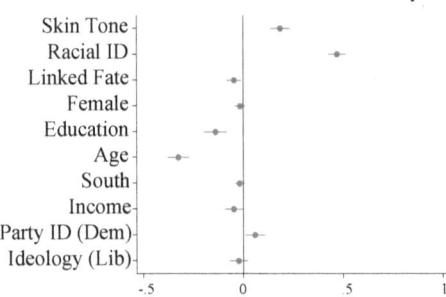

FIGURE 5.4. Coefficient Plot of Skin Tone Identity Correlates
Note: Coefficients estimated with 95 percent confidence intervals.

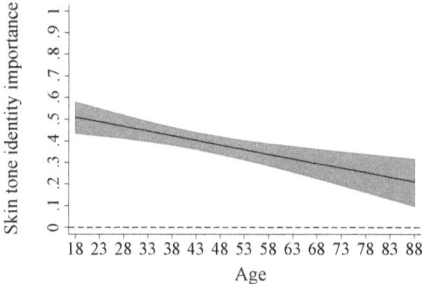

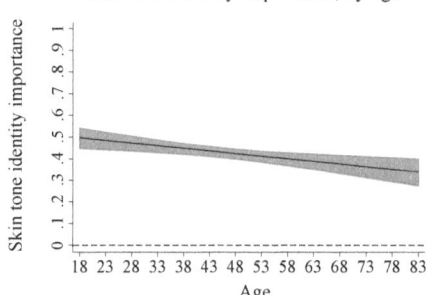

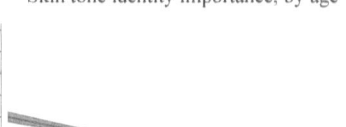

FIGURE 5.5. Skin Tone Identity Importance by Age
Note: Model estimations include 95% confidence intervals based on multivariate models from Figure 5.4.

samples suggest that higher income is associated with being less likely to identify strongly with one's skin tone group ($p < .01$; $p < .04$). With respect to education, there is no association in the AmeriSpeak sample, but the YouGov and CMPS data highlight that African Americans with more formal education may have weaker levels of skin tone identity ($p < .07$; $p < .001$). Finally, there is partisanship. There is no association between skin tone identity and partisanship in either the YouGov or AmeriSpeak samples. The CMPS data, however, suggest that African Americans who identify as Democrats are more likely to report their skin tone as important to their identity than Republicans ($p < .02$). Because of these inconsistencies, more caution should be applied in drawing overarching conclusions from these results compared with those where the same patterns are found across all three samples.

Conclusion

This chapter began by outlining how African Americans' skin color may become a politicized group identity. As noted by political scientist Efrén Pérez, "group consciousness is a phenomenon emerging under some political conditions among some individuals, rather than a mindset generally held by group members. Thus, strategies to improve a group's status follow from a politicized identity, not necessarily from identity itself. In some cases, then, the mystifying absence of an identity-to-politics link arises from not observing the 'right' people under the 'right' circumstances" (Pérez 2015, p. 160). Consistent with this, I posited that skin tone identity can be politicized, and I reviewed the two necessary components for the existence of a color-based identity: the cognitive and the affective. Drawing from social identity theory and social categorization theory, I argued that certain factors—such as proximity to a racial border, external labeling, stereotyping, and perceived similarity to group prototypes—will influence the strength of identity one reports with respect to a color-based identity. This leads to an expectation that darker-skinned African Americans will be more likely to report a stronger sense of color-based identity than their lighter-skinned Black counterparts.

The remainder of the chapter focused on assessing and measuring skin tone as an identity. The evidence found throughout this examination highlights that skin tone serves as a meaningful identity to many African Americans. Relying on a mix of in-depth interviews and survey measures, I find evidence of both cognitive and affective attachments to color-based groups. Consistent with the extant literature on colorism, socialization practices around skin tone—including cues sent by family, friends, and even media exposure—all contribute to self-categorization into skin tone groups, awareness of color-based stereotypes, and color-based status connotations. Further, participants used in-group and out-group language in open-ended survey responses and my in-depth interviews.

Deeper examination of skin tone identity was possible following the development of original survey items. Across multiple surveys I find that skin tone identity is a distinct construct from racial identity or self-assessments of skin tone. More than half of Black participants consistently report that their skin tone is important to their sense of self and that if someone insulted their skin tone group, it would feel personal. Consistent with my theoretical expectations, darker-skinned African Americans consistently indicate that their skin tone is more important to their identity, on average, than do their lighter-skinned counterparts. Younger African Americans also reliably reported their skin tone identity as more important to them than did older African Americans. This suggests that a skin tone-based identity may grow in political importance or salience—and potentially serve as a source of political mobilization—among younger generations of Black Americans.

In short, there are three primary findings from this chapter: (1) skin tone identity is a meaningful identity to a majority of African Americans; (2) skin tone identity is particularly meaningful to dark-skinned African Americans; and (3) skin tone identity can be measured using adaptations of relatively straightforward and commonly used identity measures. While this begins to answer some questions and expectations from my broader theoretical framework, it also raises other questions that are yet unanswered. How might skin tone identity influence political attitudes? And, if skin tone identity is a meaningful social identity, can it be primed in the same manner as other social identities? I begin answering these questions in the next chapter.

6

The Political Associations of Skin Tone Identity

> [Dark-skinned Black people are seen as] undesirables, unattractive, "dirty," considered to be more an "animal" than a decent human being, often considered as "thugs" or violent, dark skin children treated as adults instead of kids by racists or stereotype, seen as the lowest form of the Black community, me.
>
> DARK-SKINNED MTURK RESPONDENT

The importance of skin tone as a meaningful social identity—one that is interwoven but not interchangeable with one's racial identity—was demonstrated in the last chapter. The next step is examining how skin tone identity relates to *political views* and whether activating skin tone identity can influence subsequent views. Suggestive evidence of this relationship between skin tone identity and political views comes through in my interview conversations. For example, Anthony, a 38-year-old, dark-skinned Black man living in central Ohio underscored throughout his interview that his skin tone was important to his sense of identity given experiences he faced with respect to job opportunities, dating, and interactions with White people. On the political side, Anthony observed a connection between darker skin and anti–police brutality organizing efforts:

> Okay, I, I do believe that skin color is a focus [of the Black Lives Matter movement], which is why I think many times when I see representatives of Black Lives Matter, it's generally dark-skinned women. So, you know—And they're coming with all their facts ready to check folks on these interviews on these news networks, so I, I love it. It's like "No, sir, this is not actually how it goes down, and let me tell you why." [laughs] So seeing that makes me—It makes me happy to see that because that representation is needed. And yeah, I, absolutely [think] that's by design. To show that, you know, yes—If being the angry Black woman or man is the name that I get for being passionate about my people and educated, and can give you facts that aren't based in just opinion, then so be it. But, you know, I'll wear it proud, and you'll see my face every time.

Anthony went on to note that BLM resembled the Black Panthers movement in terms of both getting a bad reputation for being perceived as too militant, and more positively, in terms of being persistent "because the goal is to change the mindset and change the heart about your perception and that, that takes work."

Multiple points from this conversation are worth noting. In combination with Anthony's references to his experiences as a dark-skinned man throughout the earlier portions of the conversation, he expresses that his goals and passions are aligned with the dark-skinned women organizing BLM. This was based in part on a sense of shared efforts and understanding given his experiences as a darker-skinned African American man. Anthony also notes that representation is needed of darker-skinned people in higher-profile settings and media interviews, so he is happy to see the movement organizers in these venues. These feelings of joy or pride suggest an affective attachment to his skin tone identity. He also acknowledges that these efforts can result in a stronger application of stereotypes that are already laden with color-based meanings—such as being "the angry Black woman or man"—but states that he'll "wear it proud" if it means progress for his group. Although focused specifically on BLM, Anthony references an issue that he cares about (efforts against police brutality), mentions the demographic characteristics of movement organizers he respects (dark-skinned Black women), and aligns himself with them, their efforts, and the stereotypes they face as a result of being both dark-skinned and working on behalf of these goals.

Comments like Anthony's suggest a potential *politicization* of skin tone identity in the context of policing and anti-brutality movement organizing. Over the course of the last few chapters, I demonstrated that race and skin tone are associated with African Americans' political views in several domains (chapters 3 and 4), and that skin tone identity is a distinct identity meaningful to a sizable portion of African Americans (chapter 5). Importantly, however, measures of skin tone *identity* are not included on traditional political surveys such as the ANES. Consequently, those data cannot be used to assess how skin tone identity may influence preferences separately from skin tone. This leaves unanswered questions regarding whether skin tone identity is politically meaningful, or if racial identity and assessments of one's skin tone fully account for any potential political associations with skin color. Namely, what are the political associations of skin color identity? Does skin color identity influence political views in addition to the well-documented importance of racial group identity? How does activating one's skin color identity in an experimental context influence views of sociopolitical issues or behavioral outcomes?

Given the predominant focus on race and politics or political organizing, the expectations for how skin tone identity may matter politically are less clear-cut. Recognizing the importance of skin color in combination with race and other demographic characteristics is rooted in an understanding that access to power and opportunity stems from a combination of factors. Given that race is a social construction, many components influence the racialized experience (Omi and Winant 1994; Ostfeld and Yadon 2022b; Roth 2016). These include some of the same characteristics that are often studied alongside race—for example, class, religion, culture, or neighborhood. My recent work argues that these various components are not all equally meaningful in understanding race and racialized experiences. In this view, components that are "stickier" and more visible—such as skin tone—will more powerfully inform how race is experienced because these components serve as clearer markers for institutions and institutional actors to use in exerting power (Ostfeld and Yadon 2022b). In turn, an awareness around one's skin color identity can form—as demonstrated in chapter 5—and may become politicized with respect to issues perceived as highly relevant or salient. Skin tone identity, then, should be most strongly related to social and political views that explicitly center on skin tone. Moreover, skin tone identity has the potential to be activated in ways similar to other sociopolitical identities.

Recall from earlier discussions that colorism and racism coexist to maintain a hierarchy that props up Whiteness as the purported "ideal" (Banks 1999; Brown and Lemi 2021; Fanon 1952; Lemi and Brown 2020; Burch 2015). As a result, colorism operates as a feature of anti-Blackness, with color serving as a cue for racial proximity. Both historically and in the present day, darker skin signals one's closeness to Blackness and results in a stronger application of racialized stereotypes, such as those noted by Anthony at the outset of this chapter—for example, being perceived as aggressive, intimidating, or dangerous (Banks 1999; Maddox and Gray 2002; Monk 2021). The theoretical framework in chapter 2 anticipated that darker-skinned African Americans will hold more progressive political views on issues where color-based disparities are especially prominent. This expectation was based on the additional layer of marginalization that they often face in White society based on not only their race but also their darker complexion. Complementing these expectations, I argued in chapter 5 that darker-skinned African Americans should more strongly hold a color-based identity given the double marginalization they face based on both race and color, as well as the relative impermeability of group boundaries around these identities. Building from this, I expect that both racial identity and skin tone identity will be associated with political views. To be clear, my argument is not that skin tone identity will supersede racial identity in importance, but that it is an additional social identity with political associations. Skin tone identity should be most meaningful on issues where skin tone is salient or explicit. One might expect that people who identify strongly with their skin tone group would hold political preferences or support policies aimed at reducing color-based inequities. Thus, darker-skinned African Americans who identify strongly with their skin tone group should be most likely to support efforts to reduce color-based inequities.

What is less clear, however, is how the interwoven nature of race and color identities function among lighter-skinned Black people who report a strong identification with their color. On the one hand, they are also members of a marginalized racial group. This may lead to a desire to support or improve the well-being of other in-group members, especially those who may face additional stigmatization. Thus, it is possible that African Americans reporting a strong skin tone identity—regardless of their skin tone—may be most willing to acknowledge colorism and open to political remedies to reduce color-based inequities. In this scenario, one would expect skin tone identity to be a unifying identity regardless of one's self-identified color. If this is the case, there should be evidence that relative to weak skin tone identifiers, those who identify strongly with their skin tone—whether light- or dark-skinned—would be most supportive of reducing color-based inequities.

On the other hand, what is meant by holding a strong color-based identity is different for lighter- and darker-skinned African Americans. The experiences and status connotations associated with skin tone mean that light- and dark-skinned Black people experience the world in different ways. For example, a lighter complexion provides some privileges in White society and greater permeability around racial identification options, but it also presents challenges in terms of acceptance or perceived authenticity among other African Americans. Choosing to identify with one's skin tone group may mean something very different for those at the opposite end of the color spectrum, then. Just as African Americans are more likely to hold a stronger racial identity than White Americans given the power and status differentials, on average, darker-skinned Black people should be especially likely to embrace a color-based identity and acknowledge colorism. By contrast, strongly identified lighter-skinned people may identify with their skin tone because they take pride in the positive status associations of lighter skin, for example, rather than because they recognize the deleterious effects of colorism. Lighter-skinned people may be less aware or concerned about the extent of colorism's effects in certain domains such as policing or job opportunities since they do not personally face these issues. Instead, they may be more focused on addressing the racial discrimination they too face; meanwhile, their darker-skinned counterparts have the additional layer of stigmatization with which they must contend based on skin tone. This line of reasoning suggests that strongly identified light-skinned people will hold views distinctly different from those of their strongly identified dark-skinned counterparts. Thus, while dark-skinned African Americans who identify strongly with their skin tone look equivalent across these competing hypotheses, it is strongly identified light-skinned people who are expected to act in distinct ways.

Consequently, the first half of this chapter examines the political associations of skin tone identity in three large, national samples of African Americans. Here, I return to similar domains to those examined throughout chapters 3 and 4 with the addition of skin tone identity to the statistical models. In the second half of the chapter, I examine whether activation of skin tone identity can influence subsequent political views. Using a survey experiment conducted through the National Opinion Research Center at the University of Chicago's nationally representative AmeriSpeak panel, I demonstrate that skin color identity can be activated in response to reading a story about inequalities and, in turn, influence public opinion.

Skin Color Identity and Political Views

To begin examining the potential political associations of skin tone identity, I turn back to the 2018 Lucid, 2019 AmeriSpeak, and 2020 CMPS data to examine two dimensions of politically relevant attitudes where skin tone identity may have an impact. Recall that all of these surveys assessed participants' skin tone using the Yadon-Ostfeld Skin Color Scale (see chapter 3, figure 3.2). Consequently, for analyses that compare light- and dark-skinned African Americans across these three samples, I am comparing those who selected hands 1–4 (categorized as lighter-skinned) to those who selected hands 8–10 (categorized as darker-skinned).[1] First, I turn to a set of policy preferences to complement the findings from chapter 3 related to skin tone and political attitudes. Then, building from the pattern of findings in chapter 4, I examine attitudes related to policing and protest activities by skin tone identity.

POLICY PREFERENCES

My first efforts to examine how African Americans' skin tone identity is associated with political views resemble my initial examination of associations between skin tone and political attitudes in chapter 3. Unlike the 2012 ANES data examined in chapter 3, which include a wide swath of political items, the three datasets I am able to examine here include fewer policy items and, for comparable questions, the surveys use different question wording than the ANES did. Still, there are two items that can be examined from comparable political domains: income inequality and affirmative action. I begin by examining skin tone identity strength generally—looking at whether it is significantly associated with African Americans' views in the full sample while controlling for racial identity strength and other sociodemographic factors—and then broken down by participants' skin tone to examine how strongly identified lighter- and darker-skinned Black people's views compare.

All three surveys ask a question about support for efforts toward reducing growing levels of income inequality in the United States. Skin tone identity strength is associated with support for reducing income inequality in the full sample of two of three survey (see top panel figure 6.1). In the CMPS data, having a strong skin tone identity is associated with a modest 2.5 percentage-point increase in belief that the government should reduce income inequality ($p < .07$). There is a comparable effect in the Lucid data, but it is only significant with one-tailed statistical test ($p < .07$ one-tailed). In contrast, the AmeriSpeak data does not suggest any relationship between skin tone identity and views on income inequality; instead, the largest effect is driven by racial identity strength (see appendix 6.1). There is some suggestion, then, that skin tone identity is associated with attitudes about income inequality.

Now that we have some preliminary sense of how skin tone identity is associated with these views, the question remains of how the intersection of one's skin tone identity *and* skin tone may be related to these same views. Consistent with my theoretical expectations, darker-skinned Black people who identify strongly with their skin tone group are significantly more supportive of efforts to reduce income inequality (see bottom panel figure 6.1). In the CMPS sample, strongly identified darker-skinned people are 4 percentage points more likely to support the government taking steps to reduce income inequality than their weakly identified dark-skinned counterparts ($p < .07$ one-tailed). This effect is even more pronounced in the Lucid sample, in which there is a 9 percentage-point gap in support among dark-skinned Black participants at opposite ends of the skin tone identity scale ($p < .02$). Substantively, this is equivalent to weakly identified dark-skinned people "somewhat agreeing" that the government should reduce income inequality, whereas their strongly identified counterparts lean toward "strongly agreeing" with the same statement. The AmeriSpeak sample is again the only exception; here, neither light- nor dark-skinned Black participants show an association between skin tone identity strength and views on this issue. On the whole, then, there is some evidence of a meaningful association between skin tone identity and support for reducing income inequality—particularly among strongly identified dark-skinned African Americans—even when accounting for traditional measures of racial group attachment and other socioeconomic factors.[2]

Next, I turn to questions about affirmative action in the AmeriSpeak and CMPS data. The CMPS items related to affirmative action in college admissions and used a split ballot design which led to approximately half of the US-born African American sample answering each version. In neither case is there a significant relationship between skin tone identity and views about affirmative action after including controls for racial group attachment. The AmeriSpeak data included two items related to affirmative action in the workplace: a measure related to considering race in employment considerations to increase the number of Black employees at a company, and a second measure asking whether participants favored skin tone being included in hiring decisions to increase the number of dark-skinned Black employees. On the race-based affirmative action item, there is no association between skin tone identity and support for hiring more Black workers (see figure 6.2). Consistent with the theoretical expectations that skin tone identity will be most relevant to domains where skin tone is explicitly highlighted, however, there is a significant association between skin tone identity and support for considering skin tone as a means of increasing the number of darker-skinned Black employees. Strong skin tone identifiers are 7 percentage points more likely to support considering skin tone in hiring decisions than their weakly identified counterparts ($p < .05$). This is substantively equivalent to those who do not identify strongly with their skin tone slightly opposing this proposition, while those who identify strongly with their skin tone leaning toward neither favoring nor opposing this policy proposition.

When breaking these analyses down by the skin tone of respondents, there is no difference in support for either the race- or color-based affirmative action policies based on the combination of one's skin tone identity strength along with the lightness or darkness of their own skin tone. As shown in the bottom panel of figure 6.2, African Americans who identify strongly with their skin tone groups hold similar views about these affirmative action proposals regardless of their own skin tone. This may suggest that both strongly identified light- and dark-skinned African Americans hold similar perspectives on these types of policy proposals. Or, it may be an artifact of the sample sizes for these subgroup analyses being relatively small, hovering at just over two hundred cases.

There is some inconsistency, then, across measures of whether one's skin tone identity is associated with views on affirmative action in these two surveys. When affirmative action based on race is considered, racial identity strength is strongly associated with one's views. Yet the evidence suggests that when skin tone is explicitly highlighted for inclusion in a potential hiring practice, skin tone identity is associated with support for this proposition, whereas racial identity strength has no association (see appendix table A6.1B).

It is worthwhile to pause for a moment to recognize that the effects I have uncovered with respect to skin tone identity strength and views on affirmative action or income inequality are not substantively large. The prevailing literature suggests that racial identity is the primary measure associated with African Americans' political views—and that skin tone, in particular, does not carry weight in contemporary American politics. As Hochschild (2006, p. 486) summarizes, "For most blacks, in short, one form of unfairness [i.e., colorism] may be worth accepting or ignoring publicly for the sake of fighting another [i.e., racism]." Thus, the fact that not only is skin tone associated with some political views, as I demonstrated robustly in chapters 3 and 4, but that one's *skin tone identity strength* also influences these associations to some extent is noteworthy. Put differently, in addition to one's racial identity strength—which is a primary focus for scholars of race—one's skin tone identity strength is associated with some additional distinction in political views as well. While these effect sizes may be modest, they provide evidence that it is a mistake to believe that skin tone is neither a meaningful political characteristic nor a distinct social identity.

VIEWS ON POLICING

Now that I have shown that skin tone identity is associated with some political preferences in addition to racial identity, let's turn to another relevant domain: policing. Recall from chapter 4 that there was a powerful association between skin tone and criminal justice–related issues. Is it the case that skin tone identity, in addition to one's complexion itself, is associated with these views? To assess this, I return to the items examined in chapter 4; specifically, feelings of dehumanization by police, the CMPS policing battery, and perceptions that police treatment vary by skin tone.

Feelings of dehumanization were assessed by asking participants to report whether they agree or disagree that "many police officers see people like me as animals, thugs, and less than human." Recall that darker-skinned Black respondents were much more likely than their lighter-skinned counterparts to report believing that police dehumanize people like them. Is this relationship purely attributable to skin tone, or does one's skin tone identity strength also play a role? As shown in figure 6.3, Black participants with a strong skin tone identity are approximately 7 percentage points more likely than those with a

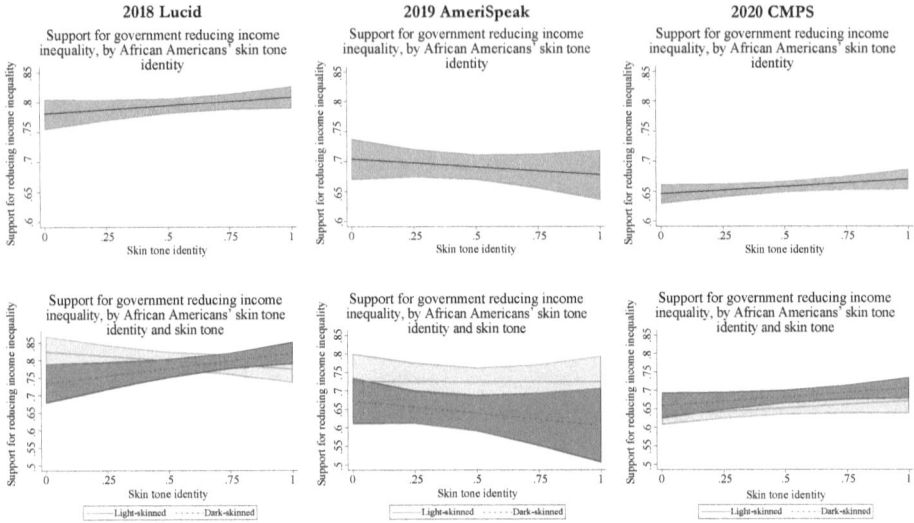

FIGURE 6.1. Association between Skin Tone Identity and Support for Reducing Income Inequality
Note: Predicted probabilities are derived from multivariate model estimations with 95% confidence intervals. Models control for gender, education, region, income, age, partisanship, ideology, and racial identity importance, linked fate (in CMPS only), Hispanic ethnicity (Lucid only), homeownership (in AmeriSpeak and CMPS), unemployment (in AmeriSpeak and CMPS) and question ordering effects (in Lucid and AmeriSpeak).

weak skin tone identity to feel dehumanized by police ($p < .001$). Holding a stronger racial identity is also associated with greater feelings of dehumanization, but skin tone identity plays a meaningful additional role with respect to understanding African Americans' feelings of dehumanization by police (see appendix table A6.1H).

When broken down by respondent's skin tone, this effect is driven by strongly identified dark-skinned participants. While there is no difference in views among lighter-skinned Black participants of varying skin tone identity strength, strongly identified dark-skinned people are 9 percentage points more likely to report feeling dehumanized by police compared with weakly identified dark-skinned participants ($p < .001$)—or their lighter-skinned counterparts of any skin tone identity strength (as shown in the middle panel of figure 6.3). Substantively, this is equivalent to strongly identified dark-skinned people "somewhat agreeing" that police dehumanize people like them, whereas their lighter-skinned counterparts are closer to "neither agreeing nor disagreeing" that police dehumanize people like them. Is the impact of skin tone identity on this item driven by dark-skinned men, in particular, as was uncovered in chapter 4? When breaking down these analyses further to also separate out gender subgroups, it is in fact strongly identified

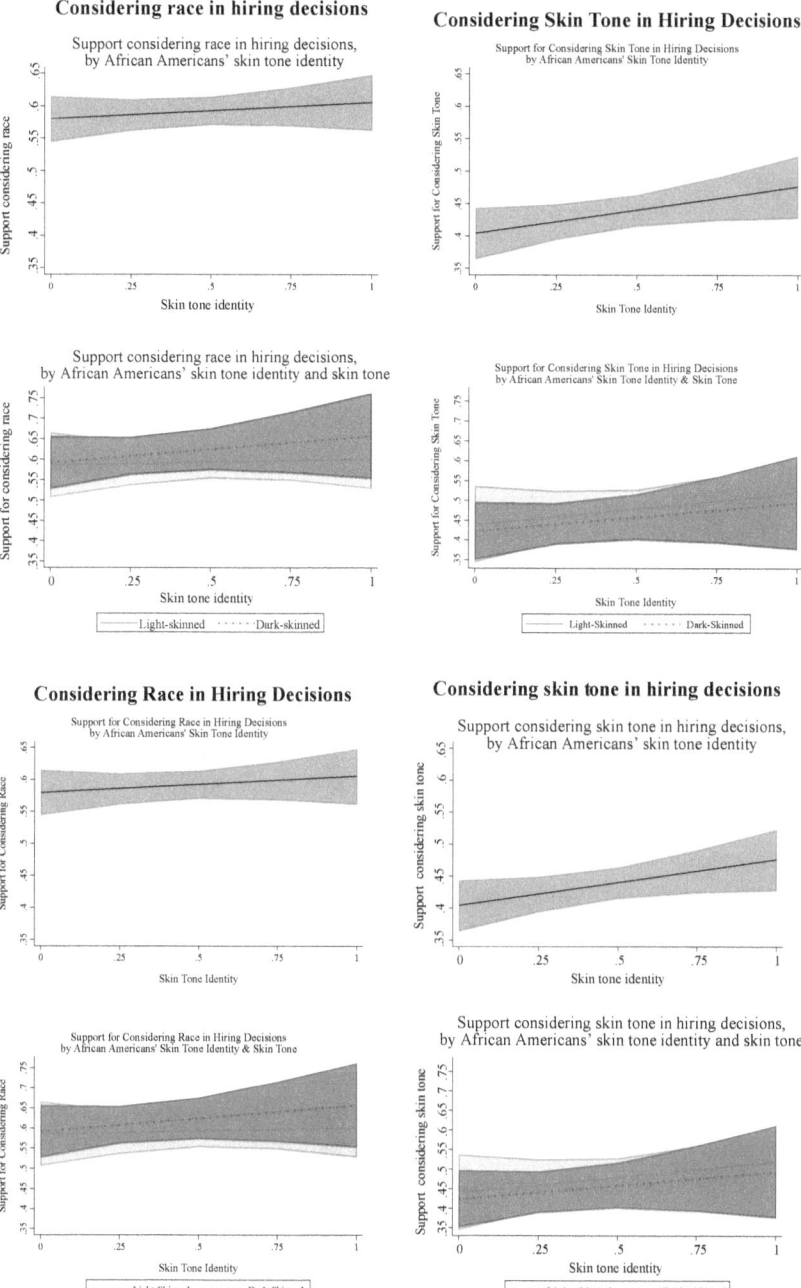

FIGURE 6.2. Association between Skin Tone Identity and Support for Two Affirmative Action Propositions (2019 AmeriSpeak)

Note: OLS regression models estimated with 95% confidence intervals and control for age, education, gender, income, region, partisanship, ideology, homeownership, unemployment, racial group importance, and survey design effects.

dark-skinned Black men who are far and away most likely to report feeling dehumanized by police (bottom panel of figure 6.3).

In combination, this pattern complements the earlier findings from chapter 4 and adds important complexity. That is, it is not just being darker-skinned that is associated with feelings of dehumanization, but the combination of one's skin tone *and* strength of skin tone identity that underlies this relationship. Put differently, lighter-skinned African Americans, regardless of their skin tone identity strength, hold similar views about whether police dehumanize them personally. For darker-skinned African Americans—and dark-skinned men in particular—their level of skin tone identity strength is powerfully associated with views on whether they are dehumanized by police; those who say their skin tone is not at all important to their identity are indistinguishable from their lighter-skinned counterparts, whereas those who say their skin tone is extremely important to their identity stand apart from everyone else in their likelihood of feeling dehumanized by police. Thus, one's perceptions on this issue are not associated with only having a darker complexion, but also one's skin tone identity strength.

Next, I turn back to the index I created in the CMPS data that combines multiple policing-related items together. Given that this index includes a mixture of policy propositions and attitudes toward police, it provides a more holistic sense of attitudes toward policing than examining any singular policing-related item (see appendix table A4.2 for details regarding this scale). I found in chapter 4 that darker-skinned African Americans, and darker-skinned men in particular, were more likely to hold a negative view of police generally. When incorporating skin tone identity into the models, I expect to see a similar pattern—that is, those higher on skin tone identity should hold a more negative view of police, and this may be especially likely for darker-skinned people.

As shown in figure 6.4, there is a statistically significant relationship between reporting a stronger skin tone identity and holding more negative views toward police ($p < .001$). While this relationship is not substantively large at 3 percentage points, it is noteworthy given that skin tone identity maintains an association with views on policing even when racial identity and linked fate are also included in the models. This signals that skin tone identity is capturing something distinct from these other measures of racial group attachment and working in complementary ways. In other words, skin tone identity is doing some additional work in explaining views of policing that are not captured by traditional measures of racial group attachment.

Here, too, intersections with skin tone are meaningful. Both lighter- and darker-skinned people who report a stronger skin tone identity report more negative views of police ($p < .01$ and $p < .001$, respectively). In contrast to the dehumanization item, then—where skin tone identity was only meaningfully associated with darker-skinned African Americans' views—when accounting for a broader range of policing-related variables, skin tone identity strength is associated with both skin tone subgroups' views. The effect of skin tone identity remains stronger among darker-skinned African Americans than among their lighter-skinned counterparts, however.

Are these effects also primarily driven by men, as found in chapter 4? As shown in the bottom panel of figure 6.4, darker-skinned women hold comparable views of police regardless of their levels of skin tone identity. Darker-skinned men, by contrast, are more likely to hold negative views of police as their skin tone identity strength increases. Dark-skinned men who say their skin tone is extremely important to their identity are 8 percentage points more likely than dark-skinned men who say their skin tone is not important to their identity to hold more negative views toward police ($p < .001$).[3] Thus, in contrast to the expectations of the skin color paradox, skin tone identity is a meaningful correlate of views toward police—among darker-skinned people, and particularly dark-skinned men—in addition to other measures of racial group attachment.

Thus far, the CMPS data has revealed the importance of skin tone, skin tone identity, and gender in more fully understanding attitudes toward policing. To examine whether this pattern holds in other datasets, I return to the 2018 Lucid and 2019 AmeriSpeak survey question asking whether police treat darker-skinned Black people worse than lighter-skinned Black people. Here, too, I find consistent evidence that skin tone identity—in addition to traditional measures of racial group attachment—is associated with views of police treatment. The intersections of skin tone identity alongside both skin tone and gender add important nuance to these findings, however.

On the whole, Black people who say their skin tone identity is extremely important to them are 7 percentage points and 14 percentage points more likely to say police treat dark-skinned people worse than those who report no attachment to a skin tone identity across both samples ($p < .04$ AmeriSpeak; $p < .001$ Lucid; see top row figure 6.5). The smaller effect size in the AmeriSpeak sample is driven by cross-cutting pressures among lighter- and darker-skinned respondents. Strongly identified dark-skinned respondents are 13 percentage points more likely to report that police treat dark-skinned people worse compared with their weakly identified dark-skinned counterparts ($p < .05$; upper-middle right figure 6.5). This effect is even stronger among men, where there is a 19 percentage-point gap between dark-skinned respondents who strongly identify with their skin tone versus those who do not ($p < .04$;

lower-middle right figure 6.5). There is suggestive evidence of the opposite effect of skin tone identity among lighter-skinned individuals in the AmeriSpeak data; that is, strongly identified light-skinned participants may be *less* likely to believe that police treat darker-skinned people worse, though this effect is not statistically significant at traditional levels.

In contrast, the Lucid data suggest that both light- and dark-skinned African Americans move in similar ways based on levels of skin tone identity strength. These parallel trends, visible in the upper-middle-left panel of figure 6.5, are driven by gender subgroups. Like the findings from the AmeriSpeak data, the effects among dark-skinned African Americans are driven primarily by men. That is, darker-skinned men who identify strongly with their skin tone are very likely to believe that police treat darker-skinned people worse. In contrast, the similar pattern of skin tone identity effects among light-skinned people are primarily driven by *women*; here, strongly identified light-skinned Black women are 18 percentage points more likely to believe that police treat darker-skinned people worse than their weakly-identified counterparts ($p < .001$). There is no association between skin tone identity and views of police treatment among light-skinned Black men. There is also no association of skin tone identity among dark-skinned Black women in this sample, but that is because this subgroup is most likely to believe police treat dark-skinned people worse regardless of their level of skin tone identity. Thus, across these two samples there is mixed evidence about how the combination of gender, skin tone, and skin tone identity operate with respect to perceptions of police treatment. A consistent pattern, however, is that strongly identified darker-skinned people are most likely to believe that dark-skinned people receive worse treatment by police.

PROTEST PARTICIPATION

Finally, I turn from attitudinal measures to a behavioral outcome: participation in protest activities since January 2020.[4] The findings in chapter 4 highlighted that darker-skinned Black Americans were more likely than their lighter-skinned counterparts to report participating in a protest, march, or rally. If there is a recognition that darker skin is associated with worse treatment in society and if darker-skinned people are more likely to report a stronger color-based identity, on average, then we might expect those with a stronger color-based identity to also be more likely to participate in protests. As shown in the leftmost panel of figure 6.6, this is precisely the pattern observed; that is, Black participants who report their skin tone as extremely important to their identity are nearly twice as likely to report protesting since

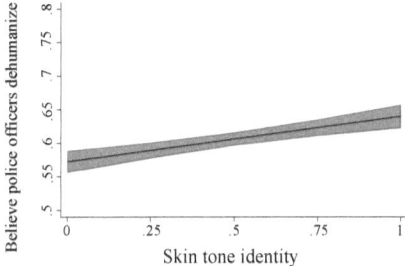

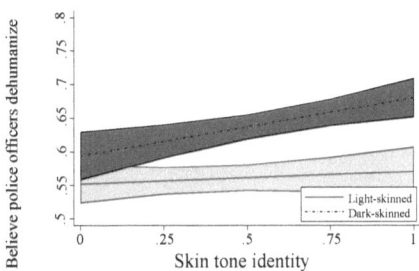

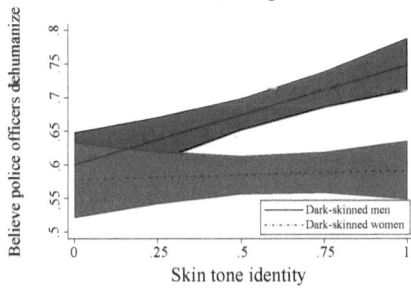

FIGURE 6.3. Belief That "Many [police] officers see people like me as animals, thugs, and less than human" (2020 CMPS)
Note: OLS regression models estimated with 95% confidence intervals and controls for gender, education, region, income, age, partisanship, ideology, homeownership, unemployment, racial group importance, and linked fate.

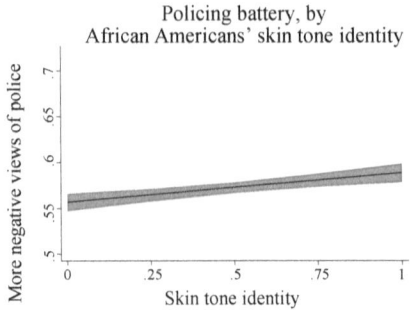

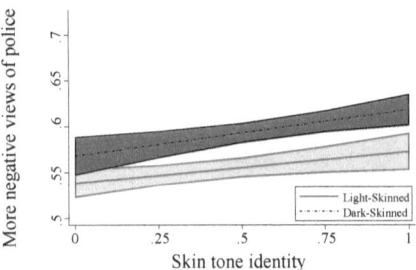

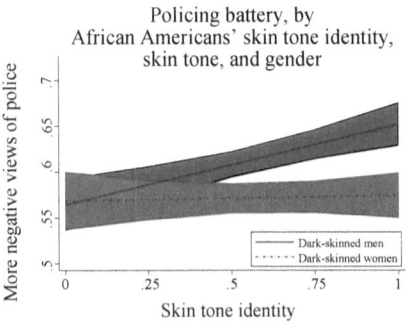

FIGURE 6.4. Index of Views toward Police (2020 CMPS)
Note: OLS regression models estimated with 95% confidence intervals and controls for gender, education, region, income, age, partisanship, ideology, homeownership, unemployment, racial group importance, and linked fate.

2018 Lucid

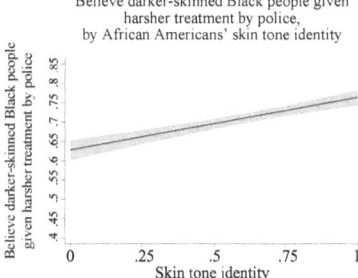

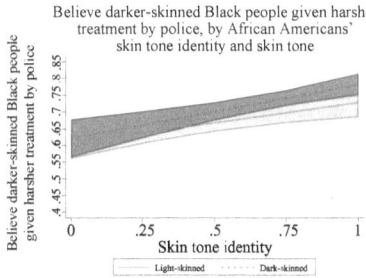

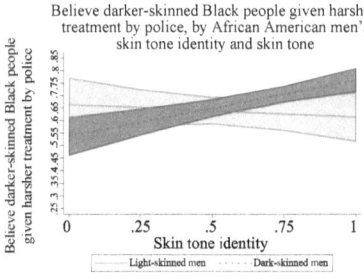

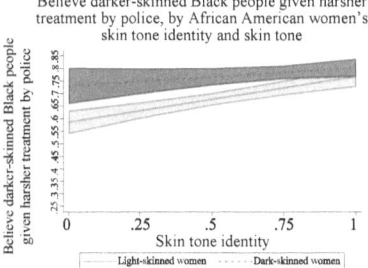

2019 AmeriSpeak

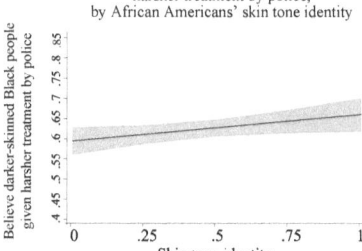

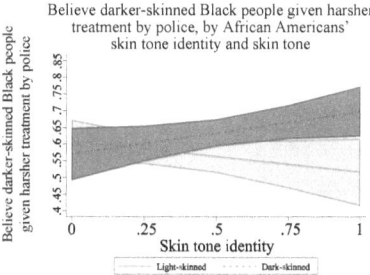

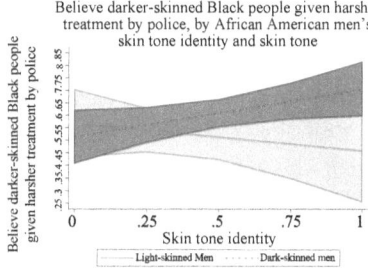

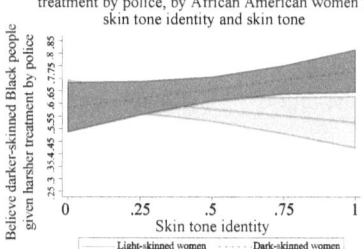

FIGURE 6.5. Belief That Police Treat Darker-Skinned People Worse

Note: OLS regression models estimated with 95% confidence intervals and control for age, education, gender, income, region, partisanship, ideology, racial group importance, and survey design effects. Estimates from 2018 Lucid also control for Hispanic ethnicity, while estimates from 2019 AmeriSpeak also control for homeownership and unemployment.

January 2020 as compared with those who said their skin tone is not at all important to their identity ($p < .001$).

When adding in one's skin tone itself to the models, skin tone identity remains meaningfully associated with likelihood of protesting for both lighter- and darker-skinned respondents ($p < .07$ and $p < .003$, respectively). The combination of one's skin tone and their level of skin tone identity is most potently associated with protest behavior among darker-skinned Black people. This provides evidence that the combination of one's skin tone and skin tone identity is meaningfully associated with not only one's political views, but also a propensity to take to the streets in protest.

Attentive readers may remember from chapter 4 that Black men were more likely than Black women to report participating in protests since January 2020. It is unclear whether these gender imbalances may reflect expressive responding by men about the issue of police brutality or, consistent with other recent work, whether men were more likely than women to have to have engaged in protests during this period (Gause and Arora, n.d.). Incorporating skin tone identity into the analyses reveals a similar pattern. As shown in the rightmost panel of figure 6.6, even when looking exclusively at Black men's protest participation, the combination of skin tone identity and skin tone is meaningful. For lighter-skinned Black men, skin tone identity is not associated with their propensity to report protesting; while light-skinned men with a stronger skin tone identity may appear slightly more likely to protest, this effect is not statistically significant ($p > .3$). Darker-skinned Black men who report their skin tone as extremely important to their identity, however, are nearly twice as likely to have participated in a protest compared with dark-skinned men who say that their skin tone is not important to their sense of self ($p < .01$). The analyses reveal that not only one's skin tone or racial group attachment but also one's *level of skin tone identity strength*, appears meaningfully associated with one's propensity to participate in protests. Thus, throughout this chapter, the combination of gender, skin tone, and skin tone identity has been repeatedly demonstrated to be associated with political views and political behavior in the form of protest.

SUMMARY OF OBSERVATIONAL ANALYSES

The pattern of findings so far complement and extend the earlier findings in the book. On political issues that are traditionally discussed in more race-focused terms, skin tone identity added relatively little explanatory power when included alongside racial identity in the statistical models. However, on issues or policy propositions that invoke skin tone—including a color-based

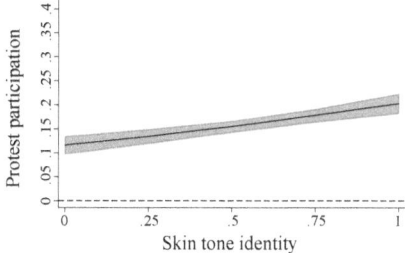

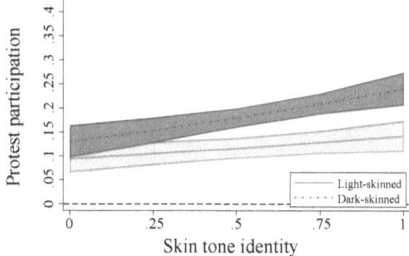

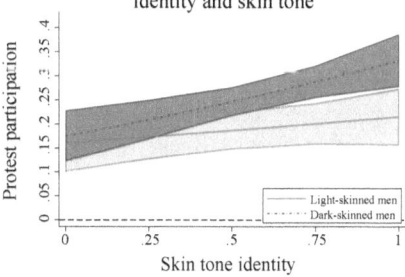

FIGURE 6.6. Likelihood of Having Participated in a Protest, March, Rally, or Demonstration since January 2020 (2020 CMPS)

Note: Logistic regression model estimated with 90% confidence intervals and controls for gender, education, region, income, age, partisanship, ideology, homeownership, unemployment, racial group importance, and linked fate.

TABLE 6.1: Summary of associations between skin tone identity and political dependent variables

	Policy preferences				
	Income inequality (2018 Lucid)	Income inequality (2019 AmeriSpeak)	Income inequality (2020 CMPS)		
Skin tone identity	*		*		
	Affirmative action: Race (2020 CMPS)	Affirmative action: race (2019 AmeriSpeak)	Affirmative action: color (2019 AmeriSpeak)		
Skin tone Identity			*		
	Policing and protest				
	Feelings of dehumanization by police (2020 CMPS)	Policing battery (2020 CMPS)	Skin tone and police treatment (2018 Lucid)	Skin tone and police treatment (2019 AmeriSpeak)	Protest participation (2020 CMPS)
Skin tone identity	*	*	*	*	*

Note: * = statistically significant at 90 percent level of confidence with one-tailed test

affirmative action item or color-based disparities in police treatment—skin tone identity was meaningfully associated with views. The largest and most consistent effects of skin tone identity were found on the policing-related items.

The evidence also suggests that skin tone identity means something different for lighter- and darker-skinned African Americans, on average. Skin tone identity was not consistently associated with lighter-skinned African Americans' political views or protest behaviors. However, the opposite was true for darker-skinned African Americans. While weakly identified darker-skinned people sometimes held indistinguishable views from their lighter-skinned counterparts, strongly identified darker-skinned African Americans had views that stood clearly apart from those of other subgroups. Additionally, given the traditional association of policing with stereotypes more consistently attributed to Black men, the associations with policing-related items were often most pronounced among strongly identified dark-skinned men. Thus, the analyses highlight several important points: (1) that skin tone identity can both complement and diverge from racial identity in its associations and impact; (2) that racialized issues may be especially salient to those group members who are disproportionately impacted, such as in the case of those affected by police brutality; and (3) in contrast to expectations from prior literature, both skin tone and skin tone identity contribute toward fully understanding racialized experiences.

Activating Skin Tone Identity

Now that skin tone identity has been shown to be associated with political views on some policies and issues in theoretically anticipated ways, I seek to investigate whether activating skin tone identity in the context of a survey experiment can influence political views. The activation of social identities has been demonstrated with respect to race, gender, class, and more, with downstream influences on various outcomes (Goff, Steele, and Davies 2008; Goren, Federico, and Kittilson 2009; Hutchings and Valentino 2004; Jardina 2019; Lewis and Sekaquaptewa 2016; Steele 2011; White 2007). Evidence throughout this chapter and chapter 5 demonstrates that skin tone is not only a meaningful social identity for African Americans, but that skin tone identity has associations with political views. A secondary question is when skin tone identity is activated, does it influence political views similar to other identities? Making this identity salient should have observable political consequences. Consequently, I attempt to activate skin tone identity through an experiment where participants read about color-based inequities in society and, in turn, examine whether this influences perceptions of colorism's influence in society or efforts to mitigate color-based inequities.

Recall from the first half of the chapter that both my theoretical framework and empirical tests highlight that strongly identifying with one's skin tone means something different to lighter- and darker-skinned African Americans. Among strongly identified darker-skinned people, there is a consistent pattern of belief that darker-skinned people are treated worse and also greater support for policies that would help the group. After exposure to the color-based inequities treatment in my experiment, I anticipate that this will continue to be the case because strongly identified dark-skinned African Americans will have the strongest reaction to this information. Specifically, one might expect that after having their color identity activated, darker-skinned individuals would increase their recognition of color-based inequities as well as their support for various policies to diminish these inequities.

The survey evidence suggests that this same pattern is not as likely to occur among lighter-skinned African Americans. That is, I did not find consistent evidence that lighter-skinned Black people—whether they identified strongly with their skin tone or said it was not at all important to them—had meaningful variation in their political views based on skin tone identity across the three surveys examined. Of course, this was not universally true; one counterexample was that lighter-skinned Black women held different views of police treatment depending on their level of skin tone identity (see figure 6.5). Still, it was not consistently the case that strongly identified light-skinned people held views that mirrored those of their strongly identified dark-skinned counterparts. Thus, the political associations of skin tone identity appear to be more nuanced for lighter-skinned Black people.

After reading about color-based disparities in an experimental context, then, it is possible that strongly identified light-skinned Black people may have two different responses. One potential response is to minimize color-based disparities when prompted to think about these issues and express less support for efforts to provide policy remedies. This response may occur for a number of reasons—for example, because strong light-skinned identifiers believe race supersedes color in terms of importance, because discussing skin color may make them more self-conscious about their authenticity within the racial group, or even because they may want to hold on to the privileges associated with light skin. Alternatively, it is possible that reading information about the extent of color-based inequities in society will lead strongly identified light-skinned participants to look more similar to their strongly identified dark-skinned counterparts. Evidence supporting this would show that people who identify strongly with their skin tone—whether light- or dark-skinned—would be most supportive of reducing color-based inequities. While the survey evidence showed that strongly identified people of different complexions often held different views, this does not necessarily preclude the possibility that reading about color-based disparities could lead to more similar views among strongly identified individuals. Again, while dark-skinned African Americans who identify strongly with their skin tone look equivalent across these two competing hypotheses, it is high-identifying light-skinned people who are expected to act in distinct ways.

I do not expect skin tone and levels of skin tone identity strength to universally inform one's political views, however. As theorized throughout this book and demonstrated in the first half of this chapter, the combination of one's skin tone and skin tone identity should be meaningful for issues where colorism is well known. The survey evidence revealed mixed evidence of associations between skin tone identity and income inequality and affirmative action, but stronger associations based on more explicitly color-based issues—for example, police treatment varying by skin tone, or a color-based affirmative action proposal. Providing information about color-based inequities to participants may also lead to greater emphasis on color-based issues or color-focused remedies. To investigate this, I include a variety of different dependent variables, some of which focus explicitly on skin tone and some of which do not.

Consequently, I examine whether skin tone can be activated as an identity in ways similar to other group-based identities. If skin color is a psychologically meaningful social identity, then making this identity salient should have meaningful consequences in terms of reported thoughts, feelings, or behaviors (Hutchings and Valentino 2004; Lewis and Sekaquaptewa 2016; Steele 2011). Thus, I examine whether skin tone can be activated through an experimental treatment and, if so, what implications this has for one's attitudes and opinions based on the combination of one's skin tone and levels of skin tone identity.

Experimental Design and Measures

To assess how skin tone identity might be activated, I draw from a body of literature that examines the activation of one's identity across a variety of contexts (e.g., Hutchings and Jardina 2009; Klar 2020; Mendelberg 2001; White 2007). Participants were randomly assigned to read one of three brief articles (see appendix 6.2 for treatments). The first article was the control, in which participants read a fictional story about a science fiction convention. This serves as a baseline for comparison against the treatments to determine what effects the treatment had on downstream political views. The second and third articles were the treatments involving a press release from an organization discussing either race-based or skin tone-based inequities in society.[5] These treatments draw estimates from actual research to demonstrate the stark differences in outcomes based on race or skin tone with specific examples of these disparities with respect to hourly wages, wealth, years of formal education, and more.[6] The only information changing across conditions was whether the inequities in the press release were attributed to racial groups or skin color groups.

This survey experiment was through the National Opinion Research Center at the University of Chicago's nationally representative AmeriSpeak panel thanks to support from Time-Sharing Experiments with the Social Sciences. The sample included 1,045 African American respondents recruited between January 16 and February 22, 2019.[7] The analyses that follow examine the interaction of three factors: (1) exposure to the treatment—that is, reading a story about color inequities or racial inequities versus the control; (2) one's self-reported skin color on the Yadon-Ostfeld Skin Color Scale; and (3) one's level of skin tone identity. For the skin color measure, I collapse across responses to the 10-point color scale for ease of interpretation. As in the first half of the chapter, hands 1–4 are categorized as light-skinned (n = 283; 27 percent of the sample) and hands 8–10 are categorized as dark-skinned (n = 260; 25 percent of the sample). The skin tone identity importance item is similarly collapsed to compare those who fall into the two highest skin tone identity importance categories (n = 370; 36 percent of the sample reported their skin tone is very or extremely important) and the two lowest skin tone identity importance categories (n = 460; 44 percent said their skin tone is not at all or not very important).

For ease of interpretation and presentation of the statistical models, I create two variables that combine skin color identity importance (low, medium, or high) crossed with self-reported skin color (light or dark). Put differently, I have one variable for light-skinned participants with low to high skin tone identity importance, and a separate variable for dark-skinned participants with low to high skin tone identity importance that I interact with the treatment variables. Estimating the models in this fashion is substantively and statistically similar to estimates from a more traditional triple interaction, but it allows for a clearer visual representation of the effects. Thus, the figures presented throughout the chapter are drawn from these truncated models, but the regression estimates from the full models with triple interactions are included in appendix 6.3. Throughout the next section, I show a side-by-side comparison of skin color identity importance crossed with self-reported skin tone.

The dependent variables fall into three categories: policies, behavioral outcome measures, and perceptions of skin tone in society (see appendix 6.2 for question wording). The policy variables include a measure of income inequality, a race-based affirmative action proposal focused on hiring more African Americans, and a color-based affirmative action proposal focused on hiring more dark-skinned African Americans. The second set of variables is related to four potential behavioral responses to the issues discussed in the treatments: interest in talking with family or friends about the issue, willingness to sign a petition, interest in volunteering, and interest in protesting about the issue. Finally, the third set of variables focuses on perceptions of skin tone in society. This is the largest set of variables included in the experiment, with questions ranging from perceptions of discrimination to feelings about whether darker-skinned Black people should occupy more positions of power in society. These original items focused on various aspects of color-based disparities that often came through in my interview conversations, including with respect to job opportunities, treatment by Whites, and police treatment.[8]

TABLE 6.2: Comparison of experimental treatment language

Race treatment language	Skin tone treatment language
New research shows **class-based** disparities are primarily driven by **race** New studies highlight how **class-based** inequalities stem primarily from **racial discrimination**.	New research shows **race-based** disparities are primarily driven by **skin tone** New studies highlight how **race-based** inequalities stem primarily from **skin tone–based discrimination**.
The Center for the Study of Race and Policy (CSRP) in Washington, DC, found dramatic differences when comparing **Black people with White people** across a number of domains.	The Center for the Study of Race and Policy (CSRP) in Washington , DC, found dramatic differences when comparing **dark-skinned Black people with both light-skinned Blacks *and* Whites** across a number of domains.
These differences based on **race** range from gaping income disparities, to vast differences in education levels, as well as shorter lives due to both worse health outcomes and criminal sentencing disparities. For example, **Black people** are twice as likely to receive the death penalty for comparable crimes, have 5 years less formal education, make about $3 less per hour worked, and have less than half the wealth of **Whites, regardless of class**. Surprisingly, the extensive research on this topic by the Center for the Study of Race and Policy dating back to early 2015 reveals that these differences persist even after taking into account levels of education, work experience, family background, and other important factors. These disparities should be especially alarming given their relationship to job and educational opportunities, various life experiences, and overall quality of life.	These differences based on **skin tone** range from gaping income disparities, to vast differences in education levels, as well as shorter lives due to both worse health outcomes and criminal sentencing disparities. For example, **darker-skinned Black people** are twice as likely to receive the death penalty for comparable crimes, have 5 years less formal education, make about $3 less per hour worked, and have less than half the wealth of **lighter-skinned Blacks and Whites**. Surprisingly, the extensive research on this topic by the Center for the Study of Race and Policy dating back to early 2015 reveals that these differences persist even after taking into account levels of education, work experience, family background, and other important factors. These disparities should be especially alarming given their relationship to job and educational opportunities, various life experiences, and overall quality of life.
The reports reveal that, on average, **lower-class Whites have better outcomes than even the most affluent Blacks**.	The reports reveal that, on average, **lighter-skinned Blacks have more similar outcomes to Whites, while darker-skinned Blacks face the most disadvantages**.
The research by the CSRP suggests that focusing on **class** alone is not enough to resolve inequalities stemming from **race**. "Most politicians aren't talking about how much worse off **Black people are than White people**," says the lead researcher at CSRP and activist, Darnell Williams. "We must acknowledge disparities based on **race** are real and are very harmful."	The research by the CSRP suggests that focusing on **race** alone is not enough to resolve inequalities stemming from **skin tone**. "Most politicians aren't talking about how much worse off **dark-skinned Black people are than lighter-skinned Black or White people**," says the lead researcher at CSRP and activist, Darnell Williams. "We must acknowledge disparities based on **skin tone** are real and are very harmful."
Only time will tell how politicians and other activists take up these disparities based on race given the CSRP's troubling findings.	Only time will tell how politicians and other activists take up these disparities based on skin tone given the CSRP's troubling findings.

Note: Bolded text denotes the differences across the treatments. Full treatment language available in appendix 6.2.

Results

Is skin tone identity strength associated with differing reactions to reading about race-based or color-based inequities? Does the combination of one's own skin tone and level of skin tone identity strength influence African Americans' political views after exposure to these treatments? Consistent with my theoretical expectations, I find that exposure to the color-based inequities treatment condition influences perceptions of skin color's impact in society (see appendix table A6.3B). On the race-based policy outcomes or behavioral responses, the expectation that there would be little association between exposure to the skin color inequities treatment, skin tone, and skin tone identity strength also holds true (appendix table A6.3A). When looking at the interaction between exposure to the race-based inequities treatment and one's racial identity strength, there is little evidence of treatment effects on these traditional policy or behavioral interest items (appendix tables A6.3C–D). This suggests that it may be difficult to move opinions on these items, either generally or at least using my specific treatment language. Thus, the only set of variables for which there is evidence that the treatment had an effect is with respect to the perceptions of skin tone's importance in society. Importantly, there is no evidence that the racial inequities treatment or the combination of one's racial identity strength combined with exposure to either of the inequities treatments results in differing perspectives on skin tone's importance in society. The color inequities treatment, in contrast, does influence perspectives of skin color in society. As I will show, this is particularly true among strongly identified dark-skinned African Americans.

The first subset of items related to perceptions of skin tone in society relates to discrimination. These questions ask participants whether lighter-skinned Black people have better job opportunities, receive better treatment by Whites, receive better treatment by police, and have more potential for upward mobility in society. Indeed, I find a significant interaction between exposure to the color-based inequities treatment, skin tone, and skin tone identity strength on three of these four items (see figure 6.7).

To begin, I examine perceptions that lighter-skinned people receive better job opportunities than darker-skinned people. Figure 6.7 highlights this effect with a direct comparison between the control and treatment groups. The dashed line at zero on the y-axis denotes the same level of agreement on a given issue in the treatment and the control. Thus, any estimate with confidence intervals not overlapping with zero represents a significant treatment effect at the $\alpha = 0.10$ level.

For example, as shown in the top left panel of figure 6.7, after viewing the color inequities treatment, strongly identified dark-skinned respondents are nearly 20 percentage points more likely than their counterparts in the control group to say that it is very common for light-skinned Black people to get better job opportunities ($p < .07$). In contrast, the racial inequities treatment does not produce an effect. Thus, reading about color-based inequities—but not race-based inequities—contributes to shifting opinions among strongly identified dark-skinned participants. How do the views of strongly identified dark-skinned participants compare with views of others who also read the color inequities treatment? Among participants randomly assigned to the color inequities treatment, strongly identified dark-skinned people believe that lighter-skinned people have better job opportunities than darker-skinned people between "half the time" and "most of the time" (0.63 on a 0 to 1 scale) relative to only "half the time" or less among weakly identified light-skinned, strongly identified light-skinned, or weakly identified dark-skinned participants (0.47, 0.50, 0.43, respectively; all $p < .05$). Even after exposure to the same information, strongly identified dark-skinned people stand apart from the other color-identity subgroup combinations in their perceptions of colorism's influence on job prospects.

There are similar effects with respect to perceptions that light-skinned Black people have greater societal mobility, beliefs that White people treat light-skinned Black people better than dark-skinned Black people, and that darker-skinned Black people receive worse treatment by police (figure 6.7). In all three cases, there is no effect of the racial inequities treatment in moving opinions on these items, but there is evidence of movement due to the color inequities treatment. With respect to perceptions of skin tone being associated with either societal mobility and treatment by Whites, there is an approximately 20 percentage-point gap between strongly identifying dark-skinned participants in the color inequities treatment relative to the control ($p < .05$ and $p < .06$ one-tailed, respectively). Similar to what was found on the job prospects question, there are also significant differences in perceptions of these two items between strongly identified dark-skinned participants and the other color-identity subgroups when comparing only participants who viewed only the color inequities treatment. Again, strongly identified dark-skinned African Americans stand apart from other color-identity subgroups in believing that skin tone influences one's treatment and potential societal mobility.

There is a weaker but similarly patterned effect on the item related to color-based differences in police treatment. In part, this seems to be driven by higher baseline agreement across all the subgroups that darker-skinned people receive worse treatment from police. After viewing the color inequities treatment, high-identifying dark-skinned participants are 13 percentage points more likely to report that police treat dark-skinned people worse than those in the control group ($p < .10$). This result should be interpreted with caution, as the triple interaction between treatment exposure, skin tone, and skin tone identity strength is not statistically significant here, unlike for the other three items in this battery. The racial inequities treatment had no impact on perceptions of police treatment, nor is there a suggestion of a meaningful relationship between treatment exposure and racial identity strength. Thus, skin tone identity strength provides explanatory power toward understanding perceptions of skin tone's influence in society, particularly for strongly identified dark-skinned Black people.

Across these color-related outcomes, then, activating skin tone identity appears to meaningfully shift the views of high-identifying dark-skinned people. There are several important takeaways from these findings. First, skin color identity works in distinct ways for strong identifiers at the lighter and darker ends of the spectrum. Indeed, it is only those with darker skin who change their views in the face of a reminder about colorism in society. Second, only reading about color-based inequities—but not race-based inequities—influenced subsequent views. This provides further evidence that talking about skin tone and race has distinct impacts and can elicit distinct responses. Moreover, references to color-based inequities have important downstream consequences on perceptions of discrimination in society, particularly for darker-skinned Black participants. Finally, a supplementary set of analyses that substitutes racial identity strength in place of skin tone identity strength in the models reveals no associations between strength of racial identity and treatment exposure on any of the variables (appendix tables A6.3C–6.3D). This further reinforces that while skin tone identity and racial identity are interrelated, they can operate in distinct ways—particularly when colorism is invoked. Put differently, even African Americans who identify strongly with their racial group do not report a heightened recognition of color-based mistreatment in society after reading about color-based inequities in society. It is only among darker-skinned African Americans who report their skin tone as being very important to their identity that there is a sizable shift in views following news of color-based inequities in society.

The second subset of color-based items included in the experiment deals with the trade-offs of discussing skin color versus race, as well as questions about power in society. These questions involve whether focusing on resolv-

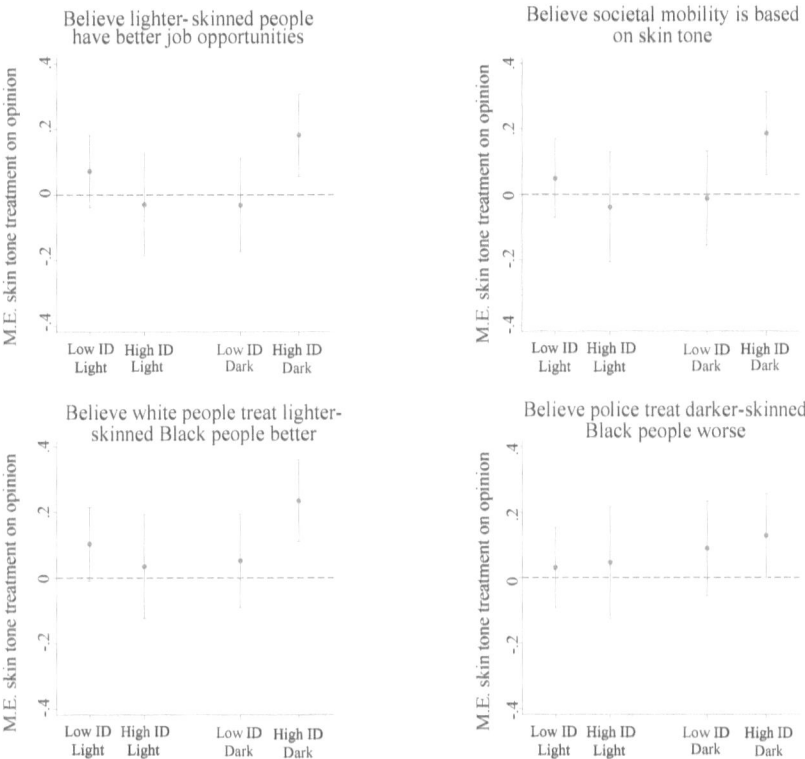

FIGURE 6.7. Treatment Effects on Colorism-Related Items by Skin Tone and Skin Tone Identity
Note: Figures depict the effect of viewing the skin color experimental treatment for each subgroup relative to the equivalent subgroup in the control with 90% confidence intervals.

ing racism will resolve colorism, whether discussing skin color is a distraction from race, whether lighter- and darker-skinned people face equal discrimination, as well as whether Black people would be better represented politically by dark-skinned politicians or whether dark-skinned individuals need more power in society. I find more mixed results on this battery of items with evidence of a meaningful relationship in two of five cases. Importantly, as with the last section, there is no evidence that reading about racial inequities influences views on any of these items, nor is there any association between the inequities treatments and levels of racial identity strength.

On two items—belief that darker-skinned people should be more fully represented in positions of power, and belief that darker-skinned politicians would better represent African Americans—there is evidence of an interactive effect of skin tone and skin tone identity in the color inequities treatment relative to the control. These effects are only significant when applying a one-tailed statistical test, but this is appropriate given the expectation that strongly identified people would be more likely to hold such views. With respect to the importance of getting dark-skinned people in positions of power, strongly identified dark-skinned people are about 17 percentage points more likely than their counterparts in the control to believe this is important ($p < .08$ one-tailed test; figure 6.8). Substantively, this is equivalent to the treatment inducing a one-category response option shift among strongly identified dark-skinned participants; that is, after viewing the treatment, this subgroup believes it would be beneficial "most of the time" to have more dark-skinned people in positions of power as opposed to believing this to be true "half of the time" in the control. There is a comparable pattern of results in terms of agreement with the statement "Black people would be better represented in politics if more dark-skinned Black people were elected." Here, there is suggestive evidence that strongly identified dark-skinned participants are about 16 percentage points more likely to agree with this statement than their counterparts in the control ($p < .09$ one-tailed; figure 6.8). This result should be interpreted with caution, though, as the triple interaction term in the full model is not significant.

In contrast to the first battery of color-based items, then, there were weaker and less consistent effects on this battery. Still, there are several useful takeaways. First, viewing the color-based inequities treatment moves participants' views more than the race treatment—and this was again due primarily to strongly identified dark-skinned Black respondents. This was true throughout the first subset of color-based outcome variables, and to the extent that there were effects in the second subset, it was only in the color-based inequities treatment. Second, the pattern of results indicates that skin color identity and racial identity may be complementary group identities, but they can also work in distinct ways. With respect to both sets of color-based outcome variables, there were essentially no association between one's racial identity strength and one's views after reading about either color-based or race-based inequities. In contrast, of course, I found that skin tone identity was associated with a number of these color-based outcome variables after reading about color-based inequities, and that these effects were driven by strongly identified dark-skinned Black respondents. Third, the significant results in this second subset of color-based items centered on getting more darker-skinned people into positions of power, be they political positions or otherwise. Although the experimental treatments did not increase participants' reported interest in protesting, it is possible that this may be more likely under other circumstances—for example, potentially related to policing or other salient power imbalances.

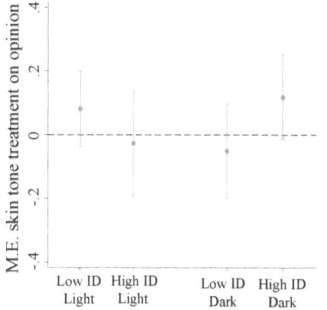
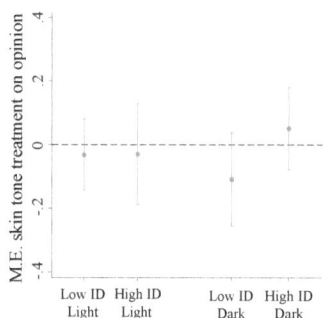

FIGURE 6.8. Treatment Effects on Power-Related Items by Skin Tone and Skin Tone Identity
Note: Figures depict the effect of viewing the skin color treatment for each subgroup relative to the equivalent subgroup in the control with 90% confidence intervals.

Conclusion

Overall, this chapter moves beyond traditional examinations of race based on Census categories by examining the multidimensionality of race by focusing on skin tone. Indeed, it represents the first attempt to examine the connection not only between skin tone and politics, but the combination of skin tone, skin tone *identity*, and politics. I find evidence that skin tone identity and self-reported skin tone are associated with several sociopolitical views and that skin tone identity can be activated like other identities to influence subsequent views. On the whole, these effects occur primarily among one color-identity subgroup: dark-skinned African Americans who are strongly identified with their skin tone group.

In the first half of the chapter, I examined three surveys and a variety of politically relevant items to examine how skin tone and skin tone identity, in addition to racial identity, influence political views. Recall that my argument is not that skin tone identity will supersede racial identity in importance but that it is an additional social identity that may have political associations. Indeed, the analyses reveal that although skin tone identity and racial identity are complementary, skin tone identity provides its own explanatory power in some cases. This is particularly true for issues explicitly invoking skin tone or colorism. Even when including racial identity strength in the statistical models, African Americans who identify strongly with their skin tone group are, for example, more supportive of policies to reduce income inequality, more likely to feel dehumanized by police, and even more likely to report participating in protests since January 2020. The survey experiment revealed that reading about color-based inequities provoked responses that differed from reading about racial inequities in society. Indeed, the racial inequities treatment had no effect on perceptions of colorism or color-based issues, whereas reading about color-based inequities did influence some views.

The results also highlight that it is not simply that skin tone identity matters; the intersection of one's skin tone *and* level of skin tone identity matters as well. The results throughout the entire chapter are largely driven by strongly identified dark-skinned African Americans. This subgroup is most likely to recognize color-based disparities at baseline. And, in a survey experiment, it is this subgroup for whom reading about color-based inequities provokes the strongest reaction in terms of further recognizing the influence of colorism in society and hoping for access to more positions of power. There was no consistent evidence that strongly identified light-skinned people held views similar to those of their strongly identified dark-skinned counterparts, nor that reading about color-based inequities in society provoked any meaningful shift in recognizing colorism's influence among this subgroup. This suggests that the interwoven nature of skin tone and race results in a nuanced relationship based not only on one's level of skin tone identity but also on one's complexion. Thus, identifying strongly with one's skin tone group is not sufficient in bridging the gap between lighter- and darker-skinned Black Americans' views or experiences, even after reading about the pervasive effects of colorism in society.

That skin tone identity provides explanatory power in addition to that of racial group attachment may be surprising given theorizing that compared with race, skin color should play little, if any, role in politics. The predominant literature suggests that racial identity is the primary marker for understanding different experiences and views (Bobo and Gilliam 1990; Dawson 1994; Harris-Lacewell and Junn 2007; McClain et al. 2009). Scholarly work addressing skin tone and public opinion argues that it will not be of any consequence to African Americans' sociopolitical views (Hochschild 2006; Hochschild and Weaver 2007). The evidence provided throughout this chapter demonstrates that skin tone can, in fact, be associated with sociopolitical views in certain circumstances—*and* that skin tone is an identity with political manifestations in terms of both attitudes and behavior. These findings suggest that asking survey questions related to color-based issues would add greater depth and nuance to our understanding of racialized experiences, particularly as they relate to understanding protest participation and criminal justice interactions.

7

Conclusion

Tina was still adjusting to college life when the COVID-19 pandemic began. The sustained summer 2020 protests against racial injustice emerged just a few months later. It was an anxiety-inducing, frustrating, and saddening time, yet somehow Tina also felt a glimmer of hope. These nationwide protests were the largest to have ever occurred, even larger than those of the civil rights era in the 1960s, and touching on issues similar to those of earlier efforts (Chudy and Jefferson 2021; Gause and Arora n.d.; Hamilton and Ture 1992; Shaw 2009). The protests captured the attention of political elites, the mass media, and many regular people—some of whom even took to the streets in support. Tina was captivated by what was happening and, in turn, regularly attended the protest demonstrations near her.

Tina identified as both African American and dark-skinned, even though she acknowledged that she had relatively lighter skin than her siblings. Complexion was both an implicit and explicit topic in Tina's household. Her siblings discussed issues related to colorism and representation with some regularity growing up, as this was a topic about which they were all passionate. But they each also faced personal challenges based on the darkness of their skin tone that were painful to discuss and, consequently, Tina felt that some stories were left untold.

The sense of hope that Tina felt during this period was due to the sheer scale of the movement and the diversity of crowds that took to the streets following the murders of George Floyd and Breonna Taylor. There was finally a political outcry related to the issues of police brutality that she, her friends, and her family had been concerned with for as long as she could remember. Still, Tina observed some familiar patterns during these protests that were exasperating. During the two months when she was attending demonstrations in summer 2020, she felt that not many dark-skinned Black people were given the opportunity to speak. She recalled witnessing multiple occasions where the people leading the protest would shut down darker-skinned people who were attempting to address the crowd. And she felt this was even more frequent if the speaker was both darker-skinned and a woman, like herself. Tina found this extremely frustrating—not only because of the frequency with which she noticed this but because she felt that some of the individuals who were given the opportunity to speak at length seemed to have relatively little to say substantively.

This pattern was disappointing but not wholly surprising to Tina given her understanding of whose voices and perspectives society deems valuable. Her observations during these protests mirrored her broader perceptions growing up regarding who was given a platform to speak on behalf of the group; whose voices and experiences were highlighted, and whose were minimized. Even in the context of protesting against police brutality—an issue that Tina felt more strongly affected darker-skinned Black individuals—there was not only a lack of conversation around skin tone but also a minimizing of opportunities for darker-skinned people to share their experiences. She expressed disappointment regarding the hesitancy to recognize and advocate on behalf of darker-skinned Black people who face additional discrimination in myriad ways within mainstream society due to their complexion.

Tina felt that people of her generation demonstrate more openness in their general willingness to discuss colorism in society. Yet these conversations often circled around issues of perceived attractiveness or dating. While such discussions were valuable, of course, Tina wished they would delve further. She noted that the systemic effects of colorism—with respect to job opportunities and income potential, police interactions and criminal sentencing—were much less likely to be recognized. Tina felt a stronger sense of urgency around these issues compared to dating, noting that these institutionalized barriers impeded the potential upward mobility of darker-skinned people like her and her siblings. While Tina was grateful that there seemed to be more openness around discussing issues of colorism within the Black community, she still felt that not enough progress had been made in addressing the wide-ranging impacts or influence of colorism. Her sense of resignation was palpable as she indicated that there was still an incredibly long way to go toward achieving any semblance of equity in society. Tina wished that someone would advocate for darker-skinned Black people, and darker-skinned Black women in particular, in the political sphere—someone who could push to develop policies and programs that would address colorism. These are the political responses she anticipated would have the biggest impact on her life.

CONCLUSION

This conversation with Tina was conducted as part of the series of interviews for this book project, underscoring several important themes that have been highlighted throughout the preceding pages. I consistently find across datasets that the combination of race and skin tone is associated with African Americans' experiences, perceptions, and opportunities in society. Moreover, African Americans, particularly those with a darker complexion, often adopt a color-based identity and feelings of psychological attachment to their skin tone group. Recall that between 50 and 70 percent of African Americans, on average, hold an attachment to their skin tone. Some African Americans also think of politics through a color-based lens, with Tina exemplifying this through her discussion of both who was permitted to speak at the anti–police brutality protests in summer 2020 and in expressing frustration at the lack of political interventions to address color-based biases in society. This final point complements community organizer Clarissa Brooks's perspective on the challenges associated with political organizing, political movements, and appearance. Brooks argues that being dark-skinned means that her activism efforts lead to harsher and more hostile responses than efforts made by light-skinned Black political organizers. She also notes that "the legacy of colorism has meant that the work of certain activists has been minimized. I am specifically thinking of Ella Baker and Fannie Lou Hamer—two dark-skinned black women who built models for decentralized leadership that community leaders like me still practice today."[1]

Importantly, however, much of this meaningful color-based nuance is overlooked by scholars interested in understanding racial dynamics because of a reliance on Census-based racial categories rather than incorporation of a multidimensional view of racialized experiences. Indeed, much of the research across the social sciences, and in political science specifically, theorizes about and studies groups by relying on categorical race alone. This book, by contrast, sets out to examine the intra-racial experiences of African Americans associated with skin tone, and in certain cases, the combination of skin tone and gender. This is especially valuable given the long-standing associations of skin tone and wealth, health, criminal justice, and more (Monk 2021). These wide-ranging impacts of skin tone in society point to the value associated with understanding potential connections between skin tone, one's sense of identity, and political views.

Across a variety of issue areas, I uncover noteworthy associations between skin tone and Black people's views of politics and power. A psychological attachment exists not only with one's racial identity group, but also in many cases with one's skin tone group. In turn, this has consequences for one's political evaluations and behavior. The evidence provided throughout this book points scholars toward skin tone and a sense of color-based identity as an important yet understudied facet of American politics.

Revisiting the Roadmap of the Book

Using a mixed-methods approach—including multiple national and nationally representative surveys, 100 original in-depth interviews, and a novel survey experiment—I demonstrated that the intersection of race and skin tone can inform one's political judgments and behavior in distinct ways. I consistently find evidence supporting my theoretical expectations that skin tone is associated with political views and behavior in areas where colorism is especially prominent. For example, I highlight the contexts in which skin color is associated with political preferences on redistributive policies, including support for welfare spending, affirmative action, and views of policing. Once color-based differences in opinion among African Americans are taken into account, the well-documented chasm in public opinion between Black and White Americans' political views appears to be driven by differences between Whites and darker-skinned African Americans. With respect to political behavior, darker-skinned African Americans appeared more likely to report engaging in protest activities than their lighter-skinned counterparts. These findings highlight the political importance of considering color-based dynamics among African Americans, particularly in domains where colorism is salient. Finally, I demonstrated that perceptions of who benefits from racialized policies vary not only on the basis of race, but also on the lightness or darkness of one's skin. The "welfare queen" stereotype, for example, is understood to be not only a Black woman but a *dark-skinned* Black woman. This adds depth to understandings of racialized policies, stereotypes, and corresponding media coverage (e.g., Brader, Valentino, and Suhay 2008; Edsall and Edsall 1991; Gilens 1996, 1999; Hancock 2004; Mendelberg 2001), as well as pointing to future directions for further scholarly interrogation.

African Americans are not only aware of but broadly concerned about skin color disparities in society. Despite a lack of questions related to color-based inequities in most mainstream research projects, I find a near unanimous sense of skin tone's importance in society among Black interview participants with 95 out of 100 indicating that skin tone remains important in society. This perceived importance of skin tone ranges across a variety of issues among both interview participants and survey respondents drawn from national samples—including treatment by police, treatment by Whites, employment opportunities, dating and social relationships, as well as opportunities for social mobility. Of course, these perceptions do not simply reflect subjective

CONCLUSION 163

opinions but are borne out empirically through administrative data sources frequently relied upon in the colorism literature. Thus, the patterns unveiled throughout this book should resonate quite strongly for those familiar with how colorism operates in society and provide empirical evidence on the corresponding political manifestations of colorism.

Beyond demonstrating the importance of skin tone in society, my interviews, surveys, and experimental data all underscore the existence of a politically meaningful and distinct *skin tone identity* for many African Americans. This expectation that a psychological attachment to one's skin tone may be undergirding potential associations between skin tone and political views is a novel contribution to the literature, which has primarily examined skin tone as a characteristic that is associated with social outcomes. Thus, the adaptation of traditional measures of identity to ask about a color-based identity provides a critical first step to begin understanding this sociopolitical identity and its potential to act as a mechanism linking skin tone and attitudes. This is an important advancement in the colorism literature and one that I hope will inspire further investigation.

Indeed, I find that skin tone is a meaningful identity to a sizable portion of the African American community. Across multiple surveys and questions, a majority of African American respondents report their skin tone as important to their sense of self. Just as I found that darker-skinned Black people are more likely to agree that colorism disadvantages them with respect to jobs, policing, criminal justice, and more, I also find that skin tone identity is stronger among darker-skinned Black people than among their lighter-skinned counterparts. This is consistent with my theory that the high visibility and stickiness of skin tone as an attribute, alongside status connotations and similarity to group prototypes, help explain why darker-skinned Black Americans are most likely to internalize color as meaningful to their identity.

After demonstrating the existence of a skin tone identity in chapter 5, I explore how skin tone identity may be associated with political views in chapter 6. I find that skin tone identity shapes the associations observed between skin tone and political views. Specifically, people who strongly identify with their skin tone group are often driving the effects found between skin tone and political views unearthed in chapters 3 and 4. I subsequently introduce a survey experiment that activates skin tone identity's importance and examines the downstream influences on views of this activation. I find that the combination of activating one's color-based identity and reading about color-based disparities in society is most likely to influence the views of the subgroup that holds the identity in the highest regard: darker-skinned Black people. The experimental evidence also underscores that skin color identity and racial identity work in sometimes complementary and sometimes crosscutting ways. Remarkably, skin tone identity appears to be more powerful than traditional measures of racial identity in its ability to predict attitudes toward color-specific issues.

Because I emphasize the multidimensional nature of racialized identities, it is worth reiterating how levels of skin tone identity compare with levels of racial identity. Given the importance of race in society, it should not be surprising that levels of racial identity are much higher, on average, than levels of skin tone identity. To be clear, my argument is *not* that skin tone identity will rival race in its relative importance. Acknowledging high levels of racial identity strength does not minimize the value of examining other identities—such as gender, class, religion, or skin tone—that work in conjunction with categorical race to influence one's experiences. Rather, examining people's unique attachments to their skin tone identity adds to and strengthens the scholarly repertoire of understanding nuanced racialized experiences.

It is also possible that this psychological attachment to one's skin tone identity may be more salient to younger generations. Indeed, in contrast to the perspective that skin color may be of declining significance today (Gullickson 2005), I find that skin tone identification is actually strongest among younger individuals. This suggests that one's sense of skin tone identity, in particular, has the potential to be of increasing importance as younger generations grow older and become more politically involved. Moreover, it may hint at a greater openness toward acknowledging or addressing skin tone and colorism in the coming decades. In turn, this may influence how political organizing and messaging take shape in search of achieving equity and justice.

Qualitative Data and Researcher Positionality

Some of the richest data in this book come from the interview conversations. While a sizable literature has emphasized the value of qualitative work toward understanding politics (e.g., Brown 2014; Cohen 1999; Cramer 2016; Harris-Lacewell 2006; Hochschild 1981; Lane 1962), contemporary research on American public opinion often builds from an assumption that people know very little about politics. This conclusion, however, hinges on a narrow conception of what represents political knowledge. If you present people with opportunities to speak in their own words about political issues that matter to them, people have incredibly insightful things to say (Abrajano 2015; Cohen and Luttig 2020; Weaver and Prowse 2020; Weaver, Prowse, and Piston 2019). Throughout the interviews conducted for this project, it was clear that people

CONCLUSION

had well-formed views related to race, skin tone, and various aspects of politics—from political candidates to racial stereotypes to racialized policies to how the media perpetuates these dynamics. These conversations provided tremendous value for understanding perceptions of how racial politics operate, far beyond what could be captured in the narrow confines of a survey.

To this point, it is worth circling back to the topic of researcher positionality that I engaged with at the outset of the book. I am a light-skinned White woman who is writing this book about the sociopolitical views and experiences of African Americans. Although I am a racial out-group member relative to the internal dynamics of colorism within Black communities, White people are largely responsible for the divisions and stereotypes based on skin tone throughout US history (see chapter 2 for a more detailed discussion). Readers should walk away from this project understanding that colorism is far from a quirky intra-racial phenomenon but instead is rooted in and maintained by racist power structures. To reduce inequities, then, I contend that it should be the task of White people alongside other communities to not only acknowledge this dark history but also work to change unjust systems. Thus, while this project contributes to an academic literature that frequently highlights White perspectives, and is conducted by a White researcher, I hope my research is viewed as building on and amplifying the voices and work of those who are directly stigmatized by colorism.

I revisit this discussion of positionality as the book concludes because it is worth explicitly noting how my background likely influenced the dynamics of the project and the data collection. This seems most pertinent with respect to the qualitative portion of the project, although my fingerprints are, of course, on every part of the project. Of the 100 interview conversations, I personally interviewed 43 people and a team of four Black women research assistants interviewed the remainder. Still, I was the one who created the advertising materials for the interviews, crafted the general interview script, and trained the research assistants. The other interviewers had latitude to provide feedback on the questions or question language—which did result in several revisions to the general script used by everyone—and they also had the ability to influence the trajectory of the conversations by deciding what follow-ups or additional points to raise during their individual conversations. Yet, the core of the qualitative data collection effort is tied to my perceptions, expectations, and interests for the project based on both my reading of the literature and my conversations with friends, family, and colleagues. If this project had been conducted by another researcher with a different set of background characteristics, the types of questions asked or the way they were asked would inevitably be different. And so, too, would be the participant's responses.

Does this mean that different patterns of findings would have been uncovered? Yes and no. This question can be answered empirically, to some extent, by looking at the race of interviewer effects present from the conversations conducted here. Each of the five interviewers had distinct experiences with the intersection of race, color, and power based on her own appearance and background, which were brought implicitly into every conversation (Brown 2012; Young 2004). The *style* of the conversations was undoubtedly distinct across interviewers—particularly between the Black and White interviewers—but the *substance* of the conversations was similar with respect to takeaways regarding skin tone's importance and influence in society. More broadly, thinking about who is an "ideal" interviewer to understand people's true feelings is a complicated question. For example, the Black interviewers more frequently reported feeling uncomfortable or sensed more hesitation from the people with whom they were speaking. This is not wholly surprising given the sensitive nature of colorism and the intra-group dynamics based on skin tone among African Americans. As a racial outsider, by contrast, I found that interviewees generally approached our conversations with an expectation that I was unfamiliar with the topic of colorism and thus needed a more foundational understanding and more detail. Even though the style of these conversations was different for me, the consistent patterns of substantive responses uncovered across all five interviewers provides confidence in the robustness of the qualitative findings. Moreover, the patterns found in my data complement those in the broader colorism literature and extend these familiar patterns more explicitly into the political sphere.

Still, it is possible—and, in fact, quite likely—that additional information could have been gleaned from these conversations had they been developed and undertaken by someone who directly faced color-based stigmatization throughout their life. This would further expand the scope of understanding of colorism's influence and impact, as well as that of skin tone identity. As with any research effort, then, a single project can contribute toward answering some research questions while also raising a number of additional questions. I hope that future researchers can continue this investigation and further transform, expand, and enhance scholarly understandings of skin tone identity's political importance.

Grappling with Intra-group Dynamics

A central takeaway from this project is the value of examining the multidimensional nature of racialized experiences. This complements other valuable work focusing on intra-group dynamics occurring within Black politics

CONCLUSION

related to gender, class, immigration status, and more (e.g., Brown and Lemi 2021; Bunyasi and Smith 2019; Carter 2019; Cohen 1999; Dawson 1994, 2001, 2001; Greer 2013; Hancock 2007; Jefferson 2023; Philpot 2017; Simien 2012; Simien and Clawson 2004; Smith 2014; Tate 1994; White and Laird 2020). My work builds from existing social scientific research on colorism to demonstrate that skin color has important implications for issues like policing, wealth inequality, political representation, and both intra- and inter-group relations. These patterns underscore the value of looking beyond the traditional Black-White racial binary on which scholars often focus and instead taking seriously intra-racial heterogeneity.

When we follow the traditional path of comparing Black and White people in terms of their political views, socioeconomic outcomes, or perceptions of the criminal justice system, we gloss over the meaningful distinctions occurring *among* African Americans based on skin tone variations that I unearthed throughout this book. Layering in further complexity, there were several cases—particularly related to issues of policing—where the combination of skin tone and gender were meaningfully associated with one's views, experiences, and sense of identity. Recall that darker-skinned Black people reported more negative experiences and perceptions of police, as well as a greater propensity to participate in protests, on average. And in several cases these patterns were driven by darker-skinned Black men.

Without examining these intra-categorical dynamics, scholars would not only misunderstand but also misrepresent them in considering potential pathways toward equity. If a primary goal of social scientific research is aiming to help inform political elites and policymakers about inequities in society, then this would be a serious error. Toward that end, intra-group examinations provide clarity as to whether certain disparities boil down to race or class, or whether there is meaningful variation based on other characteristics such as skin tone or gender. Getting this correct is especially important given that inequities between lighter- and darker-skinned African Americans can be of a similar magnitude to inequities between Black and White Americans (Monk 2021). Thus, attention to both race- and color-based inequities is necessary for any effective resolution.

This is also important because race-based efforts to reduce inequities can inadvertently exacerbate color-based inequities if those programs or policies are disproportionately used by subgroups that already have relatively more resources and power (Hochschild and Weaver 2007). Although skin tone is not often included in mainstream political considerations in the United States, this is not true across other contexts globally. One potential opportunity is for policymakers within the United States to examine the potential effectiveness of adapting programs designed to mitigate the adverse effects of colorism in Latin America. Importantly, highlighting the distinct and double-layered challenges faced by African Americans with darker skin in many corners of society should not serve to diminish the racialized challenges faced by all African Americans. Instead, it merely notes darker skin as an attribute that, in addition to race, is routinely leveraged—over time and across domains—to influence access to opportunities, power, and status (Ostfeld and Yadon 2022b; Telles 2004). As such, skin tone should be part of the conversation in terms of rectifying deep-seated inequities that cannot be helped simply by focusing on racial disparities and developing effective, policy-focused solutions. Such acknowledgments could, in turn, help avoid the entrenchment of a "pigmentocracy" whereby skin tone is used to jockey for position within a shifting racial hierarchy (Bonilla-Silva 2004a).

Overall, this project shines a spotlight on the value of taking intra-categorical dynamics around skin tone seriously and what is missed by failing to do so. The patterns throughout this book demonstrate the important contribution of studying skin tone toward understanding African Americans' sociopolitical views and experiences. More broadly, I hope that the emphasis on intra-categorical examinations will inspire other scholars to continue doing important work that moves beyond Census racial categories alone, continuing to build on the valuable projects doing exactly this in recent years (e.g., Brown and Lemi 2021; Bunyasi and Smith 2019; Carter 2019; Jefferson 2023; Philpot 2017; White and Laird 2020).

The Future of Skin Tone Identity Politics

Another central contribution of this book is demonstrating that skin tone is not simply an attribute that has been imbued with significant social meaning over time and in turn is associated with political views in certain contexts, but that a *psychological attachment* to one's skin tone has also developed as a result. Skin tone identity is found to be meaningful to a majority of African Americans across my surveys, and especially so for darker-skinned Black people. Not only is one's skin tone identity associated with how one views oneself; it is also associated with one's political views. This was true most consistently for strongly identified darker-skinned African Americans. These findings underscore not only the importance of studying racialized experiences in more fine-grained fashion, but also how variation in one's experiences influence one's sense of self and the groups with which one identifies.

Future work would benefit from greater exploration of skin tone identity as a concept and a measure. In this project, I draw from both the qualitative interviews and two survey items about identity importance that traditionally ask about racial or partisan identities but were adapted to ask about skin tone identity. A fruitful avenue for future research might include, for example, expanding the set of items tapping into skin tone identity in terms of both cognitive and affective group attachment. Recent work has begun to assess more thoroughly how complexion is relevant to one's self-concept (Harvey, Tennial, and Hudson Banks 2017). Continuing to build on these complementary efforts would provide a clearer picture of how skin tone identity operates and what its downstream sociopolitical implications are.

Pursuing such measurement strategies would also provide greater insight into how skin tone identity operates among those who strongly identify as lighter-skinned. My evidence reveals that holding a strong skin tone identity does not consistently mean the same thing for lighter- and darker-skinned African Americans. In most cases, strongly identified lighter-skinned African Americans hold views that diverge from those of their strongly identified darker-skinned counterparts despite both groups indicating the importance of their skin tone to their sense of self. This is not surprising given the status differences associated with these distinct locations on the skin tone spectrum; in other words, given that colorism privileges lighter complexions, identifying strongly as being light-skinned as opposed to identifying strongly as dark-skinned carries very different meanings. In some instances, however, a stronger skin tone identity, regardless of one's complexion, was associated with holding more negative views of police or greater likelihood of protest participation, for example. A more expansive battery of identity-related items would help shed more light on when, where, and under what conditions skin tone identity operates similarly and distinctly across the color spectrum.

I view the focus on skin tone identity in this project as being complementary to other recent examinations of racialized identities, such as a "people of color" identity (Pérez 2021). Efforts to examine identities as multidimensional do not diminish the value of studying categorical identities, but instead emphasize that people experience the world in different ways based on a variety of factors. In the case of skin tone, some people develop a meaningful skin tone identity that is associated with their political views. Similarly, a people-of-color identity extends across ethnoracial groups and suggests that there can be inter-group solidarity across communities of color in their efforts to improve their relative status and position in society (Pérez 2021). With this in mind, questions remain surrounding how exactly a skin tone identity can operate politically. For example, what are the conditions under which it is activated relative to racial identity? How might this identity or its activation influence views of political candidates? What potential might a skin tone identity have to exist across other communities of color in addition to African Americans?

It would be useful for future work to explore how skin tone and skin tone identity may operate in similar or distinct ways for other groups, including Latinos and Asian Americans. Of course these groups have histories, contexts, and political positioning distinct from those of African Americans that would require careful adaptation of the theorizing and measurement done here (e.g., Abrajano and Alvarez 2010; Fraga et al. 2010; Garcia-Bedolla 2005; Hajnal and Lee 2011; Masuoka and Junn 2013; Wong et al. 2011). Is there a sense of skin tone identity among these groups? How does skin tone identity compare, socially and politically, with that found among African Americans? Of particular importance, is there potential for a sort of cross-group solidarity based on skin tone under certain conditions, similar to a people-of color identity? Could such solidarity map onto one's social networks and, in turn, influence a propensity to participate in protests or other political activities (Frasure and Williams 2009; Simonson et al. 2024)? Given that colorism is a phenomenon that manifests across communities around the globe, with the skin bleaching industry being a billion-dollar industry in the United States alone, a color-based solidarity could be possible (Baluran 2023; Brown, Branden, and Hall 2018; Chen and Francis-Tan 2021; Craddock, Dlova, and Diedrichs 2018; Dixon and Telles 2017; Glenn 2008, 2009; Hall 2018; Herring, Keith, and Horton 2004). An exploration of this possibility would require engagement with the literature on intergroup dynamics and solidarity more broadly (e.g., Benjamin 2017; Kim 2000). Additionally, more deeply theorizing the nuanced ways that the combination of race, gender, and skin tone identities operate across contexts is a crucial area for future research given the gendered nature of racialized experiences (Hunter 2005; Lemi and Brown 2020; Threadcraft 2016; Woodly 2021). These next steps would be especially valuable to understand in an increasingly diversifying American public, as well as toward understanding the unique obstacles and opportunities of the more diverse pool of political candidates who are running for office (Dowe 2020; Holman and Schneider 2018; Lemi 2020; Meier et al. 2005; Minta and Sinclair-Chapman 2013; Scott et al. 2021; Scott, Dickinson, and Dowe 2020; Shah, Scott, and Gonzalez Juenke 2019; Smooth 2006).

Future work would also do well to have a more focused examination of the relationship between multiracialism and skin tone to understand its nuances, particularly with respect to skin tone identity. The multiracial population is of particular interest given that the value placed on skin tone is dynamic and contextual. As such, it is possible that mixed-race individuals face very different experiences based on skin tone even within their own families and other day-to-day experiences. For Black-White biracials, skin tone is likely perceived, discussed, and valued differently around one's Black family members than around White family members. Consistent with the broader colorism literature, lighter-skinned people often have access to more opportunities or positive treatment in White society, but this does not come without costs as well. There is psychological discomfort in feeling that one does not fully belong within traditional categorical racial groups (Khanna and Johnson 2010).

Understanding the patterns and associations of racial identification among multiracial individuals has received growing attention in recent years (e.g., Davenport 2018; Lemi 2020; Leslie et al. 2022; Leslie and Sears 2022; Masuoka 2017). Indeed, people from mixed-race backgrounds are understood to have the most flexible options in terms of racial identification choices (Davenport 2020). Some research suggests that multiracial individuals decide how they identify racially, in part, based on a variety of factors that may include their appearance (Roth 2016). How multiracial people may (or may not) adopt a *color-based identity* is less clear, though. Recall that younger African Americans in my samples were more likely to say their skin tone was important to their sense of identity. Multiracial people also tend to be younger, on average, than the general population. This suggests that similar sorts of considerations or interests that lead to acknowledging a mixed-race identity may also be associated with recognition of skin tone identity. Perhaps skin tone is especially salient to mixed-race people given the experiences they have faced growing up, which have placed a repeated emphasis on their skin tone across contexts. Alternatively, attachment to a skin tone identity could be less likely for multiracial individuals than among their monoracial Black peers. Recall that darker-skinned African Americans, on average, were more likely to report higher levels of skin tone identity. If mixed-race individuals are often relatively lighter-skinned than their monoracially identified Black counterparts, they may be less likely to develop a strong sense of attachment to a color-based identity. Given the growing numbers and political importance of mixed-race individuals in American politics, it would be worthwhile for future research to dig further into these dynamics among multiracial populations specifically.

Racial Group Boundaries and Political Solidarity

The extent to which skin tone identity has the potential to become more important over time also has implications for thinking about the future of racial boundaries. Historically, skin tone has been used as an important determinant of racial classification. Given the number of observed changes in the racial hierarchy in recent decades, which have expanded us beyond the Black-White binary—including significant demographic changes such as the incorporation of the sizable new ethnoracial groups and increasing levels of multiracialism—is it possible that differences in skin tone may undergird a new reshuffling of racial divisions and demarcations of identity? Skin tone may be taken up as a distinct social identity with repercussions for how we understand the boundaries around Blackness or Whiteness.

As social constructs, racial categories shift and evolve over time. This fluidity can be understood in terms of the significant changes over time in how the Census has measured racial categories—including fine-grained distinctions across categories of Blackness and more recent possibilities of selecting more than one racial category to better represent multiracial individuals (Davenport 2018; Saperstein and Gullickson 2013). For example, in the present moment, conversations are occurring around the Middle Eastern/North African (MENA) category and its potential inclusion in the Census. This group—which includes people descending from countries as diverse as Israel, Palestine, Jordan, Saudi Arabia, Iran, Sudan, Egypt, and the United Arab Emirates, among others—is currently categorized as racially "White" in many cases. Many people within this group do not feel that this categorization accurately reflects their experiences or identity, and have been pushing for a separate MENA racial category for some time (Lajevardi 2020, 2021; d'Urso 2022). Skin tone is one factor that influences how people are racialized, which in turn can influence how they perceive themselves and which aspects of their identity are meaningful to them.

Some scholars argue that racial categorization systems serve not only to reinforce unequal racial hierarchies, but also to minimize the extent to which within-group disparities are uncovered (Hochschild and Weaver 2007; Monk 2014). The maintenance and reinforcement of racial boundaries can create a double-edged sword whereby a stronger sense of Black racial unity develops in response to racial discrimination and, at the same time, efforts toward "suppressing and repressing critical vectors of inequality" such as color- or gender-based discrimination can occur (Monk 2014, p. 1332). This perspective complements theorizing about the gatekeeping that can occur regarding which group members' voices and concerns are worthy of attention and which are not (Cohen 1999; Jefferson 2023). Recall from chapter 4 the patterns of evidence that African Americans recognize that darker-skinned Black people are treated worse at the hands of police, on average, but are resistant to explicitly incorporating complexion into movement-organizing strategies. This is an example of how efforts to prioritize racial group cohesion and group-based disparities can contribute to continuing the marginalization of certain subgroups.

There are also legitimate concerns about the extent to which shifts around racial boundaries have the potential to disrupt racial group solidarity, power, and resources. Indeed, this was a concern among many civil rights organizations when the 2000 Census was considering including a multiracial option because it potentially opened the door for multiracial individuals to identify as distinct from the Black community. In turn, it was feared that this would meaningfully weaken African American coalitions and heighten disparities between Whites and monoracial Black people (Williams 2008). In a political system largely organized in terms of categorical racial groups and jockeying for position within this racial hierarchy, some scholars have rightfully noted the potential political costs associated with highlighting intra-racial disparities (e.g., Crenshaw 1990; Dawson 2001; Hochschild 2006; Monk 2014). There is concern that drawing attention to color-based inequities may increase political divisions within the categorical racial group. Such divisions may be especially straining for non-White groups, which often have less political power and access to resources. Put differently, if efforts toward highlight inequities are viewed as zero-sum, the concern is that attention devoted to intra-group disparities may limit progress toward fighting inter-group disparities.

These considerations should not be taken lightly. If social scientific research aims to shine a spotlight on inequalities experienced in society but this ultimately leads to a magnification of such inequality, then this is cause for serious concern. In this view, then, any research that focuses on intersectionality could be labeled as threatening the categorical group by virtue of focusing on intra-group dynamics. From a different perspective, however, research focusing on the complexities of any group-based dynamics—be it based on intersections of skin tone, gender, class, or sexuality—provides a lens through which we can better understand how the world operates. It is difficult to imagine, for example, arguing that men and women experience the world in the same ways; that richer and poorer people receive similar treatment; or that people who identify as heterosexual and homosexual both navigate the world similarly. Revisiting each of these examples while adding an additional layer based on race—that is, considering intersections of race and gender, race and class, or race and sexual orientation—rightfully highlights that identity is multidimensional and influences experiences, opportunities, and perspectives.

Furthermore, failing to acknowledge variation in lived experiences or outcomes simply out of fear of sowing division does little to improve the lives of those experiencing the most harm. Going back to our nation's founding, skin color has been an important tool of social division. Yet, skin color has largely avoided a deep examination with respect to scholarly theorizing and measurement within mainstream social science research. Although incorporating the intersection of race and skin tone into the conversation adds nuances to understanding race and racialized experiences, it is vital toward understanding issues of power and equity. Indeed, a number of recent calls have been made to advocate for better measurement practices such that scholars can understand these more fine-grained dynamics both within and across groups (Monk 2021; Reece 2018a; 2021; Valentino and Yadon 2023). Avoiding engagement with the importance of skin color and color-based discrimination has the potential to amplify the divisive powers of color in society rather than diminishing them. While some scholars argue that even if the racial hierarchy may shift in the face of the changing demographic characteristics of the United States, it is unlikely that African Americans, particularly those with more prototypically Black features, will stand to gain position in a reformulated hierarchy (Jardina 2019; Bobo and Hutchings 1996; Bonilla-Silva 2003).

So, why do we not see more explicit political organizing or calls to action around skin tone-based disparities in real-world politics? There is sustained evidence that African Americans continue to perceive racial discrimination as a serious obstacle in society. The evidence throughout this project underscores that Black people *also* recognize that darker-skinned people are treated worse at the hands of police and more broadly in society. Thus, there is an acknowledgment that color-based discrimination is overlayed with racial discrimination to powerfully shape lived experiences. Yet the simultaneous hesitancy expressed by many African Americans to highlight skin tone as a political issue fits with broader arguments about the challenges associated with creating inclusive political movements while also acknowledging issues that are unique to certain subgroups (Bonilla and Tillery 2020; Bunyasi and Smith 2019; Cohen 1999; hooks 2000). The recent Movement for Black Lives has explicitly acknowledged some intersectional disparities—for example, those related to Black women and Black LGBTQ individuals—but not those related to complexion. In this way, the skin color paradox seems to persist with respect to grassroots political movement organizing such that skin tone disparities are not explicitly recognized. Efforts to prioritize the racial group as a whole without emphasizing disparate subgroup impacts risk contributing to the persistence of marginalization of these subgroups (Cohen 1999).

At the same time, there are hints that attachment to one's skin tone identity *can* influence the extent to which one participates informally in politics. Even without explicit political organizing efforts, it is often recognized among

African Americans that darker-skinned Black people are more prone to police violence. And it was darker-skinned people who appeared more likely to report participating in protests and demonstrations across two separate datasets. Even without an explicit mobilizing effort based on skin tone, then, darker-skinned Black people are the color-based subgroup most likely to recognize and push back against inequities in society. This is consistent with a long-standing effort by African Americans to fight for equality and representation even when it was not historically afforded to them through institutional means (Gause 2022b; 2022a; Gillion 2013; 2020; Strolovitch 2008). Political scientist LaGina Gause argues that protest behavior by lower-resource groups sends particularly strong signals to legislators about their group's issue preferences. This is because low-resource groups have scarcer resources; in turn, using those resources to take to the streets in protest sends a strong signal about intensity of issue preferences (Gause 2022b). Consistent with Gause's argument, then, the higher rates of reported protest activity among darker-skinned Black people suggests that this subgroup takes especially seriously issues related to inequity, discrimination, and police brutality. This makes sense given the stronger application of racialized stereotypes to those with darker skin and more Afrocentric features, which can be especially detrimental to Black men in the criminal justice realm (Alexander 2020; Eberhardt et al. 2004; 2006; Smiley and Fakunle 2016). Even without formal organizing efforts, then, there are not only meaningful divides in public opinion between African Americans at the opposite end of the color spectrum but also different levels of reported protest activity.

Although skin tone is not an attribute around which there have consistently been political organizing efforts, this may change over time. Cross-racial understandings of colorism could emerge that, in turn, could help the phenomenon come to be understood as not simply existing within one's own community but having both systemic roots and far-reaching impacts across multiple communities. In that case, attachment to one's skin tone identity can potentially serve as a foundation for heightened political solidarity among members of the same racial group, or possibly even for people of similar complexions across different ethnoracial groups. While it is impossible to know what the future holds, continuing to study the conditions under which skin tone identity is activated in the real world and how this influences political views and behaviors are worthwhile next steps toward understanding the contours of the American racial landscape. Any hope for achieving racial equity hinges on recognizing and responding to color-based stigmatization.

Acknowledgments

The roots of this project date back more than a decade ago as I sat in an undergraduate lecture on political mobilization taught by Hanes Walton. Hanes was an incredible orator and lectured in a style I had never seen before. He showed up to class and started to tell a story. The story was always engaging but rarely seemed clearly tied at the outset to the specific day's topic or readings. Yet it always ended up directly linked to the subject at hand. In addition to enjoying Hanes's lecture style, I was enthralled by the course material on race, political views, and political activism. What I had anticipated was a one-off class that would fulfill a general degree requirement ended up being the first in a series of life-changing events.

It was serendipitous that the next semester a public opinion course was being offered by Vince Hutchings. I was captivated by the material in Vince's class related to group attitudes, stereotypes, and political views; I sat in the front row of every lecture and went to office hours frequently. Near the end of the semester, he asked if I had ever considered becoming a professor. The truth was I had no idea how one became a professor; I had never recognized it as an option as a first-generation college student. As would happen again countless times, Vince patiently explained about PhD programs and academia. He also suggested I consider writing an undergraduate honors thesis. Ultimately, I was fortunate enough to have both Hanes and Vince serve on my thesis examination committee. It is no understatement to say that neither my academic career nor this book project would have happened without the support and encouragement from Hanes and Vince.

As a graduate student at the University of Michigan, my intellectual curiosity was further enriched. I was thankful that one of my first classes as a graduate student was political psychology with Ted Brader. It was my first substantive introduction to the underpinnings of much of my subsequent research agenda. From that early stage, I saw that Ted was encouraging, warm, and generous with his time and feedback. I have benefited greatly from Ted's pushes to be meticulous in my attention to detail, while also zooming out to remember the bigger picture. More broadly, Ted has shaped not only my scholarly development but also my understanding of how to serve as a generous and attentive mentor.

Working with Ted and Vince as the cochairs of my dissertation was a true delight. There were inevitably highs and lows along my journey, but I always felt supported and incredibly grateful for their mentorship. It would be impossible for me to ever repay either of them for their investment in me. The best I can do is try to pay it forward by supporting the next generation of scholars.

At some point in the process of preparing my dissertation prospectus, I decided to cold email a post-doc named Mara Ostfeld to discuss some potentially shared research interests. To my surprise, Mara was interested in meeting. To my even greater surprise, that conversation blossomed into a multiyear collaboration that involved a face-to-face data collection of over 1,500 surveys, multiple publications including my first book, and a close personal friendship. Mara has been a cheerleader, a constructive critic, an excellent springboard for ideas, and an unwavering moral compass.

I was also fortunate to have an opportunity to work with Don Kinder as a graduate student. Don's dry sense of humor is one of my favorite things about him. I especially admire his ability to joke lightheartedly in one breath while giving sharp, substantive critiques in the next breath. This project has evolved a great deal thanks to his critical eye. More broadly, I learned invaluable skills about the process of writing and conducting careful research thanks to Don.

As someone who was primarily trained to work with survey and experimental data, I was eager to learn more about the process of conducting qualitative research. I am indebted to Alford Young for his support and mentorship through every stage of the in-depth interviewing process for this project. Al played a crucial role from research design to data collection to interview transcription and analysis. His perspective—both thanks to his qualitative expertise and the sociological lens he applied—was essential for improving the quality of my research. I am so grateful for the time and energy he invested into a political scientist over several years of my graduate career.

Additionally, I owe a debt of gratitude to my research team, which helped me collect the qualitative data for this project: Miriam Aggrey, Kennedi Holloway, Kamri Hudgins, and Clementine Sikpe. Recruiting, organizing, and conducting 100 in-depth interviews is a huge undertaking, but they all approached this experience with grace and enthusiasm. They also helped influence the shape of the project, giving feedback on the questions that were included in the conversations, making suggestions for other topics to consider including, and bringing their unique experiences to each conversation. I view the qualitative data as the backbone of this project and am appreciative to each of them for their steadfast commitment to collecting the best data possible.

I have been blessed to receive feedback on this project in a variety of venues, both large and small, throughout my career. Conversations and invaluable comments have been provided by participants at meetings of the American Political Science Association, Midwest Political Science Association, National Conference of Black Political Scientists, Politics of Race Ethnicity and Immigration Consortium, and the Southern Political Science Association, as well as the University of Michigan's Interdisciplinary Workshop in American Politics, Ohio State's American Politics Workshop, Ohio State's Political Psychology Workshop, UC San Diego's American Politics Workshop, LSU's Political Science Research Series, Yale's American Politics and Public Policy Workshop, Purdue's Political Science Research Workshop, and MSU's Minority Politics Lab Workshop. The NCFDD Faculty Success Program was also invaluable for helping to sustain the writing for this book.

It was an honor to host a book conference with a dream team of scholars: Marisa Abrajano, Lauren Davenport, Taeku Lee, and Ellis Monk. I left the book conference with a renewed vigor and clear vision for how to move the project forward. I also thank Charlene Stainfeld for her support in taking diligent notes and keeping the book conference on schedule. I was equally fortunate to have two reviewers for University of Chicago Press who were attentive to the project and its potential, providing clear and actionable feedback that has unquestionably served to improve the manuscript. My editor, Sara Doskow, has been amazing; she has been a steadfast supporter of the project since our very first conversation.

Countless people have contributed towards advancing my thinking for this project or my general development throughout my career. I would be remiss to not mention the support, mentorship, and friendship I have received through the years from them: Adrian Arellano, Andrea Benjamin, LaShonda Brenson, Meg Burt, Taylor Carlson, Sydney Carr, Peter Carroll, Chinbo Chong, Jenn Chudy, Kiela Crabtree, Alison Craig, Nyron Crawford, Jesse Crosson, Vanessa Cruz-Nichols, Lauren Davenport, Marty Davison, Jennifer Frentasia, LaGina Gause, Cassie Grafstrom, Maiko Heller, Portia Hemphill, Dan Hiaeshutter-Rice, Bai Linh Hoang, Kamri Hudgins, Ashley Jardina, Hakeem Jefferson, Eric Juenke, Christina Kinane, Thomas Klemm, Chryl Laird, Nazita Lajevardi, Greg Leslie, Nicky Mack, Andy Markovits,

Will Massengill, Yalidy Matos, Corrine McConnaughy, Steven Moore, Tom Nelson, Irfan Nooruddin, Angela Ocampo, Marzia Oceno, Efrén Pérez, Davin Phoenix, Spencer Piston, Eugenia Quintanilla, Lauren Ratliff-Santoro, Sinead Redmond, Amanda Robinson, LaFleur Stephens-Dougan, Nick Valentino, Hannah Walker, Julian Wamble, Carly Wayne, Ismail White, Princess Williams, Tom Wood, and Nicole Wu. Additionally, I participated in a book writing club with Taylor Carlson and Eunji Kim that significantly helped to move the revisions for this project forward. Another regular writing group with Brielle Harbin, Jamil Scott, Jessica Stewart, Carrie LeVan, Daphne Penn, Stacey Greene, Angela Ocampo, and Kelly Slay facilitated excellent feedback. LaGina Gause generously read and commented on nearly every chapter as I finalized the manuscript. LaShonda Brenson, Kiela Crabtree, Amanda d'Urso, Vince Hutchings, John Kuk, Nazita Lajevardi, Davin Phoenix, and Spencer Piston all provided valuable feedback in the final stages.

As a faculty member at Ohio State University I have been lucky to be surrounded by supportive colleagues. Tom Nelson and Tom Wood have both played a central role in mentoring me, as well as reading this entire manuscript and offering generous suggestions for improvement. Greg Leslie, Michael Neblo, and Amanda Robinson also provided valuable feedback on multiple parts of the project. In addition to supporting my research, many of my faculty colleagues have supported me as a person and a scholar. Alex Acs, Jan Box-Steffensmeier, Sarah Brooks, Greg Caldeira, Skyler Cranmer, Vlad Kogan, Marcus Kurtz, Erin Lin, Eric MacGilvray, Ben McKean, William Minozzi, Jennifer Mitzen, Michael Neblo, Julia Park, Jan Pierskalla, Philipp Rehm, Molly Ritchie, Amanda Robinson, Emma Saunders-Hastings, Alex Thompson, Ines Valdez, and Sara Watson have all provided advice and encouragement at critical moments. I could not be more thankful for having landed among such supportive colleagues.

Conducting research that involves collecting new data, particularly on hard-to-reach populations, is an expensive endeavor. I am indebted to the University of Michigan Rackham Graduate School, the University of Michigan Rackham Merit Fellows Program, the Center for Political Studies at ISR, the University of Michigan Department of Political Science, the Ohio State University Department of Political Science, the National Science Foundation, TESS, and the APSA Centennial Center for funding parts of this project. I am particularly grateful for anonymous feedback from reviewers for the NSF's Doctoral Dissertation Research Improvement Grant, as well as from anonymous TESS reviewers and the TESS PIs, Jamie Druckman and Jeremy Freese. Both sets of feedback helped in shaping the course of the project at crucial junctures. I am also deeply appreciative for the support I received from staff and administrators at Michigan and Ohio State. In particular, Kathryn Cardenas, Dave Howell, Becca Martin, Melodie McGrothers, Jeremy Mitchell, Barb Opal, Pat Preston, and Kim Smith deserve recognition for the support they provided.

I also recognize that this project is built on the shoulders of giants. Some of these giants came from the University of Michigan and legitimized the field of survey research, including creating the American National Election Study. Other giants did the vital work of bringing the study of race and politics more centrally into the social sciences, aiming to give voice to communities that were often ignored. These include Anna Julia Cooper, W. E. B. Du Bois, Ida B. Wells, and countless others who shined a spotlight on racial injustices. Within political science, this work has been done by Hanes Walton, Jewel Prestage, and the founders of the National Conference of Black Political Scientists, among others. I attempt to build from these legacies by highlighting ongoing inequities while lifting up the voices of those who are often unfairly and unjustly silenced.

On the personal side, I am blessed with love and support by family members who have poured into me over the years and shaped me into the person I am today. I am especially indebted to my parents for pushing me to never settle, to speak out against injustice, and to pull others up as I climb. They have always believed in me even when I did not believe it myself. I cannot adequately express how thankful I am for their help, time, love, and praise.

I am similarly fortunate to have a dedicated and supportive husband. He is the most kind and patient person I know, always pushing me to be the best version of myself. I am especially grateful to him for being the best father to our daughter. I was able to finish writing this book thanks to his support, my sweet daughter's nap times, and the commitment of our dog, Ned, who loyally slept beside me in my office every time I sat down to write. I hope that by adding to the chorus of research highlighting injustices and inequities in society, there may be a brighter and more equitable future on the horizon for my daughter's generation and beyond.

Appendixes

Chapter 3 Appendix

QUALITATIVE INTERVIEW METHODOLOGY

Interviews were conducted in two Midwest metropolitan areas: (1) Ann Arbor/Detroit, Michigan from October 2016 to September 2017; and (2) Columbus, Ohio from February to July 2021. Detroit has the fourth largest population of African Americans in the United States with a population of over 600,000 Black residents (Rastogi et al. 2011). For comparison purposes, the interviews were conducted in two neighboring counties in Michigan given variation in composition including population size, racial breakdown, household income, and educational differences: Washtenaw County and Wayne County. Washtenaw County has over 12 percent of the population as Black alone and 3.5 percent as two or more races, a median household income of over $65,000, and over 54 percent having a college degree. In contrast, Wayne County has a 39 percent Black population with 2.5 percent identifying as two or more races, a median household income of $43,700, and 23 percent having a college degree. Importantly, the proximity of these areas holds constant other external factors, social contexts, and political structures.

While the Michigan interviews were conducted in 2016–2017, the second round of interviews were conducted in Columbus in 2021. These interviews were delayed from their planned start date due to the COVID-19 pandemic and switched from an in-person to virtual format for health and safety reasons. This influenced the ability to recruit participants from certain backgrounds because it required individuals to have reliable internet access so the conversation could be recorded. Of course, it also meant the flow of the conversations was not as natural as being in-person. Still, this was the best option for data collection under the circumstances in another large Midwestern city with a nearly 30 percent Black population (and 6 percent identifying with two

TABLE A3.1: Descriptive statistics from survey samples of African Americans

	NSAL 2001–2003	ANES 2012	MTurk 2016	YouGov 2016	Lucid 2018	AmeriSpeak 2019	CMPS 2020
Survey mode	FTF and Phone	FTF Only	Web	Web	Web	Web	Web
% Female	68	51	51	55%	56	66	51
Age (average)	44 years	40–44 years	25–34 years	44 years	40 years	42 years	44 years
Income (average)	$18,000–$18,999	$27,500–$29,999	$30,000–$39,999	$30,000–$39,999	$40,000–$44,999	$35,000–$39,999	$40,000–$49,999
Education (average)	—	Some college	Associate's degree	Some college	Some college	Some college/ Associate's degree	Some college
% South	55	59	—	40	55	60	48
Party identity	22% Rep.	6% Rep.	13% Rep.	8% Rep.	11% Rep.	7% Rep.	8% Rep.
	2% Indep.	4% Indep.	20% Indep.	24% Indep.	12% Indep.	16% Indep.	15% Indep.
	76% Dem	90% Dem.	67% Dem.	68% Dem.	78% Dem.	77% Dem.	77% Dem.
Ideology	—	45% Cons.	20% Cons.	26% Cons.	19% Cons.	12% Cons.	17% Cons.
		8% Mod.	24% Mod.	34% Mod.	40% Mod.	27% Mod.	43% Mod.
		47% Liberal	56% Liberal	41% Liberal	42% Liberal	61% Liberal	40% Liberal
Skin tone assessment	Self-rated; 5-point (very light -very dark)	Interviewer; Massey-Martin scale	Self-rated; Massey-Martin scale	Self-rated; Massey-Martin scale	Self-rated; Yadon-Ostfeld scale	Self-rated; Yadon-Ostfeld scale	Self-rated; Yadon-Ostfeld scale
% monoracial, US-born Black Rs	92	100	97	100	92	100	77
# of observations	1,543	511	229	577	1,825	1,045	3,918

Note: ANES and CMPS samples incorporate survey weights. Partisanship and ideology calculations combine leaners and weak partisans/ideologues into the broader partisan/ideology category. 2001–2003 NSAL data does not include a question related to political ideology or levels of education received (in analyses, a proxy for college educated vs. not is used). Percent monoracial Black in NSAL data is determined by responses to questions regarding parents' race.

TABLE A3.2A: African American policy preferences in the 2012 ANES by skin tone (corresponding to figures 3.3 and 3.4)

	Support increasing welfare spending			Support affirmative action (work)			Support affirmative action (college)		
Skin tone	0.195*	0.194*	0.227**	0.323**	0.299**	0.312**	0.285**	0.263*	0.232
	(0.107)	(0.107)	(0.105)	(0.134)	(0.135)	(0.141)	(0.142)	(0.142)	(0.153)
Female	-0.082*	-0.082*	-0.080*	-0.038	-0.036	0.007	-0.054	-0.053	-0.017
	(0.044)	(0.045)	(0.041)	(0.053)	(0.053)	(0.056)	(0.055)	(0.054)	(0.058)
Age	0.010	0.011	0.008	-0.005	-0.003	0.005	0.002	0.004	0.010
	(0.007)	(0.007)	(0.007)	(0.010)	(0.010)	(0.010)	(0.009)	(0.009)	(0.010)
Income	-0.135	-0.126	-0.153	0.045	0.064	0.050	0.016	0.028	0.049
	(0.105)	(0.108)	(0.109)	(0.109)	(0.110)	(0.111)	(0.110)	(0.113)	(0.124)
Education	-0.012	-0.005	-0.068	0.206**	0.227**	0.206**	0.288***	0.318***	0.293***
	(0.103)	(0.104)	(0.101)	(0.099)	(0.096)	(0.096)	(0.089)	(0.092)	(0.110)
Democrat	0.126	0.130	-0.040	0.173	0.183	0.143	0.117	0.134	0.102
	(0.081)	(0.084)	(0.098)	(0.122)	(0.127)	(0.138)	(0.131)	(0.135)	(0.140)
South	-0.051	-0.050	-0.041	0.084*	0.096**	0.104**	0.023	0.032	0.050
	(0.042)	(0.042)	(0.040)	(0.047)	(0.047)	(0.052)	(0.051)	(0.051)	(0.057)
Own home		-0.018	0.012		-0.071	-0.066		-0.066	-0.095
		(0.050)	(0.051)		(0.056)	(0.063)		(0.058)	(0.066)
Unemployed		-0.009	-0.015		-0.073	-0.153*		-0.042	-0.147*
		(0.089)	(0.107)		(0.095)	(0.081)		(0.089)	(0.087)
Liberal			0.072			0.012			0.070
			(0.094)			(0.110)			(0.112)
Linked fate			0.073			0.143*			0.068
			(0.053)			(0.074)			(0.078)
Black identity			0.219***			-0.097			-0.064
			(0.074)			(0.084)			(0.086)
Constant	0.346***	0.340***	0.139	0.089	0.098	-0.008	0.123	0.122	0.014
	(0.125)	(0.127)	(0.137)	(0.161)	(0.166)	(0.195)	(0.163)	(0.167)	(0.211)
Observations	5,794	5,786	5,748	5,821	5,811	5,752	5,817	5,809	5,750
R-squared	0.078	0.080	0.172	0.065	0.076	0.118	0.058	0.068	0.095
N_sub	421	413	375	448	438	379	444	436	377

Notes: * p < .10; ** p < .05; *** p < .01 for two-tailed test. All variables coded 0–1. Results are based on weighted data and incorporating survey design effects. Additional controls included in the model but not shown are for interviewer skin tone and egalitarianism index. Skin color variable is a continuous ten-point scale assessed by the interviewer.

TABLE A3.2B: African American policy preferences in the 2012 ANES by skin tone (corresponding to figures 3-3 and 3-4)

	Support increasing government services		Support government reducing income inequality		Support increasing immigration levels	
Skin tone	0.152*	0.220**	0.238**	0.222**	0.285***	-0.209**	-0.206**	-0.189**
	(0.092)	(0.095)	(0.106)	(0.108)	(0.108)	(0.083)	(0.083)	(0.085)
Female	0.061*	0.048	0.027	0.031	0.042	-0.047	-0.038	-0.048
	(0.036)	(0.035)	(0.047)	(0.047)	(0.048)	(0.035)	(0.034)	(0.040)
Age	0.001	-0.003	-0.006	-0.003	-0.001	0.002	0.005	0.003
	(0.007)	(0.007)	(0.007)	(0.008)	(0.008)	(0.005)	(0.006)	(0.007)
Income	-0.019	-0.018	-0.052	-0.153	-0.144	-0.188*	-0.047	-0.052	-0.078
	(0.066)	(0.071)	(0.070)	(0.097)	(0.102)	(0.108)	(0.069)	(0.073)	(0.077)
Education	-0.125	-0.123	-0.078	-0.082	-0.054	-0.016	0.076	0.094*	0.145**
	(0.078)	(0.078)	(0.073)	(0.094)	(0.098)	(0.113)	(0.057)	(0.056)	(0.060)
Democrat	0.230***	0.226**	0.107	0.126	0.155	0.144	-0.060	-0.023	-0.047
	(0.089)	(0.103)	(0.100)	(0.106)	(0.107)	(0.114)	(0.092)	(0.089)	(0.087)
South	-0.046	-0.044	-0.052	-0.026	-0.027	-0.047	-0.078**	-0.083***	-0.070**
	(0.034)	(0.036)	(0.037)	(0.046)	(0.046)	(0.047)	(0.032)	(0.032)	(0.034)
Own home		0.001	0.018		-0.033	-0.004		0.014	0.023
		(0.045)	(0.043)		(0.050)	(0.053)		(0.039)	(0.042)
Unemployed		0.048	-0.009		0.045	0.065		0.130	0.092
		(0.056)	(0.059)		(0.072)	(0.075)		(0.080)	(0.091)
Liberal			0.083			-0.049			-0.027
			(0.077)			(0.113)			(0.074)
Linked Fate			0.008			-0.069			-0.047
			(0.052)			(0.054)			(0.050)
Black identity			0.046			0.088			-0.068
			(0.061)			(0.080)			(0.059)
Constant	0.428***	0.418***	0.463***	0.450***	0.410***	0.164	0.653***	0.577***	0.615***
	(0.094)	(0.107)	(0.144)	(0.132)	(0.142)	(0.188)	(0.099)	(0.095)	(0.109)
Observations	5,727	5,720	5,676	5,798	5,789	5,752	5,796	5,788	5,748
R-squared	0.099	0.094	0.140	0.054	0.058	0.097	0.080	0.105	0.111
N_sub	354	347	303	425	416	379	423	415	375

Notes: * p < .10; ** p < .05; *** p < .01 for two-tailed test. All variables coded 0–1. Results are based on weighted data and incorporating survey design effects. Additional controls included in the model but not shown are for interviewer skin tone and egalitarianism index. Skin color variable is a continuous ten-point scale assessed by the interviewer.

TABLE A3.2C: African American policy preferences in the 2012 ANES by skin tone (corresponding to figures 3.3 and 3.4)

	Immigrants unlikely to take jobs			Feeling thermometer: Hispanics			Feeling thermometer: Asians		
Skin tone	0.177	0.174	0.184	0.130*	0.148**	0.135*	0.057	0.065	0.042
	(0.142)	(0.143)	(0.140)	(0.074)	(0.075)	(0.069)	(0.066)	(0.065)	(0.064)
Female	0.058	0.045	0.061	0.004	0.005	-0.017	-0.010	-0.010	-0.012
	(0.056)	(0.054)	(0.056)	(0.032)	(0.032)	(0.027)	(0.026)	(0.026)	(0.027)
Age	0.001	-0.006	-0.008	-0.001	-0.000	-0.004	0.003	0.002	0.002
	(0.010)	(0.009)	(0.010)	(0.005)	(0.005)	(0.005)	(0.004)	(0.004)	(0.005)
Income	0.003	-0.003	0.013	-0.074	-0.073	-0.095	-0.047	-0.043	-0.062
	(0.104)	(0.112)	(0.104)	(0.059)	(0.062)	(0.060)	(0.057)	(0.061)	(0.063)
Education	-0.234**	-0.290***	-0.394***	0.220***	0.218***	0.232***	0.190***	0.181***	0.184***
	(0.091)	(0.093)	(0.094)	(0.051)	(0.054)	(0.057)	(0.053)	(0.053)	(0.059)
Democrat	0.051	-0.014	-0.008	0.121	0.111	-0.062	-0.002	-0.015	-0.044
	(0.121)	(0.124)	(0.130)	(0.088)	(0.095)	(0.073)	(0.064)	(0.063)	(0.065)
South	0.014	0.023	0.033	-0.044	-0.046	-0.016	-0.046	-0.046*	-0.038
	(0.050)	(0.049)	(0.050)	(0.031)	(0.032)	(0.030)	(0.028)	(0.028)	(0.028)
Own home		0.019	0.023		0.006	0.022		-0.010	0.008
		(0.059)	(0.061)		(0.032)	(0.030)		(0.030)	(0.031)
Unemployed		-0.227***	-0.190**		0.073	0.032		-0.021	-0.050
		(0.084)	(0.078)		(0.065)	(0.056)		(0.045)	(0.033)
Liberal			-0.111			0.048			0.071
			(0.098)			(0.068)			(0.054)
Linked fate			0.165**			-0.072*			-0.036
			(0.070)			(0.042)			(0.034)
Black identity			-0.054			0.114*			0.083
			(0.091)			(0.058)			(0.060)
Constant	0.402**	0.542***	0.636***	0.507***	0.496***	0.427***	0.613***	0.638***	0.551***
	(0.152)	(0.160)	(0.207)	(0.104)	(0.114)	(0.112)	(0.077)	(0.079)	(0.097)
Observations	5,806	5,799	5,757	5,806	5,796	5,755	5,806	5,796	5,755
R-squared	0.044	0.079	0.121	0.077	0.079	0.151	0.072	0.072	0.096
N_sub	433	426	384	433	423	382	433	423	382

Notes: * $p < .10$; ** $p < .05$; *** $p < .01$ for two-tailed test. All variables coded 0–1. Results are based on weighted data and incorporating survey design effects. Additional controls included in the model but not shown are for interviewer skin tone and egalitarianism index. Skin color variable is a continuous ten-point scale assessed by the interviewer.

TABLE A3.3: Examining broader sets of issues and policy opinions by skin tone (2012 ANES)

	Linked fate	Black identity	Approval of president	Anger at President Obama	Levels of political knowledge	Favor affirmative action in college	Favor affirmative action in workplace	Government assistance to Blacks
Skin tone	0.150	-0.065	-0.047	-0.111	-0.063	0.232	0.312**	0.104
	(0.160)	(0.107)	(0.052)	(0.092)	(0.077)	(0.153)	(0.141)	(0.135)
Linked fate	—	0.153***	-0.001	-0.038	0.015	0.068	0.143*	0.084
	—	(0.045)	(0.027)	(0.058)	(0.033)	(0.078)	(0.074)	(0.068)
Black identity	0.312***	—	-0.005	0.137***	-0.010	-0.064	-0.097	0.041
	(0.098)	—	(0.037)	(0.050)	(0.071)	(0.086)	(0.084)	(0.105)
Female	-0.118*	0.020	-0.011	-0.098**	-0.081***	-0.017	0.007	0.030
	(0.064)	(0.039)	(0.023)	(0.041)	(0.028)	(0.058)	(0.056)	(0.050)
Education	0.294***	-0.164	-0.025	-0.173***	0.306***	0.293***	0.206**	-0.098
	(0.095)	(0.124)	(0.040)	(0.055)	(0.068)	(0.110)	(0.096)	(0.096)
Constant	-0.328*	0.395**	0.622***	0.269**	-0.075	0.014	-0.008	0.177
	(0.180)	(0.194)	(0.112)	(0.133)	(0.131)	(0.211)	(0.195)	(0.197)
Observations	5,762	5,762	5,755	5,428	5,762	5,750	5,752	5,707
R-squared	0.224	0.210	0.281	0.605	0.324	0.095	0.118	0.140
N_sub	389	389	382	55	389	377	379	334

	Approve of Obama's handling of health care	Favor 2010 health care law	Support abortion rights	Gun ownership	Favor marijuana legalization	Support increasing federal crime spending	Support increasing federal defense spending	Know someone who has lost a job
Skin tone	−0.058	−0.108	0.043	0.042	0.199	0.016	0.206	0.364**
	(0.106)	(0.114)	(0.176)	(0.150)	(0.172)	(0.113)	(0.133)	(0.175)
Linked fate	0.005	−0.053	0.129	−0.105	0.044	−0.079*	0.075	0.235***
	(0.047)	(0.049)	(0.094)	(0.078)	(0.088)	(0.042)	(0.067)	(0.087)
Black identity	0.065	0.209***	−0.079	0.072	0.066	−0.049	0.002	−0.256**
	(0.065)	(0.065)	(0.131)	(0.071)	(0.111)	(0.084)	(0.070)	(0.122)
Female	0.043	−0.015	0.125*	−0.210***	−0.062	−0.075	0.042	0.076
	(0.038)	(0.038)	(0.074)	(0.060)	(0.068)	(0.046)	(0.054)	(0.070)
Education	0.027	0.017	0.277*	0.062	0.343***	−0.268*	−0.114	0.227
	(0.058)	(0.071)	(0.147)	(0.092)	(0.115)	(0.137)	(0.085)	(0.160)
Constant	0.328**	0.277*	0.113	−0.245	0.600***	0.915***	0.593***	0.313
	(0.147)	(0.151)	(0.279)	(0.161)	(0.223)	(0.198)	(0.196)	(0.272)
Observations	5,756	5,755	5,758	5,749	5,761	5,762	5,655	5,759
R-squared	0.266	0.223	0.092	0.184	0.115	0.074	0.124	0.119
N_sub	383	382	385	376	388	389	282	386

Notes: * p < .10; ** p < .05; *** p < .01 for two-tailed test. All variables coded 0–1. Results are based on weighted data and incorporating survey design effects. Additional controls included in the model but not shown are for interviewer skin tone, age, income, partisanship, ideology, region, egalitarian index, homeownership, and employment status. Skin color variable is a continuous ten-point scale assessed by the interviewer.

TABLE A3.4: African American policy preferences in the 2001–2003 NSAL by skin tone (corresponding to figure 3.5)

	Affirmative action in workplace	Government should guarantee jobs	Rich should pay higher taxes	Government should pay reparations for slavery	Government should help Black people
Skin tone	0.125**	0.075*	−0.032	0.005	−0.012
	(0.053)	(0.042)	(0.045)	(0.045)	(0.033)
Black identity	0.081**	0.023	0.001	0.058**	0.080***
	(0.033)	(0.027)	(0.029)	(0.028)	(0.024)
Linked fate	0.162***	0.109***	0.085**	0.151***	0.070**
	(0.037)	(0.032)	(0.035)	(0.032)	(0.028)
Female	0.024	0.037*	−0.033	0.023	0.019
	(0.023)	(0.019)	(0.022)	(0.020)	(0.016)
Democrat	0.050	0.039	0.097***	0.085***	0.099***
	(0.032)	(0.025)	(0.029)	(0.027)	(0.022)
Age	−0.015	−0.114**	0.212***	0.053	0.000
	(0.053)	(0.045)	(0.050)	(0.048)	(0.038)
Income	−0.149***	−0.195***	−0.021	−0.099**	−0.044
	(0.044)	(0.036)	(0.044)	(0.039)	(0.033)
College	−0.050**	−0.069***	0.074***	0.026	0.018
	(0.024)	(0.019)	(0.022)	(0.021)	(0.017)
Constant	0.495***	0.766***	0.512***	0.551***	0.634***
	(0.059)	(0.044)	(0.051)	(0.047)	(0.039)
Observations	1,918	2,116	2,119	2,080	2,093
R-squared	0.064	0.066	0.060	0.055	0.056
N_sub	1,262	1,460	1,463	1,424	1,437

Notes: * p < .10; ** p < .05; *** p < .01 for two-tailed test. All variables coded 0–1. Results are based on weighted analyses of the data. Skin color variable is a five-point scale from "very dark brown" to "very light brown" self-reported by the interview participant.

or more races). According to the 2020 Census, Columbus has a median income of nearly $59,000, and 38 percent of the population has a college degree. Conducting conversations in Columbus serves as a contrast to the Michigan interviews given both the different racial dynamics, including larger immigrant populations, as well as the timing following the sustained summer 2020 protests in the wake of George Floyd's murder at the hands of police.

Both sets of semi-structured interviews were advertised as a conversation about Black experiences in society via multiple methods of advertisement: student, faculty, and staff email listservs at large public universities in the areas, flyers posted at local coffee shops and libraries, postings in local church bulletins, as well as local Craigslist and other social media postings advertising the research interviews. A snowball sampling technique was also used such that upon completing an interview, participants were asked if they knew of anyone else who may be interested in participating. All participants were selected for participation only after completing a pre-screening form to ensure variation on key demographic factors of interest (e.g., age, gender, level of education). Ultimately, not everyone who completed the pre-screening form was selected for an interview.

The interview topics included discussions about everyday experiences related to race and skin tone, as well as discussions of the relationship between skin tone and various topics including politics, power, representation, stereotypes, and resources. Each interview progressed as follows: The conversation began with a discussion of the participant's reactions to a set of photos of African Americans. Participants were then prompted to discuss the key values and characteristics thought to be important to many Black people in their community or social circles. The conversation then shifted to an explicit focus on skin color—asking if they believed skin color to be important in society, if it operated differently by gender or age/generation, and asking participants to share stories about themselves or others related to color-based discrimination. Finally, there was a discussion of skin color and thoughts about potential policy or movement responses geared towards addressing colorism. At the conclusion of the study, participants answered a series of demographic questions and were asked to provide feedback to the interviewer about the interview experience or other topics they suggested as important points of discussion.

There were a total of five interviewers—two in Michigan and three in Ohio. The interviewers self-identified as a light-skinned White woman (n = 43), a light-skinned Black woman (n = 24), a dark-skinned Black woman (n = 13), a brown-skinned Black woman (n = 10), and a dark-skinned Black woman (n = 10). The variation in race and skin tone of interviewers was purposeful for allowing an examination of differences in conversational style and substance. Each interviewer has distinct experiences with the intersection of race, color, and power in America based on their own appearance and background. Each interviewer implicitly brought these differences into the conversations they had, which influenced how the conversations unfolded. The inclusion of interviewers from different backgrounds provides an opportunity to examine the dynamic nature of interviewer's insider/outsider status (Brown 2012; Young 2004). Indeed, my experiences with colorism in society are constrained by my own light skin and unearned privileges stemming from my Whiteness. In turn, this limits my ability to experience racism or colorism first-hand. Still, I argue that drawing attention to and speaking about systemic disparities based on racism or colorism should not fall solely on the shoulders of the marginalized, as it traditionally does. This is especially important as Whites continue to perpetuate colorism both implicitly and explicitly in society.

The substance of the interview conversations was relatively constant across interviews—with similar patterns in responses and views regarding skin tone's importance across interviewers. The style of the conversations, however, was distinct based on the race of the interviewer. While the White interviewer's racial outsider status required more effort towards building rapport and trust with participants, it may have also allowed room for greater extrapolation from participants because the interviewer was presumed to be unfamiliar with colorism. The Black interviewers' status as a racial insider meant that participants often signaled an expectation of mutual understanding, which sometimes inhibited the depth of responses. In turn, this required more follow-up questions from the Black interviewer to prompt further elaboration, which can create tension and a disruption to rapport (Young 2004).

In addition, the Black interviewers' racial insider status did not translate to shared insider status in all domains, including factors like gender, skin tone, education, or immigrant status. Indeed, the Black interviewers reported feeling more instances of hesitation or reluctance from participants in answering some questions related to skin tone than the White interviewer, especially if there was a skin tone mismatch between the interviewer and interviewee. This may, in part, be due to intra-racial differences in perceptions and stereotypes based on color (Banks 1999; Hunter 2005; Maddox and Gray 2002; Monk 2021). Ideally, one would not only race-match interviewers with participants, but also color- and gender-match in an effort to increase perceived insider status. From a practical perspective, this would be challenging to implement since skin tone is not observed until the interview begins, as well as the financial costs associated with maintaining such a large team of research assistants varying by race, color, and gender.

Overall, the conversations were friendly, and participants seemed mostly at ease and willing to be forthcoming with interviewers. Of course, this ebbed and flowed throughout each conversation. Interviewers felt that participants often seemed pleased that someone was interested in hearing their perspective and that they could talk at length about their experiences or views. While interviewer characteristics play an inevitable role in shaping the conversations, the qualitative analysis and feedback from interviewees at the end of every conversation provides confidence in the general themes and patterns observed.[1]

In total, the interviews lasted 70 minutes on average, ranging from 29 to 164 minutes. The average age of participants was 36 years old, with a range from 20 to 70 years. The gender breakdown of participants was nearly equal with 58 percent women, 42 percent men, and 2 percent identifying as gender non-binary, with educational attainment ranging from less than high school diploma through a doctorate. The self-identified skin color of the participants also ranged from "very light" to "dark." Participants consented to participate in this research study and to be audio-recorded at the outset of the conversation.

The interviews were transcribed by the interviewer who conducted them and formatted using a common template. The primary researcher then reviewed all 100 transcripts three times each, making notes of patterns of responses related to each item. These observations were then used to create a preliminary coding scheme of responses to the interview questions. The interviewer then used the Rapid and Rigorous Qualitative Data Analysis or "RADaR" technique (Watkins 2017) to take the detailed answers in response to any given question and winnow them down to a simplified categorical response (e.g., "believes skin color is important in society," "does not believe skin color is important in society"). After the initial coding scheme was created, the researcher re-reviewed all transcripts and coded the responses within the coding scheme along with the pertinent excerpts from the conversation. When responses fell outside of the preliminary coding scheme, a new category was added to the coding scheme and all transcripts were re-reviewed to determine whether other responses should also be recategorized.

QUALITATIVE INTERVIEW DESCRIPTIVE STATISTICS

TABLE A3.5: Distribution of interview participants' self-identified skin color

Total number by skin color (self-rating)	Total	Subtotal
Light	25	34
Light/Medium	9	
Medium	32	32
Medium/Dark	11	
Dark	23	34
Total	**100**	**100**

Note: The "subtotal" column truncates responses into light, medium, and dark categories only, combining together those who indicated they identified on the border of two groups (e.g., light/medium) along with those in the primary category (i.e., light).

TABLE A3.6: Overview of interview participants' education distribution

Highest Education	Total	Subtotal
Less than high school	3	
GED	3	
High school diploma	14	
Some college, no degree	33	53
Associate's degree	4	
Bachelor's degree	21	25
Master's degree	20	
PhD	2	22
Total	**100**	**100**

Note: The "subtotal" column provides the subtotal for 3 groups: people who do not have a college degree, those who have a 2- or 4-year college degree, and those with a post-graduate degree.

TABLE A3.7: Domains referenced as associated with skin tone among interview participants

Domain Mentioned	Number of mentions	Percent of total mentions
Beauty, relationships	84	39
Perceived violence, aggression, physical strength, targets of police	57	26
Jobs, opportunities, promotions, money	55	25
Education, intelligence, competency	11	5
Personal characteristics or personality (e.g., being loud, having an attitude, being overconfident, being trustworthy, communication style)	10	5
Total	**217**	**100**

Chapter 4 Appendix

TABLE A4.1: Relationship between skin color and reported interactions with police among Black respondents (CMPS 2020)

	Stopped by police in car	Stopped by police on foot	Charged fine or fee for noncriminal infraction	Arrested or charged with crime	Convicted of crime, even if not guilty	Charged a fine for criminal conviction	Been on probation or parole	Spent time in jail or prison	Been the victim of a crime	Close friend/family arrested or charged with crime	Close friend/family convicted of a crime, even if not guilty	Close friend/family spent time in jail, prison, probation, or parole
Skin tone	0.287* (0.152)	0.566*** (0.161)	0.422** (0.165)	0.447*** (0.167)	0.840*** (0.184)	0.784*** (0.182)	0.567*** (0.177)	0.654*** (0.174)	0.326** (0.153)	0.412*** (0.150)	0.589*** (0.156)	0.374** (0.149)
Black identity	0.302** (0.135)	0.288** (0.144)	0.217 (0.144)	0.432*** (0.149)	0.095 (0.151)	0.086 (0.152)	0.377** (0.154)	0.400*** (0.151)	0.046 (0.132)	0.224* (0.129)	0.258* (0.140)	0.320** (0.129)
Linked fate	0.198* (0.117)	−0.178 (0.121)	−0.580*** (0.119)	−0.617*** (0.121)	−1.230*** (0.132)	−0.926*** (0.129)	−0.827*** (0.126)	−0.765*** (0.122)	0.129 (0.114)	0.367*** (0.114)	−0.020 (0.116)	0.318*** (0.113)
Female	−0.992*** (0.079)	−1.490*** (0.084)	−0.760*** (0.085)	−1.046*** (0.089)	−0.781*** (0.095)	−0.880*** (0.095)	−0.909*** (0.094)	−1.186*** (0.098)	−0.494*** (0.077)	−0.242*** (0.076)	−0.360*** (0.078)	−0.267*** (0.076)
Age	−0.423* (0.253)	−1.928*** (0.265)	−1.417*** (0.272)	−0.957*** (0.269)	−2.875*** (0.326)	−2.364*** (0.311)	−1.621*** (0.291)	−1.093*** (0.284)	0.881*** (0.249)	0.330 (0.248)	−1.182*** (0.256)	0.681*** (0.248)
Income	0.073 (0.147)	−0.219 (0.154)	−0.223 (0.158)	−0.106 (0.161)	0.129 (0.169)	−0.058 (0.168)	−0.091 (0.170)	−0.300* (0.168)	0.004 (0.144)	0.274* (0.145)	0.169 (0.149)	0.115 (0.144)
Education	0.779*** (0.180)	−0.209 (0.187)	−0.431** (0.195)	−0.559*** (0.200)	−0.653*** (0.222)	−0.759*** (0.220)	−1.047*** (0.219)	−0.826*** (0.218)	0.263 (0.174)	−0.384** (0.175)	−0.375** (0.184)	−0.463*** (0.173)
Democrat	−0.710*** (0.163)	−0.265* (0.160)	−0.458*** (0.152)	−0.002 (0.157)	−0.213 (0.155)	−0.002 (0.159)	−0.311** (0.154)	−0.318** (0.155)	−0.607*** (0.151)	−0.376** (0.153)	−0.158 (0.151)	−0.212 (0.151)
Liberal	0.296** (0.146)	0.493*** (0.153)	0.451*** (0.154)	−0.035 (0.153)	0.186 (0.169)	0.124 (0.163)	0.085 (0.162)	0.023 (0.159)	0.417*** (0.143)	0.408*** (0.143)	0.180 (0.148)	0.176 (0.141)
South	0.033 (0.075)	−0.292*** (0.079)	0.020 (0.078)	0.051 (0.079)	−0.177** (0.084)	−0.061 (0.083)	0.044 (0.082)	0.150* (0.081)	−0.237*** (0.073)	0.170** (0.073)	0.118 (0.075)	0.198*** (0.073)
Constant	0.373** (0.189)	0.606*** (0.194)	0.331* (0.189)	0.032 (0.196)	0.297 (0.199)	0.115 (0.199)	0.283 (0.198)	0.192 (0.195)	−0.191 (0.184)	−0.101 (0.181)	−0.402** (0.186)	−0.154 (0.180)
Observations	3,216	3,216	3,216	3,216	3,216	3,216	3,216	3,216	3,216	3,216	3,216	3,216

Note: Logistic regression models are estimated with controls for home ownership and unemployment, but are omitted here given space constraints; *** p <0.01, ** p < 0.05, * p < 0.1

TABLE A4.2: Policing battery details

The policing battery referenced in chapter 4 (figure 4.3) is drawn from seven items included in the CMPS. These items were selected on the basis of whether they were included in the full sample, their ability to reflect general feelings toward police, and propositions that consider how police organizations could be changed. The items are as follows, with response options noted in parentheses:

1. "Many [police] officers see people like me as animals, thugs, and less than human" (7-point Likert scale from strongly agree to strongly disagree)
2. "The official rules say the police can't do certain things but, in reality, they can do whatever they want" (7-point Likert from strongly agree to strongly disagree)
3. "I do not trust the police to protect my community" (7-point Likert from strongly agree to strongly disagree)
4. "Thinking about the police department in your community, do you think that spending on policing should be:" (5-point scale from increased a lot to decreased a lot)

[Survey preamble to the final 3 items:] "Here are some things that have been proposed to reduce deadly force encounters involving the police. Which of these do you favor or oppose?" (5-point scale from strongly favor to strongly oppose)

5. "Cut funding for police departments and reinvest in community programs"
6. "Abolish the police"
7. "Create a new agency of first responders, like emergency medical services or firefighters, to deal with issues related to addiction or mental illness that need to be remedied but do not need police"

Chapter 6 Appendixes

APPENDIX 6.1: SUPPLEMENTAL TABLES FOR SURVEY ANALYSES

TABLE A6.1A: Political views by skin tone, skin tone identity, and racial identity (2018 Lucid)

	Support for reducing income inequality			Believe police treat dark-skinned people worse		
	Full Sample	Light-Skinned Rs Only	Dark-Skinned Rs Only	Full Sample	Light-Skinned Rs Only	Dark-Skinned Rs Only
Skin tone identity	0.065***	-0.050	0.086**	0.179***	0.136***	0.121***	0.162***
	(0.017)	(0.035)	(0.037)	(0.017)	(0.019)	(0.038)	(0.037)
Racial identity	—	0.149***	0.209***	—	0.144***	0.067	0.168***
	0.129***	(0.047)	(0.055)		(0.028)	(0.051)	(0.055)
	(0.027)						
Constant	0.520***	0.493***	0.300***	0.548***	0.476***	0.558***	0.373***
	(0.030)	(0.064)	(0.061)	(0.031)	(0.034)	(0.069)	(0.061)
n	1,640	404	524	1,639	1,638	403	524
R-squared	0.082	0.131	0.156	0.087	0.102	0.095	0.156

Note: Standard errors in parentheses. *** p < 0.01, ** p < 0.05, * p < 0.1 two-tailed test. Regression estimates also control for age, education, gender, income, region, partisanship, ideology, Hispanic ethnicity, racial group importance, and survey design effects, excluded here given space considerations.

TABLE A6.1B: Policy preferences by skin tone identity and racial identity (2019 AmeriSpeak)

	Support for reducing income inequality		Support for affirmative action based on race (jobs)		Support for affirmative action based on skin tone (jobs)	
Skin tone identity	0.015	−0.026	0.086***	0.026	0.086**	0.072*
	(0.029)	(0.032)	(0.030)	(0.033)	(0.033)	(0.037)
Racial identity	—	0.113***	—	0.163***	—	0.037
		(0.039)		(0.040)		(0.045)
Constant	0.371***	0.326***	0.230***	0.164***	0.338***	0.323***
	(0.058)	(0.060)	(0.061)	(0.062)	(0.067)	(0.069)
n	808	808	803	803	800	800
R-squared	0.119	0.129	0.084	0.102	0.050	0.050

TABLE A6.1C: Policy preferences by skin tone, skin tone identity, and racial identity (2019 AmeriSpeak)

	Support for reducing income inequality		Support for affirmative action based on race (jobs)		Support for affirmative action based on skin tone (jobs)	
	Light-Skinned Rs	Dark-Skinned Rs	Light-Skinned Rs	Dark-Skinned Rs	Light-Skinned Rs	Dark-Skinned Rs
Skin tone identity	−0.067	0.003	0.066	0.020	0.071	0.087
	(0.068)	(0.062)	(0.071)	(0.064)	(0.080)	(0.079)
Racial identity	0.193***	0.162*	0.108	0.311***	0.117	0.096
	(0.072)	(0.084)	(0.075)	(0.088)	(0.086)	(0.106)
Constant	0.431***	0.393***	0.352***	0.102	0.376**	0.494***
	(0.129)	(0.108)	(0.135)	(0.112)	(0.153)	(0.135)
n	202	208	202	205	202	205
R-squared	0.183	0.143	0.127	0.203	0.052	0.088

Note: Standard errors in parentheses. *** $p < 0.01$, ** $p < 0.05$, * $p < 0.1$ two-tailed test. Regression estimates also control for age, education, gender, income, region, partisanship, ideology, homeownership, unemployment, racial group importance, and survey design effects, excluded here given space considerations.

TABLE A6.1D: Political views by skin tone identity and racial group attachment (2019 AmeriSpeak)

	Lighter-skinned people receive better job opportunities		Police treat darker-skinned people worse		Whites treat lighter-skinned people better		Skin tone determines how far one can make it in society	
Skin tone identity	0.133***	0.103***	0.117***	0.068**	0.128***	0.062**	0.193***	0.152***
	(0.027)	(0.030)	(0.029)	(0.032)	(0.028)	(0.031)	(0.029)	(0.032)
Racial identity	—	0.083**	—	0.134***	—	0.181***	—	0.111***
		(0.037)		(0.039)		(0.038)		(0.039)
Constant	0.344***	0.310***	0.411***	0.356***	0.378***	0.303***	0.415***	0.369***
	(0.055)	(0.057)	(0.059)	(0.061)	(0.057)	(0.058)	(0.058)	(0.060)
n	810	810	810	810	810	810	810	810
R-squared	0.079	0.085	0.071	0.084	0.074	0.100	0.110	0.119

TABLE A6.1E: Political views by skin tone, skin tone identity, and racial group attachment (2019 AmeriSpeak)

	Lighter-skinned people receive better job opportunities		Police treat darker-skinned people worse		Whites treat lighter-skinned people better		Skin tone determines how far one can make it in society	
	Light-Skinned Rs	Dark-Skinned Rs	Light-Skinned Rs	Dark-Skinned Rs	Light-Skinned Rs	Dark-Skinned Rs	Light-Skinned Rs	Dark-Skinned Rs
Skin tone identity	−0.001	0.029	−0.090	0.128**	−0.025	−0.032	0.119*	0.129*
	(0.063)	(0.064)	(0.069)	(0.064)	(0.065)	(0.062)	(0.070)	(0.066)
Racial identity	0.076	0.288***	0.073	0.320***	0.141**	0.373***	0.055	0.193**
	(0.068)	(0.087)	(0.075)	(0.087)	(0.071)	(0.084)	(0.076)	(0.090)
Constant	0.518***	0.159	0.547***	0.183	0.452***	0.211*	0.477***	0.214*
	(0.120)	(0.112)	(0.132)	(0.112)	(0.125)	(0.108)	(0.134)	(0.116)
n	202	209	202	209	202	209	202	209
R-squared	0.109	0.153	0.117	0.196	0.076	0.195	0.121	0.142

Note: Standard errors in parentheses. *** p < 0.01, ** p < 0.05, * p < 0.1 two-tailed test. Regression estimates also control for age, education, gender, income, region, partisanship, ideology, homeownership, unemployment, racial group importance, and survey design effects, excluded here given space considerations.

TABLE A6.1F: Political views by skin tone identity and racial group attachment (2019 AmeriSpeak)

	Focusing on racism will resolve colorism		Discussing skin tone is divisive and a distraction from race		Light-skinned and dark-skinned people face equal discrimination		Black people better represented if more dark-skinned black politicians elected		Need more darker-skinned black people in positions of power	
Skin tone identity	0.082***		0.035		0.088***		0.147***		0.162***	
	(0.029)		(0.033)		(0.027)		(0.029)		(0.030)	
		0.049		−0.018		0.040		0.113***		0.104***
		(0.032)		(0.036)		(0.030)		(0.033)		(0.034)
Racial identity	—		—		—		—		—	
		0.092**		0.144***		0.130***		0.095**		0.159***
		(0.039)		(0.044)		(0.036)		(0.040)		(0.041)
Constant	0.496***		0.493***		0.459***		0.409***		0.414***	
	(0.058)		(0.066)		(0.054)		(0.059)		(0.061)	
		0.458***		0.435***		0.406***		0.369***		0.348***
		(0.060)		(0.068)		(0.056)		(0.061)		(0.063)
n	810	810	812	812	812	812	811	811	810	810
R-squared	0.080	0.086	0.025	0.038	0.025	0.041	0.107	0.113	0.108	0.125

TABLE A6.1G: Political views by skin tone, skin tone identity, and racial group attachment (2019 AmeriSpeak)

	Focusing on racism will resolve colorism		Discussing skin tone is divisive and a distraction from race		Light-skinned and dark-skinned people face equal discrimination		Black people better represented if more dark-skinned Black politicians elected		Need more darker-skinned Black people in positions of power	
	Light-Skinned Rs	Dark-Skinned Rs	Light-Skinned Rs	Dark-Skinned Rs	Light-Skinned Rs	Dark-Skinned Rs	Light-Skinned Rs	Dark-Skinned Rs	Light-Skinned Rs	Dark-Skinned Rs
Skin tone identity	−0.010	−0.020	0.015	−0.035	0.115*	0.066	−0.025	0.164**	0.025	0.157**
	(0.065)	(0.064)	(0.071)	(0.076)	(0.062)	(0.062)	(0.064)	(0.066)	(0.070)	(0.068)
Racial identity	0.150**	0.248***	0.071	0.306***	0.167**	0.094	0.063	0.231**	0.167**	0.188**
	(0.070)	(0.088)	(0.077)	(0.104)	(0.066)	(0.084)	(0.069)	(0.091)	(0.076)	(0.093)
Constant	0.561***	0.375***	0.479***	0.390***	0.394***	0.420***	0.723***	0.332***	0.429***	0.440***
	(0.124)	(0.113)	(0.136)	(0.133)	(0.118)	(0.108)	(0.123)	(0.116)	(0.135)	(0.120)
n	202	209	204	209	204	209	203	209	203	209
R-squared	0.174	0.167	0.044	0.112	0.089	0.047	0.153	0.201	0.130	0.203

Note: Standard errors in parentheses. *** $p < 0.01$, ** $p < 0.05$, * $p < 0.1$ two-tailed test. Regression estimates also control for age, education, gender, income, region, partisanship, ideology, homeownership, unemployment, racial group importance, and survey design effects, excluded here given space considerations.

TABLE A6.1H: Political views by skin tone identity and racial group attachment (2020 CMPS)

	Support for reducing income inequality		Oppose colleges excluding race in admissions (split ballot)		Support colleges considering race in admissions (split ballot)		Feel dehumanized by police		Policing scale		Protest since January 2020 (logit)	
Skin tone identity	0.057***	0.024*	-0.043**	-0.026	0.056***	0.026	0.102***	0.067***	0.056***	0.032***	0.822***	0.772***
	(0.013)	(0.014)	(0.020)	(0.021)	(0.018)	(0.019)	(0.013)	(0.014)	(0.008)	(0.008)	(0.134)	(0.152)
Racial identity	—	0.113***	—	-0.069**	—	0.092***	—	0.111***	—	0.083***	—	0.398**
		(0.022)		(0.035)		(0.029)		(0.022)		(0.013)		(0.212)
		(0.018)		(0.029)		(0.026)		(0.019)		(0.011)		(0.200)
Linked fate	—	0.041**	—	0.033	—	0.082***	—	0.113***	—	0.046***	—	-0.664***
		(0.015)		(0.023)		(0.020)		(0.015)		(0.009)		(0.139)
Constant	0.488***	0.445***	0.245***	0.260***	0.439***	0.399***	0.499***	0.442***	0.501***	0.466***	-1.383***	-1.441***
	(0.021)	(0.022)	(0.033)	(0.035)	(0.029)	(0.030)	(0.022)	(0.022)	(0.012)	(0.013)	(0.200)	(0.212)
n	3,216	3,216	1,614	1,614	1,602	1,602	3,216	3,216	3,216	3,216	3,216	3,216
R-squared	0.073	0.089	0.048	0.052	0.071	0.092	0.079	0.110	0.142	0.170		

TABLE A6.11: Political views by skin tone, skin tone identity, and racial group attachment (2020 CMPS)

	Support for reducing income inequality		Oppose colleges excluding race in admissions (split ballot)		Support colleges considering race in admissions (split ballot)		Feel dehumanized by police		Policing scale		Protest since January 2020 (logit)	
	Light-Skinned Rs	Dark-Skinned Rs	Light-Skinned Rs	Dark-Skinned Rs	Light-Skinned Rs	Dark-Skinned Rs	Light-Skinned Rs	Dark-Skinned Rs	Light-Skinned Rs	Dark-Skinned Rs	Light-Skinned Rs	Dark-Skinned Rs
Skin tone identity	0.038	0.047*	0.012	-0.034	0.026	0.015	0.019	0.087***	0.035**	0.050***	0.559*	1.022***
	(0.025)	(0.026)	(0.035)	(0.044)	(0.036)	(0.041)	(0.027)	(0.028)	(0.015)	(0.016)	(0.309)	(0.338)
Racial identity	0.123***	0.140***	-0.101**	-0.059	0.136***	0.083	0.163***	0.040	0.124***	0.035	1.152***	0.017
	(0.031)	(0.036)	(0.046)	(0.061)	(0.042)	(0.056)	(0.034)	(0.038)	(0.018)	(0.022)	(0.421)	(0.402)
Linked fate	0.011	0.035	0.039	0.034	0.096**	0.087**	0.148***	0.060*	0.050***	0.048***	-0.678*	-1.108***
	(0.029)	(0.026)	(0.042)	(0.043)	(0.039)	(0.040)	(0.031)	(0.027)	(0.017)	(0.016)	(0.351)	(0.272)
Constant	0.411***	0.523***	0.137**	0.266***	0.413***	0.383***	0.400***	0.525***	0.426***	0.531***	-1.709***	-2.183***
	(0.042)	(0.040)	(0.065)	(0.069)	(0.055)	(0.063)	(0.046)	(0.043)	(0.025)	(0.025)	(0.476)	(0.515)
n	907	902	473	463	434	439	907	902	907	902	3,216	902
R-squared	0.107	0.112	0.046	0.102	0.137	0.100	0.121	0.092	0.206	0.170		

Note: Standard errors in parentheses. *** p < 0.01, ** p < 0.05, * p < 0.1. Regression estimates also control for gender, education, age, region, income, home ownership, unemployment status, partisanship, and ideology, but are excluded here given space considerations.

APPENDIX 6.2: MATERIALS AND QUESTION WORDING FROM 2019 AMERISPEAK EXPERIMENT

Second Annual SciCon: Science Fiction, Fantasy, and People in Weird Costumes

Pittsburgh Post-Gazette
by Eric Smith
January 7, 2019

A businessman wearing a suit and carrying a briefcase in downtown Pittsburgh was passed by a group of Star Wars storm troopers. A few moments later across the street, a woman pushing her baby in a stroller casually walked by Batman standing on the edge of the sidewalk.

While this may sound out of the ordinary, it is just a normal day when a big science fiction convention like the MidAtlantic SciCon is in town. You can find an even bigger group of people dressed in increasingly elaborate costumes inside the convention. A quick stroll through the main entry of the MidAtlantic SciCon reveals hundreds of different characters from Star Wars, Harry Potter, Lord of the Rings, and superheroes from the Marvel and DC Universe. You can spot the couples in coordinated costumes—like Superman and Wonder Woman—and the groups of friends with themed costumes.

Photo: David L. Lawrence Convention Center

The MidAtlantic SciCon is the region's largest science fiction and fantasy convention. The 2nd annual convention opened last Friday at the David L. Lawrence Convention Center in Pittsburgh. Each year the convention gains more attention and attracts more participants.

This year, opening day attracted over 6,400 attendees, according to Paul Comeau, the convention's director of publicity and public relations. Comeau was confident that this year's attendance would eclipse last year's total of nearly 8,000 people. MidAtlantic SciCon has continued to attract science fiction enthusiasts from Pennsylvania, and increasingly from neighboring areas, since it was founded in 2012.

The increasing size also means more events being scheduled to meet growing demand. This year, more than 200 panels and workshops were scheduled, including "Animal People: The Drawing of Anthropomorphics," and "In an Age Before Atlantis: Sword and Sorcery Literary Influences in Gaming."

FIGURE A6.2A. Control Condition

CSRP
CENTER FOR THE STUDY OF RACE AND POLICY

New Research Shows Class-Based Disparities are Primarily Driven by Race

Press Release
January 7, 2019

New studies highlight how class-based inequalities stem primarily from racial discrimination. The Center for the Study of Race and Policy (CSRP) in Washington D.C. found dramatic differences when comparing Black people to White people across a number of domains.

These differences based on race range from gaping income disparities, to vast differences in education levels, as well as shorter lives due to both worse health outcomes and criminal sentencing disparities. For example, Black people are twice as likely to receive the death penalty for comparable crimes, have 5 years less formal education, make about $3 less per hour worked, and have less than half the wealth of Whites, regardless of class. Surprisingly, the extensive research on this topic by the Center for the Study of Race and Policy dating back to early 2015 reveals that these differences remain even after taking into account levels of education, work experience, family background, and other important factors. These disparities should be especially alarming given their relationship to job and educational opportunities, various life experiences, and overall quality of life.

Photo: Center for the Study of Race and Policy

The reports reveal that, on average, lower-class Whites have better outcomes than even the most affluent Blacks.

The research by the CSRP suggests that focusing on class alone is not enough to resolve inequalities stemming from race. "Most politicians aren't talking about how much worse off Black people are than White people," says the lead researcher at CSRP and activist, Darnell Williams. "We must acknowledge disparities based on race are real and are very harmful."

Only time will tell how politicians and other activists take up these disparities based on race given the CSRP's troubling findings.

FIGURE A6.2B. Treatment 1A: Racial Inequities Treatment (Version 1)

CENTER FOR THE STUDY OF RACE AND POLICY

Call to Action: New Research Shows Class-Based Remedies Won't Solve The Race Problem

Press Release
January 7, 2019

New studies highlight how class-based inequalities stem primarily from racial discrimination. The Center for the Study of Race and Policy (CSRP) in Washington D.C. found dramatic differences when comparing Black people to White people across a number of domains.

For example, Black people are twice as likely to receive the death penalty for comparable crimes, have 5 years less formal education, make about $3 less per hour worked, and have less than half the wealth of Whites, regardless of class.

The reports reveal that, on average, lower-class Whites have better outcomes than even the most affluent Blacks.

The research by the CSRP suggests that focusing on class alone is not enough to resolve inequalities stemming from race. "Most politicians aren't talking about how much worse off Black people are than White people," says the lead researcher at CSRP and activist, Darnell Williams. "We must acknowledge disparities based on race are real and are very harmful."

Photo: Center for the Study of Race and Policy

The CSRP recommends several immediate steps to be taken: "First, we should be in the streets protesting, in the voting booth, and in town-hall meetings telling politicians we won't accept these gaping disparities. Second, we need to follow in Brazil's footsteps and use targeted job opportunities and college admissions based not just on class, but on race. Third, the government should issue Baby Bonds at birth. Children from the poorest families would get $50,000 when they turn 18, while those from wealthy families get only $500. Together, these actions would raise awareness and drastically reduce disadvantages faced by Black people."

Only time will tell how politicians and other activists take up these disparities based on race and the CSRP's proposed solutions.

FIGURE A6.2C. Treatment 1B: Racial Inequities Treatment (Version 2)

CSRP
CENTER FOR THE STUDY OF RACE AND POLICY

New Research Shows Race-Based Disparities are Primarily Driven by Skin Tone

Press Release
January 7, 2019

New studies highlight how race-based inequalities stem primarily from skin tone-based discrimination. The Center for the Study of Race and Policy (CSRP) in Washington D.C. found dramatic differences when comparing dark-skinned Black people to both light-skinned Blacks *and* Whites across a number of domains.

These differences based on skin tone range from gaping income disparities, to vast differences in education levels, as well as shorter lives due to both worse health outcomes and criminal sentencing disparities. For example, darker-skinned Black people are twice as likely to receive the death penalty for comparable crimes, have 5 years less formal education, make about $3 less per hour worked, and have less than half the wealth of lighter-skinned Blacks and Whites. Surprisingly, the extensive research on this topic by the Center for the Study of Race and Policy dating back to early 2015 reveals that these differences remain even after taking into account levels of education, work experience, family background, and other important factors. These disparities should be especially alarming given their relationship to job and educational opportunities, various life experiences, and overall quality of life.

Photo: Center for the Study of Race and Policy

The reports reveal that, on average, lighter-skinned Blacks have more similar outcomes to Whites, while darker-skinned Blacks face the most disadvantages.

The research by the CSRP suggests that focusing on race alone is not enough to resolve inequalities stemming from skin tone. "Most politicians aren't talking about how much worse off dark-skinned Black people are than lighter-skinned Black or White people," says the lead researcher at CSRP and activist, Darnell Williams. "We must acknowledge disparities based on skin tone are real and are very harmful."

Only time will tell how politicians and other activists take up these disparities based on skin tone given the CSRP's troubling findings.

FIGURE A6.2D. Treatment 2A: Color-Based Inequities Treatment (Version 1)

CENTER FOR THE STUDY OF RACE AND POLICY

Call to Action: New Research Shows Race-Based Remedies Won't Solve The Skin Tone Problem

Press Release
January 7, 2019

New studies highlight how race-based inequalities stem primarily from skin tone-based discrimination. The Center for the Study of Race and Policy (CSRP) in Washington D.C. found dramatic differences when comparing dark-skinned Black people to both light-skinned Blacks *and* Whites across a number of domains.

For example, darker-skinned Black people are twice as likely to receive the death penalty for comparable crimes, have 5 years less formal education, make about $3 less per hour worked, and have less than half the wealth of lighter-skinned Blacks and Whites.

The reports reveal that, on average, lighter-skinned Blacks have more similar outcomes to Whites, while darker-skinned Blacks face the most disadvantages.

Photo: Center for the Study of Race and Policy

The research by the CSRP suggests that focusing on race alone is not enough to resolve inequalities stemming from skin tone. "Most politicians aren't talking about how much worse off dark-skinned Black people are than lighter-skinned Black or White people," says the lead researcher at CSRP and activist, Darnell Williams. "We must acknowledge disparities based on skin tone are real and are very harmful."

The CSRP recommends several immediate steps to be taken: "First, we should be in the streets protesting, in the voting booth, and in town-hall meetings telling politicians we won't accept these gaping disparities. Second, we need to follow in Brazil's footsteps and use targeted job opportunities and college admissions based not just on race, but on the darkness of your skin. Third, the government should issue Baby Bonds at birth. Children from the poorest families would get $50,000 when they turn 18, while those from wealthy families get only $500. Together, these actions would raise awareness and drastically reduce disadvantages faced by dark-skinned Black people."

Only time will tell how politicians and other activists take up these disparities based on skin tone and the CSRP's proposed solutions.

FIGURE A6.2E. Treatment 2B: Color-Based Inequities Treatment (Version 2)

Survey Instrument from
2019 AmeriSpeak Experiment

Key Independent Variables: As you know, human beings display a wide variety of physical characteristics. One of these is skin color. Displayed below is a skin color scale that ranges from 1 (representing the lightest possible skin color) to 10 (representing the darkest possible skin color). The 10 shades of skin color are represented by a hand of identical form, but differing in color. Please indicate which hand depicted below comes closest to your skin color. [Yadon-Ostfeld Skin Color Scale]

[*note: for the following questions, the direction of response options was randomized*]

Compared to most Black people, how would you describe your skin tone?

1. Very light
2. Light
3. Medium
4. Dark
5. Very dark

How important is your skin tone to your identity?

1. Extremely important
2. Very important
3. Moderately important
4. A little important
5. Not at all important

If someone said something bad about [light / medium / dark skinned] people, how likely is it that you would feel almost as if they said something bad about you?

1. Extremely likely
2. Very likely
3. Moderately likely
4. Slightly likely
5. Not at all likely

How important is being Black to your identity?

1. Extremely important
2. Very important
3. Moderately important
4. A little important
5. Not at all important

Key Dependent Variables: Now we would like to ask you a series of questions related to different groups and different issues in society. We want to know your opinion. There are no right or wrong answers.

The difference in incomes between the richest and poorest households in the United States has grown in the past few decades. Do you favor or oppose the government trying to make this income difference smaller?

1. Favor a great deal
2. Favor moderately

3. Favor a little
4. Neither favor nor oppose
5. Oppose a little
6. Oppose moderately
7. Oppose a great deal

Do you favor or oppose allowing companies to increase the number of darker-skinned Black workers by considering *skin tone* along with other factors when choosing employees?

1. Favor a great deal
2. Favor moderately
3. Favor a little
4. Neither favor nor oppose
5. Oppose a little
6. Oppose moderately
7. Oppose a great deal

Do you favor or oppose allowing companies to increase the number of Black workers by considering *race* along with other factors when choosing employees?

1. Favor a great deal
2. Favor moderately
3. Favor a little
4. Neither favor nor oppose
5. Oppose a little
6. Oppose moderately
7. Oppose a great deal

Please tell us how likely you are to engage in the following activities to express your opinion about inequalities in society.

RANDOMIZE GRID ITEMS:
1. Joining a protest, march, demonstration, or rally
2. Volunteering for an organization
3. Talking about these issues with family or friends
4. Signing a petition that will be sent to your political representatives

RESPONSE OPTIONS
1. Extremely likely
2. Very likely
3. Moderately likely
4. A little likely

5. Not at all likely

Next, please tell us how often you believe the following statements are true.

RANDOMIZE GRID ITEMS:
1. Black people with lighter skin are given better employment opportunities in our society than those with darker skin.
2. Black people with darker skin receive harsher treatment by police compared to those with lighter skin.
3. Black people with lighter skin are treated better than those with darker skin by White people in our society.
4. Skin tone plays a part in determining how far someone can make it in society.
5. Focusing on issues related to racial discrimination will automatically resolve any issues related to skin tone discrimination.

RESPONSE OPTIONS
1. Always
2. Most of the time
3. About half of the time
4. Some of the time
5. Never

Next, please tell us how often you believe the following statements are true.

RANDOMIZE GRID ITEMS:
1. Talking about skin tone is just a way to divide Black people and keep us from talking about the bigger issue of race.
2. Black people would be better represented in politics if more dark-skinned Black people were elected.
3. We need to get more dark-skinned Black people into positions of power in society.
4. Light-skinned Black people experience just as much discrimination and hardship in society as dark-skinned Black people.

RESPONSE OPTIONS
1. Always
2. Most of the time
3. About half of the time
4. Some of the time
5. Never

APPENDIX 6.3: REGRESSION ESTIMATES FROM SURVEY EXPERIMENT ANALYSES

TABLE A6.3A: Regression estimates for treatment, skin tone, and skin tone identity

	Income inequality	Affirmative action: skin tone	Affirmative action: race	Sign petition	Protest	Volunteer	Talk with family and friends
Skin tone treatment (vs. control)	-0.046	0.052	-0.019	-0.025	-0.129*	-0.034	-0.040
	(0.069)	(0.074)	(0.070)	(0.070)	(0.072)	(0.062)	(0.073)
Skin tone identity (high)	-0.067	0.207**	0.061	0.108	0.004	-0.059	-0.032
	(0.096)	(0.102)	(0.097)	(0.097)	(0.099)	(0.086)	(0.101)
Skin tone treatment × high skin tone identity	0.034	-0.207	-0.050	-0.111	-0.068	0.069	-0.077
	(0.121)	(0.128)	(0.123)	(0.122)	(0.124)	(0.108)	(0.126)
Dark-skinned	-0.058	0.058	-0.116	-0.019	-0.090	-0.163**	-0.179*
	(0.093)	(0.099)	(0.094)	(0.094)	(0.096)	(0.083)	(0.097)
Skin tone treatment × dark-skinned	0.138	-0.007	0.020	0.032	0.061	0.129	0.149
	(0.114)	(0.122)	(0.116)	(0.115)	(0.118)	(0.102)	(0.120)
High skin tone identity × dark-skinned	0.182	-0.108	-0.002	-0.050	0.057	0.246**	0.236
	(0.137)	(0.146)	(0.139)	(0.139)	(0.141)	(0.123)	(0.144)

(*continues*)

TABLE A6.3A: (continued)

	Income inequality	Affirmative action: skin tone	Affirmative action: race	Sign petition	Protest	Volunteer	Talk with family and friends
Skin tone treatment × high skin tone identity × dark-skinned	-0.101	0.170	0.150	0.147	0.043	-0.232	-0.032
	(0.171)	(0.182)	(0.174)	(0.172)	(0.176)	(0.152)	(0.179)
Race treatment (vs. control)	-0.004	-0.003	-0.066	-0.025	-0.182**	-0.113*	-0.027
	(0.073)	(0.078)	(0.074)	(0.074)	(0.076)	(0.066)	(0.077)
Race treatment × high skin tone identity	-0.016	0.030	0.021	-0.042	0.072	0.137	0.018
	(0.121)	(0.130)	(0.124)	(0.123)	(0.125)	(0.109)	(0.128)
Race treatment × dark-skinned	0.110	0.012	0.136	0.120	0.182	0.254**	0.171
	(0.116)	(0.124)	(0.118)	(0.118)	(0.120)	(0.104)	(0.122)
Race treatment × high skin tone identity × dark-skinned	-0.051	-0.027	-0.059	0.020	-0.109	-0.230	-0.161
	(0.169)	(0.182)	(0.173)	(0.172)	(0.175)	(0.152)	(0.178)
Constant	0.655***	0.381***	0.625***	0.348***	0.643***	0.795***	0.679***
	(0.059)	(0.063)	(0.060)	(0.060)	(0.061)	(0.053)	(0.062)
Observations	1,031	1,022	1,024	1,037	1,037	1,037	1,037
R-squared	0.032	0.064	0.032	0.044	0.031	0.043	0.030

Note: Regression estimates include 3-category skin tone and ID variables, but table is truncated to only reflect comparisons between highest and lowest categories. *** p < 0.01, ** p < 0.05, * p < 0.1, ^ p < .15 two-tailed test

TABLE A6.3B: Regression estimates for treatment, skin tone, and skin tone identity

	Job opportunities	Police treatment	Treatment by Whites	Societal mobility by color	Focusing on Race resolves colorism	Discussing color is divisive	Dark-skinned politicians represent better	Dark-skinned people need more power	Equal discrimination by color
Skin tone treatment (vs. control)	0.072	0.031	0.104	0.049	0.056	0.048	-0.031	0.082	-0.018
	(0.064)	(0.069)	(0.066)	(0.067)	(0.068)	(0.075)	(0.069)	(0.070)	(0.061)
Skin tone identity (high)	0.137	0.020	0.122	0.204**	0.203**	0.243**	0.092	0.215**	0.155*
	(0.088)	(0.095)	(0.091)	(0.092)	(0.094)	(0.104)	(0.095)	(0.097)	(0.084)
Skin tone treatment × high skin tone identity	-0.101	0.016	-0.068	-0.087	-0.177	-0.182	0.002	-0.108	0.007
	(0.111)	(0.119)	(0.114)	(0.116)	(0.117)	(0.130)	(0.119)	(0.122)	(0.106)
Dark-skinned	0.068	-0.080	0.055	0.011	0.087	-0.186*	-0.056	0.035	-0.128
	(0.085)	(0.092)	(0.088)	(0.089)	(0.090)	(0.100)	(0.091)	(0.094)	(0.081)
Skin tone treatment × dark-skinned	-0.103	0.058	-0.051	-0.061	-0.122	0.143	-0.077	-0.132	0.009
	(0.105)	(0.113)	(0.108)	(0.110)	(0.111)	(0.123)	(0.112)	(0.115)	(0.100)
High skin tone identity × dark-skinned	-0.154	0.109	-0.115	-0.144	-0.206	0.033	0.015	-0.150	0.005
	(0.126)	(0.135)	(0.130)	(0.132)	(0.134)	(0.148)	(0.135)	(0.138)	(0.120)

(continues)

TABLE A6.3B: (continued)

	Job opportunities	Police treatment	Treatment by Whites	Societal mobility by color	Focusing on Race resolves colorism	Discussing color is divisive	Dark-skinned politicians represent better	Dark-skinned people need more power	Equal discrimination by color
Skin tone treatment × high skin tone identity × dark-skinned	0.314**	0.023	0.251^	0.285*	0.301*	-0.085	0.158	0.277^	-0.041
	(0.157)	(0.168)	(0.162)	(0.164)	(0.166)	(0.184)	(0.168)	(0.172)	(0.150)
Race treatment (vs. control)	0.019	-0.009	0.039	0.057	-0.067	0.064	-0.070	-0.006	-0.055
	(0.067)	(0.072)	(0.070)	(0.071)	(0.072)	(0.079)	(0.072)	(0.074)	(0.064)
Race treatment × high skin tone identity	-0.076	-0.027	-0.072	0.003	-0.061	-0.262**	-0.046	-0.056	-0.021
	(0.112)	(0.120)	(0.115)	(0.117)	(0.118)	(0.131)	(0.120)	(0.123)	(0.107)
Race treatment × dark-skinned	0.036	0.074	0.105	0.063	0.053	0.064	0.105	0.017	0.147
	(0.107)	(0.115)	(0.110)	(0.111)	(0.113)	(0.125)	(0.114)	(0.117)	(0.102)
Race treatment × high skin tone id × dark-skinned	0.143	0.070	0.111	0.031	0.134	0.037	0.107	0.179	-0.123
	(0.156)	(0.168)	(0.161)	(0.163)	(0.165)	(0.184)	(0.168)	(0.172)	(0.149)
Constant	0.393***	0.554***	0.393***	0.384***	0.268***	0.580***	0.438***	0.491***	0.536***
	(0.054)	(0.058)	(0.056)	(0.057)	(0.058)	(0.064)	(0.058)	(0.060)	(0.052)
Observations	1,036	1,036	1,036	1,036	1,036	1,036	1,035	1,034	1,036
R-squared	0.062	0.054	0.076	0.103	0.050	0.028	0.074	0.073	0.042

Note: Regression estimates include 3-category skin tone and ID variables, but table is truncated to only reflect comparisons between highest and lowest categories. *** p < 0.01, ** p < 0.05, * p < 0.1, ^ p < .15 two-tailed test

TABLE A6.3C: Regression estimates for treatment, skin tone, and racial identity

	Income inequality	Affirmative action: skin tone	Affirmative action: race	Sign petition	Protest	Volunteer	Talk with family and friends
Skin tone treatment (vs. control)	0.067	0.148*	0.066	-0.002	-0.100	0.124*	0.089
	(0.076)	(0.083)	(0.077)	(0.078)	(0.078)	(0.068)	(0.080)
Racial identity (high)	0.114	0.142*	0.215***	0.061	0.058	0.237***	0.191**
	(0.071)	(0.078)	(0.071)	(0.072)	(0.073)	(0.063)	(0.074)
Skin tone treatment × high race identity	-0.035	-0.111	-0.025	-0.013	0.013	-0.153**	-0.128
	(0.083)	(0.090)	(0.083)	(0.084)	(0.084)	(0.073)	(0.086)
Race treatment (vs. control)	0.090	0.101	0.098	-0.009	-0.171**	0.085	0.076
	(0.082)	(0.089)	(0.083)	(0.083)	(0.084)	(0.073)	(0.086)
Race treatment × high race identity	-0.052	-0.096	-0.123	0.067	0.139	-0.076	-0.056
	(0.088)	(0.096)	(0.088)	(0.089)	(0.090)	(0.078)	(0.092)
Constant	0.553***	0.295***	0.394***	0.307***	0.534***	0.545***	0.477***
	(0.066)	(0.072)	(0.067)	(0.068)	(0.068)	(0.059)	(0.069)
Observations	1,034	1,025	1,027	1,040	1,040	1,040	1,040
R-squared	0.014	0.009	0.037	0.020	0.035	0.048	0.027

Note: Regression estimates include 3-category racial ID variables, but table is truncated to only reflect comparisons between highest and lowest categories. *** $p < 0.01$, ** $p < 0.05$, * $p < 0.1$

TABLE A6.3D: Regression estimates for treatment, skin tone, and racial identity

	Job opportunities	Police treatment	Treatment by Whites	Societal mobility by color	Focusing on race resolves colorism	Discussing color is divisive	Dark-skinned politicians represent Better	Dark-skinned people need more power	Equal discrimination by color
Skin tone treatment (vs. control)	0.078	0.041	0.104	0.083	-0.057	0.104	0.069	0.031	-0.088
	(0.071)	(0.076)	(0.073)	(0.076)	(0.075)	(0.083)	(0.077)	(0.078)	(0.068)
Racial identity (high)	0.168**	0.164**	0.230***	0.221***	0.020	0.138*	0.203***	0.159**	0.032
	(0.066)	(0.071)	(0.068)	(0.070)	(0.070)	(0.077)	(0.072)	(0.073)	(0.063)
Skin tone treatment × high race identity	-0.062	-0.029	-0.065	-0.081	0.057	-0.103	-0.078	-0.033	0.083
	(0.077)	(0.082)	(0.079)	(0.082)	(0.081)	(0.089)	(0.083)	(0.085)	(0.073)
Race treatment (vs. control)	0.007	-0.002	0.006	0.072	-0.111	0.005	0.063	-0.022	-0.101
	(0.076)	(0.082)	(0.078)	(0.081)	(0.081)	(0.089)	(0.083)	(0.084)	(0.072)
Race treatment × high race identity	-0.008	0.003	0.006	-0.055	0.124	0.000	-0.060	0.035	0.074
	(0.082)	(0.087)	(0.084)	(0.087)	(0.087)	(0.095)	(0.088)	(0.090)	(0.077)
Constant	0.352***	0.477***	0.330***	0.318***	0.318***	0.477***	0.273***	0.443***	0.500***
	(0.062)	(0.066)	(0.063)	(0.066)	(0.065)	(0.072)	(0.067)	(0.068)	(0.059)
Observations	1,039	1,039	1,039	1,039	1,039	1,039	1,038	1,037	1,039
R-squared	0.027	0.032	0.056	0.033	0.015	0.010	0.026	0.038	0.018

Note: Regression estimates include 3-category racial ID variables, but table is truncated to only reflect comparisons between highest and lowest categories. *** $p < 0.01$, ** $p < 0.05$, * $p < 0.1$

Notes

Chapter One

1. Pseudonyms are used for all interview participants throughout the book.
2. Throughout this book I use the terms Black and African American interchangeably.
3. I use the terms skin tone, skin color, color, and complexion interchangeably throughout this book.
4. Some scholars may take issue with the statistical models controlling for downstream factors related to skin tone, such as income or education. Instead, they might prefer to see that only factors unrelated to skin tone included in the model (i.e., "causal priors" such as gender and age). Other scholars might be concerned about omitted variable bias leading to a misleading representation of skin tone's effects—for example, if factors like income or racial group attachment are not accounted for in the models, then we might falsely conclude that there is a skin tone effect when it is truly an income-driven or group attachment-driven effect. The models presented throughout the book are more extensive in their controls, but as discussed in chapter 3 and elsewhere these models have also been estimated with varying sets of controls and similar patterns remain (see chapter 3 appendix, table A3.2).

Chapter Two

1. Of course, skin tone is one of a constellation of factors—for example, features, hair, accent—associated with how one is racialized (Ostfeld and Yadon 2022b). In this project, I focus on skin color given that it is relatively "sticky" (i.e., difficult to change), easy to assess, and influential in shaping one's experiences.
2. Eduardo Bonilla-Silva (2004b; 2004a) argues this middle category includes light-skinned Latinos, certain Asian ethnic groups (e.g., Japanese, Koreans, Chinese, Asian Indians), Middle Eastern Americans, and multiracial individuals. The "collective Black" category includes dark-skinned Latinos, Blacks, other Asian ethnic groups (e.g., Filipinos, Vietnamese, Hmong, Laotians), and both West Indian and African immigrants. I extend this argument by noting that skin color may influence the placement of African Americans into the racial hierarchy similar to Bonilla-Silva's argument regarding Latinos.
3. The privileges and opportunities associated with this group also varied by context. For example, there were differences in perceptions of mixed-race individuals and the system of

slavery in the upper South vs. the lower South. Specifically, there was less distinguishing between mixed-race and Black people in the upper South compared with the lower South, where color served as a more meaningful marker (Berlin 1974, p.162). For a more detailed historical discussion of these points, see Berlin 1974, Menke 1979, and Williamson 1980.

4. Malcolm X, "Who Taught You to Hate Yourself?" (excerpt from May 5, 1962 speech at the funeral of Ronald Stokes), *Genius*, https://genius.com/Malcolm-x-who-taught-you-to-hate-yourself-annotated.

5. The Pew Research Center reviews the language and Census forms used from 1790 to 2010 (2020a, 2020b).

Chapter Three

1. National social surveys like the GSS and ANES started incorporating measures of skin color into their data collection in the 2010s, which presents a promising opportunity for exploration. Still, issues with the number of political items asked may be limited to relatively small samples of non-Whites, and may overlook the nuances associated with interpreting different measures of skin color (Ostfeld and Yadon 2022b).

2. See Coppock and McClellan (2019) for a discussion of survey data from Lucid as comparable to MTurk.

3. The specific controls in the models vary to some extent across datasets given differences in survey items and are noted under each figure.

4. This examination also complements Wilkinson, Garand, and Dunaway's (2015) findings. Using 2010 CCES data, the authors find that lighter-skinned Black people are less likely to perceive commonality with Latinos—which is consistent with my results. However, they also find that lighter-skinned Blacks perceive greater employment competition with Latinos than those with dark skin. This suggests important nuance when invoking "Latinos" vs. "immigrants" (Pérez 2016).

5. Recall that skin tone was assessed in the NSAL using a five-point word scale ranging from "very dark" to "very light."

6. For ease of comparison across groups, the analyses corresponding to figure 3.6 rely on the trichotomized measure of skin color, as opposed to the full 10-point scale that was used in prior sections.

7. Jessica Guynn, "White Women Benefit Most from Affirmative Action. So Why Do They Oppose it, *USA Today*, June 29, 2023.

Chapter Four

1. This pattern has received attention from some Black media sources, however (e.g., Jones 2014; Roberts 2018).

2. Consistent with the broader colorism literature (Hunter 2002; 2007), the most frequently mentioned domain overall in the interviews involved interpersonal interactions related to dating or perceived attractiveness (appendix table A3.7). Such challenges were also mentioned more often by Black women.

3. The 2018 Lucid analyses include all respondents who identified as African American as at least one of their racial identities. The results remain similar when the analyses are limited to monoracial African Americans.

4. These distributions are unweighted. Survey weights are not employed with AmeriSpeak sample because the size of the weights are outside the standard recommended range and based on the independent variables in the models, thereby introducing bias into the OLS regression estimates (Thomas 2017; Winship and Radbill 1994).

5. As noted in chapter 3, the analyses presented throughout the book are drawn from regression estimates with extensive controls. The pattern of results remain similar if using a more limited set of control variables.

6. This includes 13 Black-identified participants who reported being born in Puerto Rico. Of the 3,918 US-born respondents, 77 percent identify as monoracial African American.

7. This question was added amid the 2016-2017 interview data collection and was not explicitly asked of participants during the first half of data collection. Ultimately, 36 of 67 interview participants were asked this item. In the 2021 interviews, this question was asked of 32 of 33 participants because one participant left the interview early due to a family emergency.

8. I examine the general participation item here to mirror the question used in the 2012 ANES. The 2020 CMPS also includes a follow-up question about different types of protests potentially participated in. Darker-skinned African Americans were more likely to report participating in protests related to wages and economic inequality as well as the Women's March, for example. While there are high levels of reported BLM participation across the skin tone spectrum, lighter-skinned Black respondents are more likely to report participating in BLM protests than darker-skinned respondents. This may point to the distinct nature of the BLM movement protests since, unlike the civil rights movement, the majority of protesters were non-Black, and evidence suggests that participants had weaker attachment to the movement (Gause and Arora, n.d.). Further investigation of these patterns would be valuable for future work.

Chapter Five

1. There were 229 Black participants in the MTurk survey. With respect to the stereotypes question related to light-skinned Black people, only 2 percent of participants (n = 5) left the textbox blank. Similarly, on the stereotypes question for dark-skinned Black people, 3.5 percent of participants (n = 8) did not provide any response.

2. MTurk survey participants are paid as soon as they complete a given task, which creates an incentive for finishing tasks quickly. Still, the average length of open-ended responses to these color-based stereotypes questions was equivalent to writing two or more sentences. This signals that this is an issue which the vast majority of participants have some perspective to share, and that this perspective is both easily assessed and summarized.

3. See appendix table A3.1 for descriptive statistics from each of the survey samples.

4. Survey weights are not employed with AmeriSpeak sample because the size of the weights provided by AmeriSpeak are outside the standard recommended range and based on the independent variables in the models, thereby introducing bias into the statistical models (Thomas 2017; Winship and Radbill 1994).

5. The linked fate survey question included in the YouGov and CMPS surveys was not identical. The YouGov language mirrors the two-question linked fate language used in the ANES. The CMPS version, however, measures linked fate with a single question and using a different set of response options.

Chapter Six

1. Subgroup sample sizes by skin tone across datasets are as follows:

Lighter-skinned Black participants (hands 1–4): 2018 Lucid n = 445; 2019 AmeriSpeak n = 283; 2020 CMPS n = 1,145;

Darker-skinned Black participants (hands 8–10): 2018 Lucid n = 592; 2019 AmeriSpeak n = 260; 2020 CMPS n = 1,068.

2. Similar to the analyses from earlier chapters, the statistical models estimated here include a fairly extensive set of controls. The general patterns hold when re-estimating the models with sparser controls.

3. Interestingly, there is some suggestion that the opposite pattern is true among lighter-skinned individuals; light-skinned women who strongly identify with their skin tone hold more negative views of police than their weakly identified light-skinned female counterparts ($p < .07$), but skin tone identity has no association with light-skinned men's views of policing. There is no evidence of a similar pattern on the singular dehumanization item.

4. This CMPS item is coded as a binary variable, with responses of "yes" recorded as 1 and "no" recorded as zero.

5. Within these broader treatment categories, participants were assigned to view one of two versions of the article (see appendix 6.2). In both treatment categories, the information regarding inequities was presented, but one condition had additional information that suggested potential policy solutions. To increase power in my analyses, I combine across these conditions as the policy solutions intervention did not influence responses.

6. Because I wanted to keep the text presented constant across conditions, I looked up the statistics based on both race- and color-based inequalities and included an average of these numbers for both conditions. Although this means that the specific numbers presented to participants are not entirely accurate, they provide a realistic approximation of these disparities. Making these disparities concrete is valuable given that Americans routinely underestimate disparities between groups (Kraus, Rucker, and Richeson 2017; Onyeador et al. 2020; Valentino and Yadon 2023).

7. While the full AmeriSpeak panel is nationally representative, there are a number of inconsistencies between AmeriSpeak's African American subsample and Census estimates. Specifically, the sample is skewed toward women and more educated participants (see appendix table A3.1 for descriptive statistics).

8. Inspiration for these items came from my in-depth interviews, as well as work by Richard Harvey et al. (2017) on creating a colorism scale. Specifically, the question wording for my societal mobility item was adapted from a similar item used by Harvey and colleagues.

Chapter Seven

1. Clarissa Brooks, "'Cops Only Tackled Me and My Friend': Why a Dark Skin Tone Makes Activism Dangerous," *The Guardian*, April 10, 2019.

Appendixes

1. At the conclusion of each interview, participants were asked to provide feedback on how they felt the interview went or if there was anything the interviewer could do better going forward. Some participants commented on the race of the White interviewer specifically during this time and inquired about her interest in this topic. Below are some examples of these comments:

"I thought it was like a really cool and fun experience . . . I will say this one thing. I was really surprised that you were White. [laughs] . . . For me, it wouldn't influence the honesty level or anything. But it was surprising, and I also think I'm always interested in why people are interested in their research. And I think had it been a Black person, I would have just made assumptions about why I thought they were interested in the research. But with you I just wasn't sure."—26-year-old, light-skinned woman

"You're gonna ambush those white people [by making them confront the issue of colorism], aren't ya? You really are. [laughs]"—67-year-old, brown-skinned man

References

Abrajano, Marisa. 2015. "Reexamining the 'Racial Gap' in Political Knowledge." *Journal of Politics* 77 (1): 44–54. https://doi.org/10.1086/678767.

Abrajano, Marisa A., Christopher S. Elmendorf, and Kevin M. Quinn. 2018. "Labels vs. Pictures: Treatment-Mode Effects in Experiments About Discrimination." *Political Analysis* 26 (1): 20–33. https://doi.org/10.1017/pan.2017.36.

Abrajano, Marisa, and R. Michael Alvarez. 2010. *New Faces, New Voices: The Hispanic Electorate in America*. Princeton University Press.

Abrams, Dominic, and Michael A. Hogg. 1988. "Comments on the Motivational Status of Self-Esteem in Social Identity and Intergroup Discrimination." *European Journal of Social Psychology* 18 (4): 317–34. https://doi.org/10.1002/ejsp.2420180403.

Adames, Alexander. 2023. "The Cumulative Effects of Colorism: Race, Wealth, and Skin Tone." *Social Forces*, March, soad038. https://doi.org/10.1093/sf/soad038.

Alexander, Michelle. 2020. *The New Jim Crow: Mass Incarceration in the Age of Colorblindness*. New Press.

Allen, Walter, Edward Telles, and Margaret Hunter. 2000. "Skin Color, Income, and Education: A Comparison of African Americans and Mexican Americans." *National Journal of Sociology* 12 (1): 129–80.

Anderson, Claud, and Rue L. Cromwell. 1977. "'Black Is Beautiful' and the Color Preferences of Afro-American Youth." *Journal of Negro Education* 46 (1): 76–88. https://doi.org/10.2307/2966874.

Austin, Sharon D. Wright. 2018. *The Caribbeanization of Black Politics: Race, Group Consciousness, and Political Participation in America*. State University of New York Press.

Bailenson, J., S. Iyengar, N. Yee, and N. Collins. 2008. "Facial Similarity between Voters and Candidates Causes Influence." *Public Opinion Quarterly* 72 (5): 935–61. https://doi.org/10.1093/poq/nfn064.

Bailey, Stanley, Aliya Saperstein, and Andrew Penner. 2014. "Race, Color, and Income Inequality across the Americas." *Demographic Research* 31 (September): 735–56. https://doi.org/10.4054/DemRes.2014.31.24.

Baluran, Darwin A. 2023. "Differential Racialization and Police Interactions among Young Adults of Asian Descent." *Sociology of Race and Ethnicity* 9 (2): 220–34. https://doi.org/10.1177/23326492221125121.

Banks, Antoine J., Ismail K. White, and Brian D. McKenzie. 2019. "Black Politics: How Anger Influences the Political Actions Blacks Pursue to Reduce Racial Inequality." *Political Behavior* 41 (4): 917–43. https://doi.org/10.1007/s11109-018-9477-1.

Banks, Taunya Lovell. 1999. "Colorism: A Darker Shade of Pale." *UCLA Law Review* 47: 1705–46.

Banton, Michael. 2012. "The Colour Line and the Colour Scale in the Twentieth Century." *Ethnic and Racial Studies* 35 (7): 1109–31. https://doi.org/10.1080/01419870.2011.605902.

Barker, Lucius J., Mack Jones, and Katherine Tate. 1998. *African Americans and the American Political System*. 4th edition. Pearson.

Bartels, Larry M. 2013. "Political Effects of the Great Recession." *Annals of the American Academy of Political and Social Science* 650 (1): 47–76. https://doi.org/10.1177/0002716213496054.

Barth, Fredrik. 1981. *Process and Form in Social Life*. Routledge & Kegan Paul.

Benjamin, Andrea. 2017. *Racial Coalition Building in Local Elections: Elite Cues and Cross-Ethnic Voting*. Cambridge University Press.

Berlin, Ira. 1974. *Slaves without Masters; the Free Negro in the Antebellum South*. Pantheon Books.

Blair, Irene, Charles Judd, and Kristine Chapleau. 2004. "The Influence of Afrocentric Facial Features in Criminal Sentencing." *Psychological Science* 15 (10): 674–79. https://doi.org/10.1111/j.0956-7976.2004.00739.x.

Blair, Irene, Charles Judd, Melody Sadler, and Christopher Jenkins. 2002. "The Role of Afrocentric Features in Person Perception: Judging by Features and Categories." *Journal of Personality and Social Psychology* 83 (1): 5–25. https://doi.org/10.1037//0022-3514.83.1.5.

Blake, Jamilia J., Verna M. Keith, Wen Luo, Huong Le, and Phia Salter. 2017. "The Role of Colorism in Explaining African American Females' Suspension Risk." *School Psychology Quarterly* 32 (1): 118–30. https://doi.org/10.1037/spq0000173.

Bobo, Lawrence. 2004. "Inequalities That Endure? Racial Ideology, American Politics, and the Peculiar Role of the Social Sciences." In *The Changing Terrain of Race and Ethnicity*, edited by Maria Krysan and Amanda E. Lewis. Russell Sage Foundation.

Bobo, Lawrence, Camille Zubrinsky Charles, Maria Krysan, and Alicia D. Simmons. 2012. "The Real Record on Racial Attitudes." In *Social Trends in American Life: Findings from the General Social Survey since 1972*, edited by Peter V. Marsden, 38–83. Princeton University Press.

Bobo, Lawrence, and Franklin D. Gilliam. 1990. "Race, Sociopolitical Participation, and Black Empowerment." *American Political Science Review* 84 (2): 377. https://doi.org/10.2307/1963525.

Bobo, Lawrence, and Vincent Hutchings. 1996. "Perceptions of Racial Group Competition: Extending Blumer's Theory of Group Position to a Multiracial Social Context." *American Sociological Review* 61 (6): 951. https://doi.org/10.2307/2096302.

Bobo, Lawrence, James Johnson, Melvin Oliver, Reynolds Farley, Barry Bluestone, Irene Browne, Sheldon Danziger, et al. 1998. "Multi-City Study of Urban Inequality, 1992–1994: [Atlanta, Boston, Detroit, and Los Angeles]: Version 3." https://doi.org/10.3886/icpsr02535.v3.

Bodenhorn, Howard. 2006. "Colorism, Complexion Homogamy, and Household Wealth: Some Historical Evidence." *American Economic Review* 96 (2): 256–60. https://doi.org/10.1257/000282806777211883.

Bodenhorn, Howard. 2011. "Manumission in Nineteenth-Century Virginia." *Cliometrica* 5 (2): 145–64. https://doi.org/10.1007/s11698-010-0056-x.

Bodenhorn, Howard, and Christopher S. Ruebeck. 2007. "Colourism and African–American Wealth: Evidence from the Nineteenth-Century South." *Journal of Population Economics* 20 (3): 599–620. https://doi.org/10.1007/s00148-006-0111-x.

REFERENCES

Boepple, Leah, and J. Kevin Thompson. 2016. "A Content Analytic Study of Appearance Standards for Women of Color in Magazines." *Psychology of Popular Media Culture.* https://doi.org/10.1037/ppm0000136.

Bonilla, Tabitha, and Alvin Tillery. 2020. "Which Identity Frames Boost Support for and Mobilization in the #BlackLivesMatter Movement? An Experimental Test." *American Political Science Review* 114 (4): 947–62. https://doi.org/10.1017/S0003055420000544.

Bonilla, Yarimar, and Jonathan Rosa. 2015. "#Ferguson: Digital Protest, Hashtag Ethnography, and the Racial Politics of Social Media in the United States." *American Ethnologist* 42 (1): 4–17. https://doi.org/10.1111/amet.12112.

Bonilla-Silva, Eduardo. 2003. *Racism Without Racists: Color-Blind Racism and the Persistence of Racial Inequality in the United States.* Rowman & Littlefield.

Bonilla-Silva, Eduardo. 2004a. "We Are All Americans!: The Latin Americanization of Racial Stratification in the USA." *Race and Society* 5 (1): 3–16. https://doi.org/10.1016/j.racsoc.2003.12.008.

Bonilla-Silva, Eduardo. 2004b. "From Bi-Racial to Tri-Racial: Towards a New System of Racial Stratification in the USA." *Ethnic and Racial Studies* 27 (6): 931–50. https://doi.org/10.1080/0141987042000268530.

Bowman, P., R. Muhammad, and M. Ifatunji. 2004. "Skin Tone, Class, and Racial Attitudes among African Americans." In *Skin Deep: How Race and Complexion Matter in the "Color-Blind" Era,* edited by Cedric Herring, Verna Keith, and H. Horton, 128–58. University of Illinois Press.

Brader, Ted, Nicholas A. Valentino, and Elizabeth Suhay. 2008. "What Triggers Public Opposition to Immigration? Anxiety, Group Cues, and Immigration Threat." *American Journal of Political Science* 52 (4): 959–78. https://doi.org/10.1111/j.1540-907.2008.00353.x.

Brewer, Marilynn B. 1991. "The Social Self: On Being the Same and Different at the Same Time." *Personality and Social Psychology Bulletin* 17 (5): 475–82. https://doi.org/10.1177/0146167291175001.

Broady, Kristen E., Curtis L. Todd, and William A. Darity. 2018. "Passing and the Costs and Benefits of Appropriating Blackness." *Review of Black Political Economy,* August, 003464461878918. https://doi.org/10.1177/0034644618789182.

Brown, Donna, Karen Branden, and Ronald E Hall. 2018. "Native American Colorism: From Historical Manifestations to the Current Era." *American Behavioral Scientist* 62 (14): 2023–36.

Brown, Nadia. 2012. "Negotiating the Insider/Outsider Status: Black Feminist Ethnography and Legislative Studies." *Journal of Feminist Scholarship* 3 (3): 19–34.

Brown, Nadia. 2014a. "'It's More than Hair . . . That's Why You Should Care': The Politics of Appearance for Black Women State Legislators." *Politics, Groups, and Identities* 2 (3): 295–312. https://doi.org/10.1080/21565503.2014.925816.

Brown, Nadia. 2014b. *Sisters in the Statehouse: Black Women and Legislative Decision Making.* Oxford University Press.

Brown, Nadia, and Danielle Lemi. 2021. *Sister Style: The Politics of Appearance for Black Women Political Elites.* 1st edition. Oxford University Press.

Brunsma, David L., and Kerry Ann Rockquemore. 2001. "The New Color Complex: Appearances and Biracial Identity." *Identity* 1 (3): 225–46. https://doi.org/10.1207/S1532706XID0103_03.

Bunyasi, Tehama Lopez, and Candis Watts Smith. 2019. "Do All Black Lives Matter Equally to Black People? Respectability Politics and the Limitations of Linked Fate." *Journal of Race, Ethnicity and Politics* 4 (1): 180–215. https://doi.org/10.1017/rep.2018.33.

Burch, Traci. 2013. *Trading Democracy for Justice: Criminal Convictions and the Decline of Neighborhood Political Participation*. University of Chicago Press.

Burch, Traci. 2015. "Skin Color and the Criminal Justice System: Beyond Black-White Disparities in Sentencing: Skin Color and the Criminal Justice System." *Journal of Empirical Legal Studies* 12 (3): 395–420. https://doi.org/10.1111/jels.12077.

Burge, Camille, Julian Wamble, and Rachel Cuomo. 2020. "A Certain Type of Descriptive Representative?: Understanding How the Skin Tone and Gender of Candidates Influences Black Politics." *Journal of Politics* 82 (4): 1596–1601. https://doi.org/10.1086/708778.

Burke, Peter J. 1980. "The Self: Measurement Requirements from an Interactionist Perspective." *Social Psychology Quarterly* 43 (1): 18–29. https://doi.org/10.2307/3033745.

Burnett, Myra N., and Kimberly Sisson. 1995. "Doll Studies Revisited: A Question of Validity." *Journal of Black Psychology* 21 (1): 19–29. https://doi.org/10.1177/00957984950211003.

Cameron, James E. 2004. "A Three-Factor Model of Social Identity." *Self and Identity* 3 (3): 239–62. https://doi.org/10.1080/13576500444000047.

Campbell, Angus, University of Michigan Survey Research Center, Philip E. Converse, Warren E. Miller, and Donald E. Stokes. 1960. *The American Voter*. University of Chicago Press.

Carter, Niambi. 2019. *American While Black: African Americans, Immigration, and the Limits of Citizenship*. Oxford University Press.

Carter, Prudence L. 2003. "'Black' Cultural Capital, Status Positioning, and Schooling Conflicts for Low-Income African American Youth." *Social Problems* 50 (1): 136–55. https://doi.org/10.1525/sp.2003.50.1.136.

Chandra, Kanchan. 2006. "What Is Ethnic Identity and Does It Matter?" *Annual Review of Political Science* 9 (1): 397–424. https://doi.org/10.1146/annurev.polisci.9.062404.170715.

Chen, Jacqueline M., and Andrew Francis-Tan. 2021. "Setting the Tone: An Investigation of Skin Color Bias in Asia." *Race and Social Problems*, May. https://doi.org/10.1007/s12552-021-09329-0.

Chudy, Jennifer, and Hakeem Jefferson. 2021. "Support for Black Lives Matter Surged Last Year. Did It Last?" Opinion, *New York Times*, May 22, 2021. https://www.nytimes.com/2021/05/22/opinion/blm-movement-protests-support.html.

Citrin, Jack, and David Sears. 2009. "Balancing National and Ethnic Identities." In *Measuring Identity: A Guide for Social Scientists*, edited by R. Abdelal, M. Herrera, I. Johnston, and R. McDermott, 145–74. New York: Cambridge University Press.

Citrin, Jack, Cara Wong, and Brian Duff. 2001. "The Meaning of American National Identity: Patterns of Ethnic Conflict and Consensus." In *Social Identity, Intergroup Conflict, and Conflict Reduction*, chapter 4. Cambridge University Press.

Clark, Kenneth B., and Mamie K. Clark. 1940. "Skin Color as a Factor in Racial Identification of Negro Preschool Children." *Journal of Social Psychology* 11 (1): 159–69. https://doi.org/10.1080/00224545.1940.9918741.

Cohen, Cathy. 1999. *The Boundaries of Blackness: AIDS and the Breakdown of Black Politics*. University of Chicago Press.

Cohen, Cathy, and Matthew Luttig. 2020. "Reconceptualizing Political Knowledge: Race, Ethnicity, and Carceral Violence." *Perspectives on Politics* 18 (3): 805–18. https://doi.org/10.1017/S1537592718003857.

Cole-Frowe, Carol, and Richard Fausset. 2015. "Jarring Image of Police's Use of Force at Texas Pool Party." *New York Times*, June 8, 2015. https://www.nytimes.com/2015/06/09/us/mckinney-tex-pool-party-dispute-leads-to-police-officer-suspension.html.

Collins, Patricia Hill. 1989. "The Social Construction of Black Feminist Thought." *Signs: Journal of Women in Culture and Society* 14 (4): 745–73. https://doi.org/10.1086/494543.
Combahee River Collective. 1977. "The Combahee River Collective Statement." https://www.blackpast.org/african-american-history/combahee-river-collective-statement-1977/.
Conover, Pamela Johnston. 1988. "Feminists and the Gender Gap." *Journal of Politics* 50 (4): 985–1010. https://doi.org/10.2307/2131388.
Conover, Pamela Johnston, and Stanley Feldman. 1984. "Group Identification, Values, and the Nature of Political Beliefs." *American Politics Quarterly* 12 (2): 151–75. https://doi.org/10.1177/1532673X8401200202.
Coppock, Alexander, and Oliver A. McClellan. 2019. "Validating the Demographic, Political, Psychological, and Experimental Results Obtained from a New Source of Online Survey Respondents." *Research & Politics* 6 (1): 1–14. https://doi.org/10.1177/2053168018822174.
Cottom, Tressie McMillan. 2019. *Thick: And Other Essays*. The New Press.
Crabtree, Kiela. 2022. "Forged in the Fire: Racially-Targeted Violence and Implications for Political Behavior in the United States." PhD diss., University of Michigan–Ann Arbor. http://deepblue.lib.umich.edu/handle/2027.42/175638.
Crabtree, Kiela, and Nicole Yadon. 2024. "Remaining Neutral?: White Americans' Reactions to Police Violence and Policing." *Political Behavior* 46: 355–75. https://doi.org/10.1007/s11109-022-09831-0.
Craddock, Nadia, Ncoza Dlova, and Phillippa C. Diedrichs. 2018. "Colourism: A Global Adolescent Health Concern." *Current Opinion in Pediatrics*, May, 1. https://doi.org/10.1097/MOP.0000000000000638.
Cramer, Katherine J. 2016. *The Politics of Resentment: Rural Consciousness in Wisconsin and the Rise of Scott Walker*. University of Chicago Press.
Crenshaw, Kimberle. 1990. "Mapping the Margins: Intersectionality, Identity Politics, and Violence against Women of Color." *Stanford Law Review* 43 (6): 1241–1300.
Davenport, Lauren. 2016. "The Role of Gender, Class, and Religion in Biracial Americans' Racial Labeling Decisions." *American Sociological Review* 81 (1): 57–84. https://doi.org/10.1177/0003122415623286.
Davenport, Lauren. 2018. *Politics beyond Black and White: Biracial Identity and Attitudes in America*. Cambridge University Press. https://doi.org/10.1017/9781108694605.
Davenport, Lauren. 2020. "The Fluidity of Racial Classifications." *Annual Review of Political Science* 23 (1): 221–40. https://doi.org/10.1146/annurev-polisci-060418-042801.
Davis, Darren W., and Ronald E. Brown. 2002. "The Antipathy of Black Nationalism: Behavioral and Attitudinal Implications of an African American Ideology." *American Journal of Political Science* 46 (2): 239–52. https://doi.org/10.2307/3088374.
Davis, F. James. 1991. *Who Is Black?: One Nation's Definition*. Pennsylvania State University Press.
Dawson, Michael C. 1994. *Behind the Mule: Race and Class in African-American Politics*. Princeton University Press.
Dawson, Michael C. 2001. *Black Visions*. University of Chicago Press.
Dixon, Angela, and Edward Telles. 2017. "Skin Color and Colorism: Global Research, Concepts, and Measurement." *Annual Review of Sociology* 43 (1): 405–24. https://doi.org/10.1146/annurev-soc-060116-053315.
Dixon, Travis L., and Keith B. Maddox. 2005. "Skin Tone, Crime News, and Social Reality Judgments: Priming the Stereotype of the Dark and Dangerous Black Criminal." *Journal of Applied Social Psychology* 35 (8): 1555–70. https://doi.org/10.1111/j.1559-1816.2005.tb02184.x.

Dowe, Pearl K. Ford. 2020. "Resisting Marginalization: Black Women's Political Ambition and Agency." *PS: Political Science & Politics* 53 (4): 697–702. https://doi.org/10.1017/S1049096520000554.

Drake, St. Clair, and Horace R. Cayton. 1945. *Black Metropolis: A Study of Negro Life in a Northern City*. University of Chicago Press.

Duster, Troy. 2003. *Backdoor to Eugenics*. Psychology Press.

Eberhardt, Jennifer, Paul Davies, Valerie Purdie-Vaughns, and Sheri-Lynn Johnson. 2006. "Looking Deathworthy: Perceived Stereotypicality of Black Defendants Predicts Capital-Sentencing Outcomes." *Psychological Science* 17 (5): 383–86. https://doi.org/10.1111/j.1467-9280.2006.01716.x.

Eberhardt, Jennifer, Phillip Atiba Goff, Valerie J. Purdie, and Paul G. Davies. 2004. "Seeing Black: Race, Crime, and Visual Processing." *Journal of Personality and Social Psychology* 87 (6): 876–93. https://doi.org/10.1037/0022-3514.87.6.876.

Edsall, T. B., and M. D. Edsall. 1991. *Chain Reaction: The Effect of Race, Rights, and Taxes on American Politics*. Norton.

Ellemers, Naomi. 1993. "The Influence of Socio-Structural Variables on Identity Management Strategies." *European Review of Social Psychology* 4 (1): 27–57. https://doi.org/10.1080/14792779343000013.

Ellemers, Naomi, Ad van Knippenberg, Nanne De Vries, and Henk Wilke. 1988. "Social Identification and Permeability of Group Boundaries." *European Journal of Social Psychology* 18 (6): 497–513. https://doi.org/10.1002/ejsp.2420180604.

Ellemers, Naomi, Ad van Knippenberg, and Henk Wilke. 1990. "The Influence of Permeability of Group Boundaries and Stability of Group Status on Strategies of Individual Mobility and Social Change." *British Journal of Social Psychology* 29 (3): 233–46. https://doi.org/10.1111/j.2044-8309.1990.tb00902.x

Fanon, Frantz. 1952. *Black Skin, White Masks*. Grove Press.

Foote, Nelson N. 1951. "Identification as the Basis for a Theory of Motivation." *American Sociological Review* 16 (1): 14–21. https://doi.org/10.2307/2087964.

Fraga, Luis, John A. Garcia, Gary M. Segura, Michael Jones-Correa, Rodney Hero, and Valerie Martinez-Ebers. 2010. *Latino Lives in America: Making It Home*. Temple University Press.

Frasure, Lorrie Ann, and Linda Faye Williams. 2009. "Racial, Ethnic, and Gender Disparities in Political Participation and Civic Engagement." In *Emerging Intersections: Race, Class, and Gender in Theory, Policy, and Practice*, edited by Bonnie Thornton Dill and Ruth Enid Zambrana, 203–28. Rutgers University Press. https://doi.org/10.36019/9780813546513-011.

Frazier, E. Franklin. 1930. "The Negro Slave Family." *Journal of Negro History* 15 (2): 198–259. https://doi.org/10.2307/2714011.

Frazier, E. Franklin. 1932. *The Free Negro Family: A Study of Family Origins before the Civil War*. Fisk University Press.

Frazier, E. Franklin. 1965. *Black Bourgeoisie*. Free Press.

Gaines, Kevin K. 1996. *Uplifting the Race: Black Leadership, Politics, and Culture in the Twentieth Century*. University of North Carolina Press.

Garcia-Bedolla, Lisa. 2005. *Fluid Borders: Latino Power, Identity, and Politics in Los Angeles*. University of California Press.

Garcia-Bedolla, Lisa. 2007. "Intersections of Inequality: Understanding Marginalization and Privilege in the Post–Civil Rights Era." *Politics & Gender* 3 (2): 232–48.

REFERENCES

Garcia-Rios, Sergio, Francisco Pedraza, and Bryan Wilcox-Archuleta. 2019. "Direct and Indirect Xenophobic Attacks: Unpacking Portfolios of Identity." *Political Behavior* 41 (3): 633–56. https://doi.org/10.1007/s11109-018-9465-5.

Gatewood, Willard B. 1990. *Aristocrats of Color: The Black Elite, 1880–1920*. University of Arkansas Press.

Gause, LaGina. 2022a. "Revealing Issue Salience via Costly Protest: How Legislative Behavior Following Protest Advantages Low-Resource Groups." *British Journal of Political Science* 52 (1): 259–79. https://doi.org/10.1017/S0007123420000423.

———. 2022b. *The Advantage of Disadvantage: How Protest Drives Legislative Support for the Politically Marginalized*. Cambridge University Press.

Gause, LaGina, and Maneesh Arora. n.d. "Unaligned Activists: How Digital Technologies, Decentralized Leadership, Post-Materialism, and Self-Identification Facilitate Unaligned Participation in Contemporary Social Movements." Unpublished Manuscript.

Gay, Claudine. 2004. "Putting Race in Context: Identifying the Environmental Determinants of Black Racial Attitudes." *American Political Science Review* 98 (4): 547–62. https://doi.org/10.1017/S0003055404041346.

Gelman, Andrew, Boris Shor, Joseph Bafumi, and David Park. 2007. "Rich State, Poor State, Red State, Blue State: What's the Matter with Connecticut?" *Quarterly Journal of Political Science* 2: 345–67. https://doi.org/10.1561/100.00006026.

Gilens, Martin. 1996. "'Race Coding' and White Opposition to Welfare." *American Political Science Review* 90 (03): 593–604. https://doi.org/10.2307/2082611.

Gilens, Martin. 1999. *Why Americans Hate Welfare: Race, Media, and the Politics of Antipoverty Policy*. University of Chicago Press.

Gillion, Daniel. 2013. *The Political Power of Protest: Minority Activism and Shifts in Public Policy*. Cambridge University Press.

Gillion, Daniel. 2016. *Governing with Words: The Political Dialogue on Race, Public Policy, and Inequality in America*. Cambridge University Press.

Gillion, Daniel. 2020. *The Loud Minority: Why Protests Matter in American Democracy*. Princeton University Press.

Gilroy, Paul. 1993. *The Black Atlantic: Modernity and Double Consciousness*. Harvard University Press.

Glenn, Evelyn Nakano. 2008. "Yearning for Lightness: Transnational Circuits in the Marketing and Consumption of Skin Lighteners." *Gender & Society* 22 (3): 281–302. https://doi.org/10.1177/0891243208316089.

Glenn, Evelyn Nakano. 2009. *Shades of Difference: Why Skin Color Matters*. Stanford University Press.

Goering, John M. 1972. "Changing Perceptions and Evaluations of Physical Characteristics among Blacks: 1950–1970." *Phylon (1960-)* 33 (3): 231–41. https://doi.org/10.2307/273523.

Goff, Phillip Atiba, Jennifer L. Eberhardt, Melissa J. Williams, and Matthew Christian Jackson. 2008. "Not Yet Human: Implicit Knowledge, Historical Dehumanization, and Contemporary Consequences." *Journal of Personality and Social Psychology* 94 (2): 292–306. https://doi.org/10.1037/0022-3514.94.2.292.

Goff, Phillip Atiba, Claude M. Steele, and Paul G. Davies. 2008. "The Space between Us: Stereotype Threat and Distance in Interracial Contexts." *Journal of Personality and Social Psychology* 94 (1): 91–107. https://doi.org/10.1037/0022-3514.94.1.91.

Goldsmith, Arthur, Darrick Hamilton, and William Darity. 2006. "Shades of Discrimination: Skin Tone and Wages." *American Economic Review* 96 (2): 242–45. https://doi.org/10.1257/000282806777212152.

Goldsmith, Arthur, Darrick Hamilton, and William Darity. 2007. "From Dark to Light: Skin Color and Wages among African-Americans." *Journal of Human Resources* 42 (4): 701–38. https://doi.org/10.3368/jhr.XLII.4.701.

Goren, Paul, Christopher M. Federico, and Miki Caul Kittilson. 2009. "Source Cues, Partisan Identities, and Political Value Expression." *American Journal of Political Science* 53 (4): 805–20. https://doi.org/10.1111/j.1540-907.2009.00402.x.

Graham, Lawrence Otis. 1999. *Our Kind of People: Inside America's Black Upper Class*. Harper Perennial.

Gravlee, Clarence C., and William W. Dressler. 2005. "Skin Pigmentation, Self-Perceived Color, and Arterial Blood Pressure in Puerto Rico." *American Journal of Human Biology* 17 (2): 195–206.

Green, Tiffany L., and Tod G. Hamilton. 2013. "Beyond Black and White: Color and Mortality in Post-Reconstruction Era North Carolina." *Explorations in Economic History* 50 (1): 148–59. https://doi.org/10.1016/j.eeh.2012.06.002.

Greer, Christina. 2013. *Black Ethnics: Race, Immigration, and the Pursuit of the American Dream*. Oxford University Press.

Gullickson, Aaron. 2005. "The Significance of Color Declines: A Re-Analysis of Skin Tone Differentials in Post–Civil Rights America." *Social Forces* 84 (1): 157–80. https://doi.org/10.1353/sof.2005.0099.

Gurin, Patricia. 1985. "Women's Gender Consciousness." *Public Opinion Quarterly* 49 (2): 143–63. https://doi.org/10.1086/268911.

Hajnal, Zoltan L., and Taeku Lee. 2011. *Why Americans Don't Join the Party: Race, Immigration, and the Failure (of Political Parties) to Engage the Electorate*. Princeton University Press.

Hall, Ronald. 1995. "The Bleaching Syndrome: African Americans' Response to Cultural Domination vis-à-vis Skin Color." *Journal of Black Studies* 26 (2): 172–84.

Hall, Ronald. 2018. "The Globalization of Light Skin Colorism: From Critical Race to Critical Skin Theory." *American Behavioral Scientist*, November, 0002764218810755. https://doi.org/10.1177/0002764218810755.

Hall, Ronald. 2021. "Women of Color Spend More than $8 Billion on Bleaching Creams Worldwide Every Year." The Conversation. 2021. http://theconversation.com/women-of-color-spend-more-than-8-billion-on-bleaching-creams-worldwide-every-year-153178.

Hamilton, Charles V., and Kwame Ture. 1992. *Black Power: Politics of Liberation in America*. Knopf Doubleday.

Hancock, Ange-Marie. 2004. *The Politics of Disgust: The Public Identity of the Welfare Queen*. New York University Press.

Hancock, Ange-Marie. 2007. "When Multiplication Doesn't Equal Quick Addition: Examining Intersectionality as a Research Paradigm." *Perspectives on Politics* 5 (1): 63–79. https://doi.org/10.1017/S1537592707070065.

Hancock, Ange-Marie. 2016. *Intersectionality: An Intellectual History*. Oxford University Press.

Haney Lopez, Ian. 1997. *White by Law: The Legal Construction of Race*. New York University Press.

Hannon, Lance, Robert DeFina, and Sarah Bruch. 2013. "The Relationship between Skin Tone and School Suspension for African Americans." *Race and Social Problems* 5 (4): 281–95. https://doi.org/10.1007/s12552-013-9104-z.

Harburg, Ernest, Lillian Gleibermann, Peter Roeper, Anthony Schork, and William J. Schull. 1978. "Skin Color, Ethnicity, and Blood Pressure I: Detroit Blacks." *American Journal of Public Health* 68 (12): 1177–83.

Hargrove, Taylor W. 2018. "Light Privilege? Skin Tone Stratification in Health among African Americans." *Sociology of Race and Ethnicity*, September. https://doi.org/10.1177/2332649 218793670.

Harris, Cheryl I. 1993. "Whiteness as Property." *Harvard Law Review* 106 (8): 1707. https://doi.org/10.2307/1341787.

Harris, Fredrick C., Valeria Sinclair-Chapman, and Brian D. McKenzie. 2005. "Macrodynamics of Black Political Participation in the Post–Civil Rights Era." *Journal of Politics* 67 (4): 1143–63. https://doi.org/10.1111/j.1468-2508.2005.00354.x.

Harris-Lacewell, Melissa. 2006. *Barbershops, Bibles, and BET: Everyday Talk and Black Political Thought*. Princeton University Press.

Harris-Lacewell, Melissa, and Jane Junn. 2007. "Old Friends and New Alliances: How the 2004 Illinois Senate Race Complicates the Study of Race and Religion." *Journal of Black Studies* 38 (1): 30–50. https://doi.org/10.1177/0021934707304953.

Harvey, Richard D., Nicole LaBeach, Ellie Pridgen, and Tammy M. Gocial. 2005. "The Intragroup Stigmatization of Skin Tone among Black Americans." *Journal of Black Psychology* 31 (3): 237–53. https://doi.org/10.1177/0095798405278192.

Harvey, Richard D., Rachel E. Tennial, and Kira Hudson Banks. 2017. "The Development and Validation of a Colorism Scale." *Journal of Black Psychology* 43 (7): 740–64. https://doi.org/10.1177/0095798417690054.

Hebl, Michelle, Melissa Williams, Jane Sundermann, Harrison Kell, and Paul Davies. 2012. "Selectively Friending: Racial Stereotypicality and Social Rejection." *Journal of Experimental Social Psychology* 48 (6): 1329–35. https://doi.org/10.1016/j.jesp.2012.05.019.

Herring, Cedric, Verna Keith, and Hayward Derrick Horton. 2004. *Skin Deep: How Race and Complexion Matter in the "Color-Blind" Era*. University of Illinois Press.

Hess, Robert, and Judith Torney. 1967. *The Development of Political Attitudes in Children*. Aldine.

Hickman, Christine B. 1997. "The Devil and the One Drop Rule: Racial Categories, African Americans, and the U.S. Census." *Michigan Law Review* 95 (5): 1161–265. https://doi.org/10.2307/1290008.

Hochschild, Jennifer. 1981. *What's Fair?: American Beliefs about Distributive Justice*. Harvard University Press.

Hochschild, Jennifer. 2005. "Looking Ahead: Racial Trends in the United States." *Daedalus* 134 (1): 70–81. https://doi.org/10.1162/0011526053124343.

Hochschild, Jennifer. 2006. "When Do People Not Protest Unfairness? The Case of Skin Color Discrimination." *Social Research: An International Quarterly* 73 (2): 473–98.

Hochschild, Jennifer, and Brenna Powell. 2008. "Racial Reorganization and the United States Census 1850–1930: Mulattoes, Half-Breeds, Mixed Parentage, Hindoos, and the Mexican Race." *Studies in American Political Development* 22 (01). https://doi.org/10.1017/S0898588 X08000047.

Hochschild, Jennifer, and Vesla Weaver. 2007. "The Skin Color Paradox and the American Racial Order." *Social Forces* 86 (2): 643–70. https://doi.org/10.1093/sf/86.2.643.

Hochschild, Jennifer, Vesla Weaver, and Traci Burch. 2012. *Creating a New Racial Order: How Immigration, Multiracialism, Genomics, and the Young Can Remake Race in America*. Princeton University Press.

Hogg, Michael. 1996. "Intragroup Processes, Group Structure and Social Identity." In *Social Groups and Identities: Developing the Legacy of Henri Tajfel*, edited by W. Peter Robinson, 65–93. Butterworth Heinemann.

Hogg, Michael. 2001a. "From Prototypicality to Power: A Social Identity Analysis of Leadership." *Advances in Group Processes* 18: 1–30. https://doi.org/10.1016/S0882-6145(01)18002-1

Hogg, Michael. 2001b. "A Social Identity Theory of Leadership." *Personality and Social Psychology Review* 5 (3): 184–200. https://doi.org/10.1207/S15327957PSPR0503_1.

Hollinger, David A. 2006. *Postethnic America: Beyond Multiculturalism*. Hachette UK.

Holman, Mirya R., and Monica C. Schneider. 2018. "Gender, Race, and Political Ambition: How Intersectionality and Frames Influence Interest in Political Office." *Politics, Groups, and Identities* 6 (2): 264–80. https://doi.org/10.1080/21565503.2016.1208105.

hooks, bell. 2000. *Feminist Theory: From Margin to Center*. Pluto Press.

Hooper, Michael. 1976. "The Structure and Measurement of Social Identity." *Public Opinion Quarterly* 40 (2): 154–64. https://doi.org/10.1086/268284.

Hornsey, Matthew J., and Jolanda Jetten. 2004. "The Individual within the Group: Balancing the Need to Belong with the Need to Be Different." *Personality and Social Psychology Review* 8 (3): 248–64. https://doi.org/10.1207/s15327957pspr0803_2.

Horowitz, Donald L. 1985. *Ethnic Groups in Conflict*. University of California Press.

Huddy, Leonie. 2001. "From Social to Political Identity: A Critical Examination of Social Identity Theory." *Political Psychology* 22 (1): 127–56. https://doi.org/10.1111/0162-895X.00230.

Huddy, Leonie, and Nadia Khatib. 2007. "American Patriotism, National Identity, and Political Involvement." *American Journal of Political Science* 51 (1): 63–77. https://doi.org/10.1111/j.1540-907.2007.00237.x.

Hughes, Michael, and Bradley R. Hertel. 1990. "The Significance of Color Remains: A Study of Life Chances, Mate Selection, and Ethnic Consciousness among Black Americans." *Social Forces* 68 (4): 1105–20. https://doi.org/10.2307/2579136.

Hunter, Margaret. 2002. "'If You're Light You're Alright': Light Skin Color as Social Capital for Women of Color." *Gender & Society* 16 (2): 175–93. https://doi.org/10.1177/08912430222104895.

Hunter, Margaret. 2005. *Race, Gender, and the Politics of Skin Tone*. Routledge.

Hunter, Margaret. 2007. "The Persistent Problem of Colorism: Skin Tone, Status, and Inequality." *Sociology Compass* 1 (1): 237–54. https://doi.org/10.1111/j.1751-9020.2007.00006.x.

Hunter, Margaret. 2021. "Colorism and the Racial Politics of Beauty." In *The Routledge Companion to Beauty Politics*. ed. Maxine Leeds Craig. Routledge.

Hutchings, Vincent, and Ashley Jardina. 2009. "Experiments on Racial Priming in Political Campaigns." *Annual Review of Political Science* 12 (1): 397–402. https://doi.org/10.1146/annurev.polisci.12.060107.154208.

Hutchings, Vincent, and Hakeem Jefferson. 2014. "Out of Options? Blacks and Support for the Democratic Party." Presentation Delivered at the World Congress of the International Political Science Association, Montreal.

Hutchings, Vincent, Hakeem Jefferson, Neil Lewis, and Nicole Yadon. 2016. "The Color of Our Skin and the Content of Our Politics: Exploring the Effects of Skin Tone on Policy Preferences Among African Americans." Presentation Delivered at the 2016 APSA Annual Meeting.

Hutchings, Vincent L., and Nicholas A. Valentino. 2004. "The Centrality of Race in American Politics." *Annual Review of Political Science* 7: 383–408.

Jablonski, Nina. 2021. "Skin Color and Race." *American Journal of Physical Anthropology* 175 (2): 437–47. https://doi.org/10.1002/ajpa.24200.

Jablonski, Nina, and George Chaplin. 2000. "The Evolution of Human Skin Coloration." *Journal of Human Evolution* 39 (1): 57–106. https://doi.org/10.1006/jhev.2000.0403.

Jackman, Mary. 1994. *The Velvet Glove: Paternalism and Conflict in Gender, Class, and Race Relations*. University of California Press.

Jackson, James S., and Gerald Gurin. 1987. "National Survey of Black Americans, 1979–1980: Version 1." https://doi.org/10.3886/icpsr08512.v1.

Jardina, Ashley. 2019. *White Identity Politics*. Cambridge University Press.

Jefferson, Hakeem. 2023. "The Politics of Respectability and Black Americans' Punitive Attitudes." *American Political Science Review*, January, 1–17. https://doi.org/10.1017/S0003055422001289.

Johnson, J., W. Farrell, and J. Stoloff. 1998. "The Declining Social and Economic Fortunes of African American Males: A Critical Assessment of Four Perspectives." *Review of Black Political Economy* 25 (4): 17–40.

Jones, Mack H. 2015. *Knowledge, Power, and Black Politics*. State University of New York Press.

Jones, Solomon. 2014. "Michael Brown and the Deadly Effects of Colorism." *PBS Philadelphia* (blog). October 30, 2014. https://whyy.org/articles/michael-brown-and-the-deadly-effects-of-colorism/.

Junn, Jane, and Natalie Masuoka. 2008. "Asian American Identity: Shared Racial Status and Political Context." *Perspectives on Politics* 6 (4): 729–40. https://doi.org/10.1017/S1537592708081887.

Keith, Verna, and Cedric Herring. 1991. "Skin Tone and Stratification in the Black Community." *American Journal of Sociology* 97 (3): 760–78.

Kerr, A.E. 2006. "The History of Color Prejudice at Howard University—ProQuest." *Journal of Blacks in Higher Education* 54: 82–87.

Khanna, Nikki, and Cathryn Johnson. 2010. "Passing as Black: Racial Identity Work among Biracial Americans." *Social Psychology Quarterly* 73 (4): 380–97. https://doi.org/10.1177/0190272510389014.

Kim, Claire Jean. 2000. *Bitter Fruit: The Politics of Black-Korean Conflict in New York City*. Revised edition. Yale University Press.

Kim, Eunji, Rasmus Pedersen, and Diana Mutz. 2016. "What Do Americans Talk about When They Talk about Inequality?" MPSA Annual Meeting. https://sites.duke.edu/preferencesoverredistribution/files/2016/04/MPSA2016_Understanding-Inequality-1.pdf.

Kinder, Donald, and Lynn Sanders. 1996. *Divided by Color: Racial Politics and Democratic Ideals*. University of Chicago Press.

Kinder, Donald, and Nicholas Winter. 2001. "Exploring the Racial Divide: Blacks, Whites, and Opinion on National Policy." *American Journal of Political Science* 45 (2): 439. https://doi.org/10.2307/2669351.

King, Ryan, and Brian Johnson. 2016. "A Punishing Look: Skin Tone and Afrocentric Features in the Halls of Justice." *American Journal of Sociology* 122 (1): 90–124. https://doi.org/10.1086/686941.

Kizer, Jessica. 2017. "Arrested by Skin Color: Evidence from Siblings and a Nationally Representative Sample." *Socius* 3: 1–12. https://doi.org/10.1177/2378023117737922.

Klandermans, Bert, Jose Manuel Sabucedo, Mauro Rodriguez, and Marga De Weerd. 2002. "Identity Processes in Collective Action Participation: Farmers' Identity and Farmers' Protest in the Netherlands and Spain." *Political Psychology* 23 (2): 235–51. https://doi.org/10.1111/0162-895X.00280.

Klar, Samara. 2020. "Turn and Face the Strange Ch-Ch-Changes: How an Evolving America Activates Identity Politics." *Journal of Politics* 82 (1): e1–6. https://doi.org/10.1086/706456.

Kluegel, James R., and Eliot R. Smith. 1986. *Beliefs about Inequality: Americans' Views of What Is and What Ought to Be*. A. de Gruyter.

Korgen, Kathleen Odell. 1998. *From Black to Biracial: Transforming Racial Identity among Americans*. Greenwood.

Kraus, Michael, Julian Rucker, and Jennifer Richeson. 2017. "Americans Misperceive Racial Economic Equality." *Proceedings of the National Academy of Sciences* 114 (39): 10324–31. https://doi.org/10.1073/pnas.1707719114.

Krieger, Nancy, Stephen Sidney, and Eugenie Coakley. 1998. "Racial Discrimination and Skin Color in the CARDIA Study: Implications for Public Health Research." *American Journal of Public Health* 88 (9): 1308–13.

Kuryla, P., and G. Jaynes. 2005. "Blue Vein Society." In *Encyclopedia of African American Society*, edited by G. Jaynes. Sage.

Lacy, Karyn R. 2007. *Blue-Chip Black: Race, Class, and Status in the New Black Middle Class*. University of California Press.

Laidley, Thomas, Benjamin Domingue, Piyapat Sinsub, Kathleen Mullan Harris, and Dalton Conley. 2019. "New Evidence of Skin Color Bias and Health Outcomes Using Sibling Difference Models: A Research Note." *Demography*. https://doi.org/10.1007/s13524-018-0756-6.

Lajevardi, Nazita. 2020. *Outsiders at Home: The Politics of American Islamophobia*. Cambridge University Press.

Lajevardi, Nazita. 2021. "The Media Matters: Muslim American Portrayals and the Effects on Mass Attitudes." *Journal of Politics* 83 (3): 1060–79. https://doi.org/10.1086/711300.

Lakoff, George. 2008. *Women, Fire, and Dangerous Things: What Categories Reveal about the Mind*. University of Chicago Press.

Lane, Robert E. 1962. *Political Ideology: Why the American Common Man Believes What He Does*. Free Press of Glencoe.

Lee, Sharon. 1993. "Racial Classifications in the US Census: 1890–1990." *Ethnic and Racial Studies* 16 (1): 75–94. https://doi.org/10.1080/01419870.1993.9993773.

Lee, Taeku. 2002. *Mobilizing Public Opinion: Black Insurgency and Racial Attitudes in the Civil Rights Era*. University of Chicago Press.

Lee, Taeku. 2007. "From Shared Demographic Categories to Common Political Destinies: Immigration and the Link from Racial Identity to Group Politics." *Du Bois Review: Social Science Research on Race* 4 (2): 433–56. https://doi.org/10.1017/S1742058X07070245.

Lemi, Danielle. 2020. "Do Voters Prefer Just Any Descriptive Representative? The Case of Multiracial Candidates." *Perspectives on Politics* 19 (4): 1061–81. https://doi.org/10.1017/S1537592720001280.

Lemi, Danielle, and Nadia Brown. 2019. "Melanin and Curls: Evaluation of Black Women Candidates." *Journal of Race, Ethnicity and Politics* 4 (2): 259–96. https://doi.org/10.1017/rep.2019.18.

Lemi, Danielle, and Nadia Brown. 2020. "The Political Implications of Colorism Are Gendered." *PS: Political Science & Politics* 53 (4): 669–73. https://doi.org/10.1017/S1049096520000761.

Lerman, Amy, Katherine McCabe, and Meredith Sadin. 2015. "Political Ideology, Skin Tone, and the Psychology of Candidate Evaluations." *Public Opinion Quarterly* 79 (1): 53–90. https://doi.org/10.1093/poq/nfu055.

Lerman, Amy, and Vesla Weaver. 2014. *Arresting Citizenship: The Democratic Consequences of American Crime Control*. University of Chicago Press.

Leslie, Gregory John, Natalie Masuoka, Sarah E. Gaither, Jessica D. Remedios, and A. Chyei Vinluan. 2022. "Voter Evaluations of Biracial-Identified Political Candidates." *Social Sciences* 11 (4): 171. https://doi.org/10.3390/socsci11040171.

Leslie, Gregory John, and David O. Sears. 2022. "The Heaviest Drop of Blood: Black Exceptionalism among Multiracials." *Political Psychology*, March. https://doi.org/10.1111/pops.12806.

Lewis, Neil A., and Denise Sekaquaptewa. 2016. "Beyond Test Performance: A Broader View of Stereotype Threat." *Current Opinion in Psychology*, Intergroup relations, 11 (October): 40–43. https://doi.org/10.1016/j.copsyc.2016.05.002.

Lindsey, Treva B. 2015. "Post-Ferguson: A 'Herstorical' Approach to Black Violability." *Feminist Studies* 41 (1): 232–37. https://doi.org/10.15767/feministstudies.41.1.232.

Maddox, Keith. 2004. "Perspectives on Racial Phenotypicality Bias." *Personality and Social Psychology Review* 8 (4): 383–401. https://doi.org/10.1207/s15327957pspr0804_4.

Maddox, Keith, and Stephanie Gray. 2002. "Cognitive Representations of Black Americans: Reexploring the Role of Skin Tone." *Personality and Social Psychology Bulletin* 28 (2): 250–59. https://doi.org/10.1177/0146167202282010.

Major, Brenda, and Laurie T. O'Brien. 2005. "The Social Psychology of Stigma." *Annual Review of Psychology* 56: 393–421. https://doi.org/10.1146/annurev.psych.56.091103.070137.

Masuoka, Natalie. 2017. *Multiracial Identity and Racial Politics in the United States*. Oxford University Press.

Masuoka, Natalie, and Jane Junn. 2013. *The Politics of Belonging: Race, Public Opinion, and Immigration*. University of Chicago Press.

McCall, Leslie. 2005. "The Complexity of Intersectionality." *Signs: Journal of Women in Culture and Society* 30 (3): 1771–1800. https://doi.org/10.1086/426800.

McCall, Leslie, and Jeff Manza. 2011. "Class Differences in Social and Political Attitudes in the United States." In *The Oxford Handbook of American Public Opinion and the Media*. Vol. 34. Oxford University Press.

McCarty, Nolan, Keith T Poole, and Howard Rosenthal. 2006. *Polarized America: The Dance of Ideology and Unequal Riches*. MIT Press.

McClain, Paula D., Jessica D. Johnson Carew, Eugene Walton, and Candis S. Watts. 2009. "Group Membership, Group Identity, and Group Consciousness: Measures of Racial Identity in American Politics?" *Annual Review of Political Science* 12 (1): 471–85. https://doi.org/10.1146/annurev.polisci.10.072805.102452.

Mears, Bill. 2014. "Michigan's Ban on Affirmative Action Upheld by Supreme Court." *CNN*, April 22, 2014. https://www.cnn.com/2014/04/22/justice/scotus-michigan-affirmative-action/index.html.

Medow, Herman, and Alvin Zander. 1965. "Aspirations for the Group Chosen by Central and Peripheral Members." *Journal of Personality and Social Psychology* 1 (3): 224–28. https://doi.org/10.1037/h0021876.

Meier, Kenneth J., Eric Gonzalez Juenke, Robert D. Wrinkle, and J. L. Polinard. 2005. "Structural Choices and Representational Biases: The Post-Election Color of Representation." *American Journal of Political Science* 49 (4): 758–68. https://doi.org/10.1111/j.1540-907.2005.00153.x.

Mendelberg, Tali. 2001. *The Race Card: Campaign Strategy, Implicit Messages, and the Norm of Equality*. Princeton University Press.

Menke, John G. 1979. *Mulattoes and Race Mixture: American Attitudes and Images, 1865–1918*. University of Michigan Press.

Miller, Arthur H., Patricia Gurin, Gerald Gurin, and Oksana Malanchuk. 1981. "Group Consciousness and Political Participation." *American Journal of Political Science* 25 (3): 494. https://doi.org/10.2307/2110816.

Minta, Michael D., and Valeria Sinclair-Chapman. 2013. "Diversity in Political Institutions and Congressional Responsiveness to Minority Interests." *Political Research Quarterly* 66 (1): 127–40. https://doi.org/10.1177/1065912911431245.

Monk, Ellis. 2014. "Skin Tone Stratification among Black Americans, 2001–2003." *Social Forces* 92 (4): 1313–37. https://doi.org/10.1093/sf/sou007.

Monk, Ellis. 2015. "The Cost of Color: Skin Color, Discrimination, and Health among African-Americans." *American Journal of Sociology* 121 (2): 396–444. https://doi.org/10.1086/682162.

Monk, Ellis. 2018. "The Color of Punishment: African Americans, Skin Tone, and the Criminal Justice System." *Ethnic and Racial Studies* 42 (10): 1593–1612. https://doi.org/10.1080/01419870.2018.1508736.

Monk, Ellis. 2021. "The Unceasing Significance of Colorism: Skin Tone Stratification in the United States." *Daedalus* 150 (2): 76–90. https://doi.org/10.1162/daed_a_01847.

Montoya, Celeste, Christina Bejarano, Nadia Brown, and Sarah Allen Gershon. 2021. "The Intersectional Dynamics of Descriptive Representation." *Politics & Gender*, 1–30. https://doi.org/10.1017/S1743923X20000744.

Mora, G. Cristina. 2014. *Making Hispanics: How Activists, Bureaucrats, and Media Constructed a New American*. University of Chicago Press.

Mummendey, Amélle, and Hans-Joachim Schreiber. 1983. "Better or Just Different? Positive Social Identity by Discrimination against, or by Differentiation from Outgroups." *European Journal of Social Psychology* 13 (4): 389–97. https://doi.org/10.1002/ejsp.2420130406.

Myrdal, Gunnar. 1944. *An American Dilemma: The Negro Problem and Modern Democracy*, Volume 1. Routledge. https://doi.org/10.4324/9781315082417.

Myrdal, Gunnar. 1996. *An American Dilemma: The Negro Problem and Modern Democracy*, Volume 2. Routledge.

Nunnally, Shayla. 2012. *Trust in Black America: Race, Discrimination, and Politics*. New York University Press.

Ogorzalek, Thomas, Spencer Piston, and Luisa Godinez Puig. 2019. "Nationally Poor, Locally Rich: Income and Local Context in the 2016 Presidential Election." *Electoral Studies*, September, 102068. https://doi.org/10.1016/j.electstud.2019.102068.

Olsen, M.E. 1970. "Social and Political Participation of Blacks." *American Sociological Review* 35 (4): 682–97. https://www.jstor.org/stable/pdf/2093944.pdf.

Omi, M., and H. Winant. 1994. *Racial Formation in the United States: From the 1960s to the 1990s*. 2nd ed. Routledge.

Onyeador, Ivuoma, Natalie Daumeyer, Julian Rucker, Ajua Duker, Michael Kraus, and Jennifer Richeson. 2020. "Disrupting Beliefs in Racial Progress: Reminders of Persistent Racism Alter Perceptions of Past, but Not Current, Racial Economic Equality." *Personality and Social Psychology Bulletin*, August, 014616722094262. https://doi.org/10.1177/0146167220942625.

Orey, Byron D'Andra, and Yu Zhang. 2019. "Melanated Millennials and the Politics of Black Hair." *Social Science Quarterly* 100 (6): 2458–76. https://doi.org/10.1111/ssqu.12694.

Ostfeld, Mara, and Nicole Yadon. 2022a. "¿Mejorando La Raza?: The Political Undertones of Latinos' Skin Color in the United States." *Social Forces* 100 (4): 1806–32. https://doi.org/10.1093/sf/soab060.

Ostfeld, Mara, and Nicole Yadon. 2022b. *Skin Color, Power, and Politics in America*. Russell Sage Foundation Press.
Parker, Christopher. 2009. *Fighting for Democracy: Black Veterans and the Struggle against White Supremacy in the Postwar South*. Princeton University Press.
Parrish, Charles H. 1946. "Color Names and Color Notions." *Journal of Negro Education* 15 (1): 13. https://doi.org/10.2307/2966307.
Pérez, Efrén. 2015. "Ricochet: How Elite Discourse Politicizes Racial and Ethnic Identities." *Political Behavior* 37 (1): 155–80. https://doi.org/10.1007/s11109-013-9262-0.
Pérez, Efrén 2016. *Unspoken Politics: Implicit Attitudes and Political Thinking*. Cambridge University Press.
Pérez, Efrén. 2021. *Diversity's Child: People of Color and the Politics of Identity*. University of Chicago Press.
Pérez, Efrén, and Bianca V. Vicuna. 2023. "The Gaze from Below: Toward a Political Psychology of Minority Status." In *The Oxford Handbook of Political Psychology*, edited by Leonie Huddy, David O. Sears, Jack S. Levy, and Jennifer Jerit, Oxford University Press. https://doi.org/10.1093/oxfordhb/9780197541296.013.24.
Pew. 2007. "Blacks See Growing Values Gap between Poor and Middle Class." *Pew Research Center's Social & Demographic Trends Project* (blog). November 13, 2007. https://www.pewresearch.org/social-trends/2007/11/13/blacks-see-growing-values-gap-between-poor-and-middle-class/.
Pew. 2008. "One in 100: Behind Bars in America 2008." Pew Center on the States. https://www.pewtrusts.org/-/media/legacy/uploadedfiles/pcs_assets/2008/one20in20100pdf.pdf.
Pew. 2020a. "What Census Calls Us." *Pew Research Center* (blog). February 6, 2020. https://www.pewresearch.org/interactives/what-census-calls-us/.
Pew. 2020b. "The Changing Categories the U.S. Census Has Used to Measure Race." *Pew Research Center* (blog). February 25, 2020. https://www.pewresearch.org/fact-tank/2020/02/25/the-changing-categories-the-u-s-has-used-to-measure-race/.
Pew. 2023. "Racial Disparities Persist in Many U.S. Jails." https://pew.org/44DtVUh.
Philpot, Tasha S. 2017. *Conservative but Not Republican*. Cambridge University Press.
Phoenix, Davin. 2019. *The Anger Gap: How Race Shapes Emotion in Politics*. Cambridge University Press.
Piston, Spencer. 2018. *Class Attitudes in America: Sympathy for the Poor, Resentment of the Rich, and Political Implications*. Cambridge University Press.
Prestage, Jewel L. 1991. "In Quest of African American Political Woman." *Annals of the American Academy of Political and Social Science* 515 (1): 88–103. https://doi.org/10.1177/0002716291515001008.
Ransford, H. Edward. 1970. "Skin Color, Life Chances, and Anti-White Attitudes." *Social Problems* 18 (2): 164–79. https://doi.org/10.2307/799579.
Reece, Robert. 2018a. "Color Crit: Critical Race Theory and the History and Future of Colorism in the United States." *Journal of Black Studies* 50 (1): 24. http://doi.org/10.1177/0021934718803735.
Reece, Robert. 2018b. "Genesis of U.S. Colorism and Skin Tone Stratification: Slavery, Freedom, and Mulatto-Black Occupational Inequality in the Late 19th Century." *Review of Black Political Economy* 45 (1): 3–21. https://doi.org/10.1177/0034644618770761
Reece, Robert. 2021. "The Future of American Blackness: On Colorism and Racial Reorganization." *Review of Black Political Economy* 48 (4): 481–505. https://doi.org/10.1177/00346446211017274.

Reichel, Philip L. 1988. "Southern Slave Patrols as a Transitional Police Type." *American Journal of Police* 7 (2): 51–78.

Reuter, Edward B. 1918. *The Mulatto in the United States*. Negro Universities Press.

Rickford, Russell. 2016. "Black Lives Matter: Toward a Modern Practice of Mass Struggle." *New Labor Forum* 25 (1): 34–42. https://doi.org/10.1177/1095796015620171.

Roberts, Nailah. 2018. "How Colorism Impacts the Response to Dark-Skinned Black Women Victims of Violence." AFROPUNK. May 1, 2018. https://afropunk.com/2018/05/how-colorism-impacts-the-response-to-dark-skinned-black-women-victims-of-violence/.

Robinson, Amanda Lea. 2023. "Ethnic Visibility." *American Journal of Political Science*. https://doi.org/10.1111/ajps.12795.

Robinson, Tracy L., and Janie V. Ward. 1995. "African American Adolescents and Skin Color." *Journal of Black Psychology* 21 (3): 256–74. https://doi.org/10.1177/00957984950213004.

Roth, Wendy. 2016. "The Multiple Dimensions of Race." *Ethnic and Racial Studies* 39 (8): 1310–38. https://doi.org/10.1080/01419870.2016.1140793.

Russell, Kathy, Midge Wilson, and Ronald Hall. 1993. *The Color Complex: The Politics of Skin Color among African Americans*. Anchor.

Russell, Kathy, Midge Wilson, and Ronald Hall. 2013. *The Color Complex (Revised): The Politics of Skin Color in a New Millennium*. Knopf Doubleday.

Saperstein, Aliya, and Aaron Gullickson. 2013. "A 'Mulatto Escape Hatch' in the United States? Examining Evidence of Racial and Social Mobility during the Jim Crow Era." *Demography* 50 (5): 1921–42. https://doi.org/10.1007/s13524-013-0210-8.

Saperstein, Aliya, and Andrew M. Penner. 2012. "Racial Fluidity and Inequality in the United States." *American Journal of Sociology* 118 (3): 676–727. https://doi.org/10.1086/667722.

Schuman, Howard, Charlotte Steeh, Lawrence Bobo, and Maria Krysan. 1997. *Racial Attitudes in America: Trends and Interpretations*. Harvard University Press.

Schwartzman, Luisa Farah. 2007. "Does Money Whiten? Intergenerational Changes in Racial Classification in Brazil." *American Sociological Review* 72 (6): 940–63.

Scott, Jamil, Nadia Brown, Lorrie Frasure, and Dianne Pinderhughes. 2021. "Destined to Run? The Role of Political Participation on Black Women's Decision to Run for Elected Office." *National Review of Black Politics* 2 (1): 22–52. https://doi.org/10.1525/nrbp.2021.2.1.22.

Scott, Jamil, Kesicia Dickinson, and Pearl Dowe. 2020. "Who Is Stacey Abrams? An Examination of Gender and Race Dynamics in State-Level Candidacy." In *Good Reasons to Run: Women and Political Candidacy*, edited by Shauna Lani Shames et al., 56–67. Temple University Press.

Sears, David. 1983. "The Persistence of Early Political Predispositions: The Roles of Attitude Object and Life Stage." In *Review of Personality and Social Psychology* 4:79–116. Sage.

Sears, David O., Mingying Fu, P. J. Henry, and Kerra Bui. 2003. "The Origins and Persistence of Ethnic Identity among the 'New Immigrant' Groups." *Social Psychology Quarterly* 66 (4): 419–37. https://doi.org/10.2307/1519838.

Seltzer, Richard, and Robert Smith. 1991. "Color Differences in the Afro-American Community and the Differences They Make." *Journal of Black Studies* 21 (3): 279–86. https://doi.org/10.1177/002193479102100303.

Shah, Paru, Jamil Scott, and Eric Gonzalez Juenke. 2019. "Women of Color Candidates: Examining Emergence and Success in State Legislative Elections." *Politics, Groups, and Identities* 7 (2): 429–43.

Shaw, Todd C. 2009. *Now Is the Time!: Detroit Black Politics and Grassroots Activism*. Duke University Press.

Shelby, Tommie. 2005. *We Who Are Dark: The Philosophical Foundations of Black Solidarity*. Harvard University Press.

Shingles, Richard D. 1981. "Black Consciousness and Political Participation: The Missing Link." *American Political Science Review* 75 (1): 76–91. https://doi.org/10.2307/1962160.

Shoichet, Catherine, Ashley Fantz, and Holly Yan. 2015. "Texas Officer's Attorney: He Let His Emotions Get the Better of Him." CNN. June 10, 2015. https://www.cnn.com/2015/06/10/us/mckinney-texas-pool-party-video/index.html.

Sidanius, Jim, and Felicia Pratto. 2001. *Social Dominance: An Intergroup Theory of Social Hierarchy and Oppression*. Cambridge University Press.

Sigelman, Lee, and Susan Welch. 1991. *Black Americans' Views of Racial Inequality: The Dream Deferred*. Cambridge University Press.

Simien, Evelyn M. 2012. *Black Feminist Voices in Politics*. State University of New York Press.

Simien, Evelyn M., and Rosalee A. Clawson. 2004. "The Intersection of Race and Gender: An Examination of Black Feminist Consciousness, Race Consciousness, and Policy Attitudes." *Social Science Quarterly* 85 (3): 793–810. https://doi.org/10.1111/j.0038-4941.2004.00245.x.

Simon, Bernd, Michael Loewy, Stefan Stürmer, Ulrike Weber, Peter Freytag, Corinna Habig, Claudia Kampmeier, and Peter Spahlinger. 1998. "Collective Identification and Social Movement Participation." *Journal of Personality and Social Psychology* 74 (3): 646–58. https://doi.org/10.1037/0022-3514.74.3.646.

Simonson, Matthew David, Ray Block Jr, James N. Druckman, Katherine Ognyanova, and David M. J. Lazer. 2024. "Black Networks Matter: The Role of Interracial Contact and Social Media in the 2020 Black Lives Matter Protests." *Elements in Contentious Politics*, January. https://doi.org/10.1017/9781009415842.

Slaughter, Christine. 2021. "No Strangers to Hardship: African Americans, Inequality, and the Politics of Resilience." PhD diss., University of California–Los Angeles. https://escholarship.org/content/qt2mx8k909/qt2mx8k909_noSplash_0f20f0f85f171486137fc346643c3623.pdf.

Slaughter, Christine, and Nadia E. Brown. 2022. "Intersectionality and Political Participation." In *The Oxford Handbook of Political Participation*, edited by Marco Giugni and Maria Grasso, 725–43. Oxford University Press. https://doi.org/10.1093/oxfordhb/9780198861126.013.42.

Smiley, CalvinJohn, and David Fakunle. 2016. "From 'Brute' to 'Thug:' The Demonization and Criminalization of Unarmed Black Male Victims in America." *Journal Of Human Behavior in the Social Environment* 26 (3–4): 350–66. https://doi.org/10.1080/10911359.2015.1129256.

Smith, Candis Watts. 2014. *Black Mosaic: The Politics of Black Pan-Ethnic Diversity*. New York University Press.

Smith, Rogers M. 1997. *Civic Ideals: Conflicting Visions of Citizenship in US History*. Yale University Press.

Smooth, Wendy. 2006. "Intersectionality in Electoral Politics: A Mess Worth Making." *Politics & Gender* 2 (3): 400–414. https://doi.org/10.1017/S1743923X06261087.

Spencer, Margaret B. 1982. "Personal and Group Identity of Black Children: An Alternative Synthesis." *Genetic Psychology Monographs* 106 (1): 59–84.

Steele, Claude M. 2011. *Whistling Vivaldi: How Stereotypes Affect Us and What We Can Do*. W.W. Norton

Stewart, Jessica Lynn. 2018. "Regional Blackness: Regional Differences in Black Views on Racial Progress and Government Assistance." *National Political Science Review* 19 (1): 144–68. https://papers.ssrn.com/sol3/papers.cfm?abstract_id=2537541.

Streeter, Shea. 2019a. "The Racial Politics of Police Violence in the United States." PhD. diss., Stanford University. https://www.proquest.com/docview/2466285591/abstract/ED29401D416C4586PQ/1.

Streeter, Shea. 2019b. "Lethal Force in Black and White: Assessing Racial Disparities in the Circumstances of Police Killings." *Journal of Politics* 81 (3): 1124–32.

Stonecash, Jeffrey. 2000. *Class and Party in American Politics*. Routledge.

Strolovitch, Dara Z. 2008. *Affirmative Advocacy: Race, Class, and Gender in Interest Group Politics*. University of Chicago Press.

Stryker, Sheldon. 1968. "Identity Salience and Role Performance: The Relevance of Symbolic Interaction Theory for Family Research." *Journal of Marriage and Family* 30 (4): 558–64. https://doi.org/10.2307/349494.

Stryker, Sheldon. 1980. *Symbolic Interactionism: A Social Structural Version*. Benjamin-Cummings.

Stryker, Sheldon, and Richard T. Serpe. 1982. "Commitment, Identity Salience, and Role Behavior: Theory and Research Example." In *Personality, Roles, and Social Behavior*, edited by William Ickes and Eric S. Knowles, 199–218. Springer Series in Social Psychology. Springer. https://doi.org/10.1007/978-1-4613-9469-3_7.

Tajfel, Henri. 1972. "Social Categorization. (English Manuscript of 'La catégorisation sociale')." In *Introduction à la psychologie sociale*, edited by S. Moscovici, 1:272–302. Larousse.

Tajfel, Henri. 1974. "Social Identity and Intergroup Behaviour." *Social Science Information* 13 (2): 65–93. https://doi.org/10.1177/053901847401300204.

Tajfel, Henri. 1981. *Human Groups and Social Categories: Studies in Social Psychology*. Cambridge University Press.

Tajfel, Henri, and John Turner. 1979. "An Integrative Theory of Intergroup Conflict." In *The Social Psychology of Intergroup Relations*, edited by W. G. Austin and S. Worchel, 33–47. Brooks/Cole.

Tajfel, Henri. 1986. "The Social Identity Theory of Intergroup Behavior." In *Psychology of Intergroup Relations*, edited by S. Worchel and W. G. Austin, 7–24. Nelson-Hall.

Tate, Katherine. 1994. *From Protest to Politics*. Harvard University Press.

Tate, Katherine. 1998. *Black Faces in the Mirror: African Americans and Their Representatives in the U.S. Congress*. Princeton University Press.

Tate, Katherine. 2010. *What's Going On?: Political Incorporation and the Transformation of Black Public Opinion*. Georgetown University Press.

Taylor, Keeanga-Yamahtta. 2023. "Black Class Matters." *Hammer & Hope*, 2023. https://hammerandhope.org/article/black-america-2020-protests.

Telles, Edward. 2004. *Race in Another America: The Significance of Skin Color in Brazil*. Princeton University Press.

Telles, Edward, and René Flores. 2013. "Not Just Color: Whiteness, Nation, and Status in Latin America." *Hispanic American Historical Review* 93 (3): 411–49. https://doi.org/10.1215/00182168-2210858.

Terkildsen, Nayda. 1993. "When White Voters Evaluate Black Candidates: The Processing Implications of Candidate Skin Color, Prejudice, and Self-Monitoring." *American Journal of Political Science* 37 (4): 1032. https://doi.org/10.2307/2111542.

Terry, Deborah, and Michael Hogg. 1996. "Group Norms and the Attitude-Behavior Relationship: A Role for Group Identification." *Personality and Social Psychology Bulletin* 22 (8): 776–93.

Tharps, Lori L. 2016. *Same Family, Different Colors: Confronting Colorism in America's Diverse Families*. Beacon Press.

Thomas, Jerry. 2017. "To Weight, or Not to Weight (A Primer on Survey Data Weighting)." May 10, 2017. http://decisionanalyst.com/blog/dataweighting/.
Threadcraft, Shatema. 2016. *Intimate Justice: The Black Female Body and the Body Politic*. Oxford University Press.
Tillery, Alvin. 2019. "What Kind of Movement Is Black Lives Matter? The View from Twitter." *Journal of Race, Ethnicity, and Politics* 4 (2): 297–323. https://doi.org/10.1017/rep.2019.17.
Toplin, Robert Brent. 1979. "Between Black and White: Attitudes toward Southern Mulattoes, 1830–1861." *Journal of Southern History* 45 (2): 185. https://doi.org/10.2307/2208151.
Torres, Michelle. 2019. "A Visual Political World: Determinants and Effects of Visual Content." PhD diss., Washington University. https://openscholarship.wustl.edu/art_sci_etds/1767.
Torres, Michelle, and Alex Pugh. 2024. "Beyond Prediction: Identifying and Accounting for Latent Treatments in Images." Presented at the Research Workshop, Ohio State University, April.
Towler, Christopher, and Christopher Parker. 2018. "Between Anger and Engagement: Donald Trump and Black America." *Journal of Race, Ethnicity, and Politics* 3 (1): 219–53. https://doi.org/10.1017/rep.2017.38.
Turner, John, Michael Hogg, Penelope Oakes, Stephen Reicher, and Margaret Wetherell. 1987. *Rediscovering the Social Group: A Self-Categorization Theory*. Basil Blackwell.
Urso, Amanda Sahar d'. 2022. "A Boundary of White Inclusion: The Role of Religion in Ethnoracial Assignment." *Perspectives on Politics*, December, 1–18. https://doi.org/10.1017/S1537592722003309.
Valentino, Lauren, and Nicole Yadon. 2023. "Intersectional Wealth Gaps: Contemporary and Historical Trends in Wealth Stratification among Single Households by Race and Gender." *Social Currents* 10 (1): 3–16. https://doi.org/10.1177/23294965221139845.
Valenzuela, Ali A., and Melissa R. Michelson. 2016. "Turnout, Status, and Identity: Mobilizing Latinos to Vote with Group Appeals." *American Political Science Review* 110 (4): 615–30. https://doi.org/10.1017/S000305541600040X.
Verba, Sidney, and Norman H. Nie. 1972. *Participation in America: Political Democracy and Social Equality*. New York: Harper & Row.
Walker, Alice. 1983. *In Search of Our Mothers' Gardens—Womanist Prose*. Harvest / Harcourt.
Walker, Hannah. 2020. *Mobilized by Injustice: Criminal Justice Contact, Political Participation, and Race*. Oxford University Press.
Walsh, James, and Christopher O'Connor. 2019. "Social Media and Policing: A Review of Recent Research." *Sociology Compass* 13 (1): e12648. https://doi.org/10.1111/soc4.12648.
Walton, Hanes. 1985. *Invisible Politics: Black Political Behavior*. SUNY Press.
Walton, Hanes, Robert C. Smith, and Sherri L. Wallace. 2017. *American Politics and the African American Quest for Universal Freedom*. Taylor & Francis.
Waters, Mary C. 1999. *Black Identities*. Harvard University Press.
Weaver, Vesla. 2012. "The Electoral Consequences of Skin Color: The 'Hidden' Side of Race in Politics." *Political Behavior* 34 (1): 159–92. https://doi.org/10.1007/s11109-010-9152-7.
Weaver, Vesla, and Gwen Prowse. 2020. "Racial Authoritarianism in U.S. Democracy." *Science* 369 (6508): 1176–78. https://doi.org/10.1126/science.abd7669.
Weaver, Vesla, Gwen Prowse, and Spencer Piston. 2019. "Too Much Knowledge, Too Little Power: An Assessment of Political Knowledge in Highly Policed Communities." *The Journal of Politics* 81 (3): 1153–66. https://doi.org/10.1086/703538.

White, Ariel. 2019. "Misdemeanor Disenfranchisement? The Demobilizing Effects of Brief Jail Spells on Potential Voters." *American Political Science Review* 113 (2): 311–24. https://doi.org/10.1017/S000305541800093X.

White, Ismail K. 2007. "When Race Matters and When It Doesn't: Racial Group Differences in Response to Racial Cues." *American Political Science Review* 101 (2): 339–54. https://doi.org/10.1017/S0003055407070177.

White, Ismail K., and Chryl N. Laird. 2020. *Steadfast Democrats*. Princeton, N.J: Princeton University Press. https://press.princeton.edu/books/hardcover/9780691199511/steadfast-democrats.

White, Karletta. 2015. "The Salience of Skin Tone: Effects on the Exercise of Police Enforcement Authority." *Ethnic and Racial Studies* 38 (6): 993–1010. https://doi.org/10.1080/01419870.2014.952752.

Wilder, JeffriAnne. 2010. "Revisiting 'Color Names and Color Notions': A Contemporary Examination of the Language and Attitudes of Skin Color Among Young Black Women." *Journal of Black Studies* 41 (1): 184–206. https://doi.org/10.1177/0021934709337986.

Wilder, JeffriAnne. 2015. *Color Stories: Black Women and Colorism in the 21st Century*. ABC-CLIO.

Wilder, JeffriAnne, and Colleen Cain. 2011. "Teaching and Learning Color Consciousness in Black Families: Exploring Family Processes and Women's Experiences With Colorism." *Journal of Family Issues* 32 (5): 577–604. https://doi.org/10.1177/0192513X10390858.

Wilkinson, Betina Cutaia, James Garand, and Johanna Dunaway. 2015. "Skin Tone and Individuals' Perceptions of Commonality and Competition with Other Racial and Ethnic Groups." *Race and Social Problems* 7 (3): 181–97. https://doi.org/10.1007/s12552-015-9151-8.

Williams, Kim M. 2008. *Mark One or More: Civil Rights in Multiracial America*. University of Michigan Press.

Williams, Princess. 2021. "The Politics of Place: How Southern Identity Shapes Americans' Political Beliefs." PhD diss., University of Michigan–Ann Arbor. https://deepblue.lib.umich.edu/bitstream/handle/2027.42/171439/princesh_1.pdf?sequence=1.

Williams, Sherri. 2016. "#TeamLightSkin vs. #TeamDarkSkin: Colorism on Twitter." In *Women's Magazines in Print and New Media*, edited by Noliwe Rooks, Victoria Pass, and Ayana Weekley. Routledge.

Williamson, Joel. 1980. *New People: Miscegenation and Mulattoes in the United States*. Free Press.

Winship, Christopher, and Larry Radbill. 1994. "Sampling Weights and Regression Analysis." *Sociological Methods & Research* 23 (2): 230–57. https://doi.org/10.1177/0049124194023002004.

Winter, J. Alan. 1996. "Symbolic Ethnicity or Religion among Jews in the United States: A Test of Gansian Hypotheses." *Review of Religious Research* 37 (3): 233–47. https://doi.org/10.2307/3512276.

Winter, Nicholas J. G. 2008. *Dangerous Frames: How Ideas about Race and Gender Shape Public Opinion*. University of Chicago Press.

Womack, Gabrielle C. 2017. "From 'Mulatto' To 'Negro': How Fears of 'Passing' Changed the 1930 United States Census." MA diss., Simmons College. https://www.proquest.com/docview/1954049630/abstract/9E9B3AB887094EC1PQ/1.

Wong, Cara, and Grace Cho. 2005. "Two-Headed Coins or Kandinskys: White Racial Identification." *Political Psychology* 26 (5): 699–720. https://doi.org/10.1111/j.1467-9221.2005.00440.x.

Wong, Janelle S., S. Karthick Ramakrishnan, Taeku Lee, Jane Junn, and Janelle Wong. 2011. *Asian American Political Participation: Emerging Constituents and Their Political Identities*. Russell Sage Foundation.

REFERENCES

Woodly, Deva R. 2021. *Reckoning: Black Lives Matter and the Democratic Necessity of Social Movements*. Transgressing Boundaries: Studies in Black Politics and Black Communities. Oxford University Press.

Yadon, Nicole. 2020. "The Politics of Skin Color." PhD diss., University of Michigan–Ann Arbor.

Yadon, Nicole. 2022. "'They Say We're Violent': The Multidimensionality of Race in Perceptions of Police Brutality and BLM." *Perspectives on Politics* 20 (4): 1209–25. https://doi.org/10.1017/S1537592722001013.

Yadon, Nicole, and Mara Ostfeld. 2020. "Shades of Privilege: The Relationship between Skin Color and Political Attitudes among White Americans." *Political Behavior* 42 (4): 1369–92. https://doi.org/10.1007/s11109-020-09635-0.

Yadon, Nicole, and Mara Ostfeld. 2024. "Measuring Color: The Role of Physics, History, Identity, and Politics in How We Understand Skin Color." In *The Oxford Handbook of Methodological Pluralism in Political Science*, edited by Janet M. Box-Steffensmeier, Dino P. Christenson, and Valeria Sinclair-Chapman. Oxford University Press. https://doi.org/10.1093/oxfordhb/9780192868282.013.52.

Young, Alford A. 2004. "Experiences in Ethnographic Interviewing about Race." In *Researching Race and Racism*, edited by Martin Bulmer and John Solomos, 187–202. Routledge.

Zepeda-Millán, Chris, and Sophia Jordán Wallace. 2013. "Racialization in Times of Contention: How Social Movements Influence Latino Racial Identity." *Politics, Groups, and Identities* 1 (4): 510–27. https://doi.org/10.1080/21565503.2013.842492.

Index

Page numbers followed by "f" or "t" refer to figures or tables, respectively.

abortion rights, 54–55, 189t
activism. *See* protest participation
affirmative action: in education, 49–52, 50f, 51t, 61f, 134, 185t; in employment, 49–50, 50f, 51t, 55–56, 56f, 61f, 134–35, 137f, 185t, 190t, 198t; perceptions of beneficiaries, 62–65, 63t; policy preferences, 49–52, 50f, 51t, 55–56, 56f, 59, 61f, 134–35, 137f, 162, 185t, 190t, 198t
African American men: incarceration rates for, 69; policing and, 2, 67, 69–70, 72, 76–77, 138–40, 222n3; protest participation by, 87–88, 144; skin tone stereotype, 2, 69, 71, 72, 81, 129
African Americans: civil rights movement and, 31, 80, 122, 159, 173, 221n8; free Black people, 19–20; interactions with Whites, 18, 38, 128, 153, 155f, 162; LGBTQ community and, 79, 174; one-drop rule and, 8, 20–21, 35, 40, 57; political cohesion/solidarity among, 23, 30, 34, 57, 89; public opinion divide with Whites, 34, 59, 62, 162; racial hierarchy and, 16–17, 26, 219n2 (ch. 2); skin bleaching by, 21, 106, 170; skin tone hierarchy among, 22–24, 26. *See also* African American men; African American women; Blackness; darker-skinned African Americans; lighter-skinned African Americans; racism; skin tone; skin tone politics; slavery and enslaved people
African American women: Black feminism, 6, 30; Black Lives Matter campaigns for, 79; club movement and, 22; incarceration rate of, 69; policing and, 67, 69, 72, 77, 139–40, 222n3; protest participation by, 88, 144, 159–60; rape by White slaveholders, 3, 19; school suspensions among, 21; skin tone stereotype, 2, 62–64, 72, 129; welfare queen stereotype, 62–64, 72, 162

African Methodist Episcopal Church, 24
Afrocentric features, 16, 22, 68, 69, 109, 175
American National Election Study (ANES): correlates of skin tone in, 46–48, 48t; descriptive statistics from, 184t; distribution of skin tone in, 46–47; on linked fate and racial identity, 58; measurement of skin tone in, 27, 43, 46, 220n1 (ch. 3); on policy preferences, 48–55, 50f, 51f, 53f, 57, 185–89t, 198t; on protest participation, 86, 86f
American Voter, The (Campbell et al.), 35
AmeriSpeak survey: dependent variables in, 150, 210–12; descriptive statistics from, 73, 149, 184t, 222n7; independent variables in, 209–10; lack of survey weights with, 221n4 (ch. 4), 221n4 (ch. 5); measurement of skin tone in, 44, 73, 121, 132, 149; on policing, 73–74, 74t, 75f, 139–40, 143f; on policy preferences, 133–35, 136–37f; on racial identity, 121–22; on skin tone as distraction from broader issues of race, 83–84, 84f, 84t; on skin tone identity, 114–17, 116–17f, 119–26, 120f, 124–25f; subgroup sample sizes by skin tone, 222n1 (ch. 6)
ANES. *See* American National Election Study (ANES)
anti–police brutality movement, 68, 79–81, 85, 88–90, 128–29, 159–61, 175
arrests, 3, 15, 25, 68, 77t, 81, 195t
Asian Americans: African American views of, 53f, 54, 187t; skin tone politics and, 28, 170; sociodemographic shifts and, 8, 32, 41
authenticity. *See* racial authenticity

Baker, Ella, 161
Birth of a Nation (film), 69

Black Americans. *See* African Americans; Blackness
Black feminism, 6, 30
"Black Is Beautiful" movement, 16, 83
Black Lives Matter (BLM) movement, 79–83, 85, 89–90, 128–29, 221n8
Blackness: anti-Blackness, 15, 130; boundaries between Whiteness and, 32, 35, 172; criminalization of, 69; dark skin as epitome of, 109–10; one-drop rule and, 8, 20–21, 35, 40, 57; signaling of, 102; skin tone and proximity to, 6, 8, 15, 17, 25, 92, 95, 130
Black Panthers movement, 128–29
bleaching of skin, 21, 106, 170
BLM. *See* Black Lives Matter (BLM) movement
blue vein societies, 23
Bonilla, Tabitha, 79
Bonilla-Silva, Eduardo, 16–17, 219n2 (ch. 2)
Brooks, Clarissa, 161
brown paper bag tests, 23, 92, 94
brutality. *See* policing and police brutality

Casebolt, Eric, 67
Census, US: Pew Research Center reviews of, 220n5 (ch. 2); racial categories for, 20, 32, 92, 161, 168, 172, 173; on sociodemographic shifts, 32, 33f
civil rights movement, 31, 80, 122, 159, 173, 221n8
class: intersectionality and, 30, 101, 173; lower, 22, 23; middle, 1, 22, 23, 35, 57, 58; racial identity and, 30, 94; skin tone and, 11, 22–23, 26, 28, 31–32, 36, 40–41; tax policy and, 56; upper, 22; working, 58
Cohen, Cathy, 22, 81, 97
Collaborative Multiracial Post-Election Survey (CMPS): descriptive statistics from, 184t, 221n6; on linked fate, 123, 221n5 (ch. 5); measurement of skin tone in, 27, 44, 76, 121, 132; on policing, 76–78, 77t, 78f, 138–39, 141–42f, 195–96t; on policy preferences, 133–35, 136f; on protest participation, 86–88, 87f, 145f, 221n8, 222n4; on racial identity, 118, 119t, 122; on skin tone identity, 114–26, 116–17f, 119t, 120f, 124–25f; subgroup sample sizes by skin tone, 222n1 (ch. 6)
color. *See* skin tone
color-based identity. *See* skin tone identity
color-based politics. *See* skin tone politics
color-based stereotypes: of beauty/attractiveness, 2, 98, 108, 110; of criminality, 69, 71, 72, 108; disparate impacts of, 21; institutionalization of, 10; multiracialism and, 19; perpetuation of, 65, 108; policing and, 68, 69, 81; proximity to Blackness and, 6, 8, 15, 130; skin tone identity and, 92, 95, 100, 102–3, 108–13, 129; welfare queen and, 62–64, 72, 162
color-blindness, 28, 34–36, 41–42

Colored Methodist Episcopal Church, 24
colorism: anti-colorist policies, 96, 102, 168; in Black communities, 22–24, 122–23; creation and perpetuation of by Whites, 10–11, 15, 19–22, 165, 192; cross-racial understandings of, 175; dating and, 107, 160; defined, 4, 14; education and, 9, 23, 36, 41; employment and, 9, 41, 53, 68, 131, 153, 160; income and, 36, 68, 160; lack of minimization efforts, 34–35, 42; legacy in United States, 16–25, 161; linked fate and, 39; in media, 34, 66, 91, 99, 108, 109; movement organizing around, 79–85, 172; policing and, 8, 9, 36, 41, 68, 131, 160; political manifestations of, 29, 163; racism and, 8, 14–16, 21, 102, 130, 155, 165, 174; religion and, 23–24; skin tone politics and, 26–27, 34, 36, 39, 41, 52, 55, 88, 162; stigmatization and, 10, 165, 166, 175; wealth and, 41. *See also* color-based stereotypes
Combahee River Collective, 6
comb tests, 23
complexion. *See* skin tone
complexion homogamy, 23, 93
Cottom, Tressie McMillan, 101
COVID-19 pandemic, 45, 159, 183
criminal justice system: Black-White divide in public opinion on, 34; death penalty and, 4, 15, 54, 68, 80; incarceration and, 15, 68–69, 72, 76, 77t, 195t; skin tone and, 4–5, 15, 27, 29, 39, 68–71, 102, 161; stigmatization within, 70. *See also* policing and police brutality

darker-skinned African Americans: arrests among, 3, 15, 25, 77t; Black Lives Matter movement and, 128–29; class status and, 11, 26; contextual assessments of, 2, 4, 16, 18, 94, 98, 101–2; dating and, 2, 18, 94, 107; death penalty given to, 4, 15; as doubly marginalized, 29, 34, 41, 49, 52, 130, 168; education and, 15, 21, 25, 39; election to political office, 26, 39; employment and, 12, 15, 25; health and, 3, 4, 15, 25; homeownership among, 47; income and, 4, 15, 25, 39, 47; policing and, 2, 4, 12, 18, 71–79, 74t, 75f, 77t, 78f, 89, 136, 138–40, 141–43f, 167, 175; policy preferences of, 12, 49–56, 50f, 51t, 53f, 56, 60–62, 60–61f, 133–34, 136–37f; protest participation by, 85–89, 86–87f, 140, 144–46, 145f, 159–62, 167, 175, 221n8; racial authenticity and, 4, 16, 18, 94, 98, 100, 102, 109–10; racial identity and, 58, 98, 100, 131; on skin tone as distraction from broader issues of race, 84, 84f; skin tone identity and, 12–13, 29, 92–103, 106–21, 116–17f, 120f, 126–32, 147, 161, 163, 168–69; slavery and, 3, 16, 19; stereotypes of, 2, 6, 8, 15, 21, 63–65, 68, 71–73, 81, 92, 100, 108–12; stigmatization of, 1, 2, 70, 95, 103, 131; wealth and, 4, 15
dating, 2, 18, 38–39, 91–92, 94, 107, 128, 160, 162

Dawson, Michael, 31, 89
death penalty, 4, 15, 54, 68, 80
dehumanization, 76–77, 77t, 78f, 135–36, 138, 141f, 157
discrimination: gender-based, 172; perceptions of, 26, 27, 57, 150, 154. *See also* colorism; racism
Dunaway, Johanna, 220n4 (ch. 3)

education: access to opportunities, 17; affirmative action in, 49–52, 50f, 51t, 61f, 134, 185t; Black-White divide in public opinion on, 34; colorism and, 9, 23, 36, 41; HBCUs, 23, 94; skin tone and, 15, 21, 25, 27, 39, 62; skin tone identity and, 102, 123, 126; suspensions, 21, 25
employment: affirmative action in, 49–50, 50f, 51t, 55–56, 56f, 61f, 134–35, 137f, 185t, 190t, 198t; Black-White divide in public opinion on, 34; class divides and, 22; colorism and, 9, 41, 53, 68, 131, 153, 160; government-guaranteed jobs, 51t, 55–56, 56f, 190t; immigration's impact on, 53, 53f, 60–62, 61f, 187t; skin tone and, 12, 25, 29, 32, 38, 39, 62, 152–53, 155f; unemployment, 15, 31
ethnicity. *See* race and ethnicity
eugenics, 3, 15–16, 19, 42

feeling thermometers, 51t, 54, 113, 187t
feminism, Black, 6, 30
Floyd, George, 70, 159, 190
free Black people, 19–20

Garand, James, 220n4 (ch. 3)
Gause, LaGina, 175
gender: Black Lives Matter movement and, 79, 80; discrimination based on, 172; identities based on, 30; intersectionality and, 6, 30, 65, 72, 76, 89, 101, 139, 173; policing and, 69–73, 75–76, 89, 139–40, 167; protest participation and, 12, 87–88, 87f, 144; race-based policies and, 62–65, 63t; racial identity and, 30, 94; school suspensions and, 21; skin tone and, 47, 63, 170. *See also* African American men; African American women
General Social Survey (GSS), 26–27, 39, 40, 220n1 (ch. 3)
government: income inequality reduction by, 50f, 52, 59–60, 60f, 133–35, 136f, 186t, 197–98t; jobs guaranteed by, 51t, 55–56, 56f, 190t; spending on services, 50f, 51t, 60, 60f. *See also* welfare programs
Gray, Stephanie, 7
gun rights, 54–55, 189t

Hamer, Fannie Lou, 161
Harris, Kamala, 4
Harvey, Richard, 222n8
HBCUs (historically Black colleges and universities), 23, 94

health: access to resources, 17; multiracialism and, 19; skin tone and, 3, 4, 15, 25, 31, 161
hierarchy: of colorism and racism, 8, 15, 16, 130, 174; of groups, 96, 97; of skin tone, 11, 15, 17, 22–24, 26, 40. *See also* racial hierarchy
Hispanics. *See* Latinos/Latinas
historically Black colleges and universities (HBCUs), 23, 94
Hochschild, Jennifer, 25–26, 39–40, 57–58, 135
homeownership, 47, 49, 62
Huddy, Leonie, 100

identity: dynamic nature of, 93–94; gender-based, 30; political, 8–10, 13, 16, 93, 130, 163. *See also* racial identity; skin tone identity; social identity
identity centrality measures, 113–15, 116f
immigrants and immigration: employment effects of, 53, 53f, 60–62, 61f, 187t; feelings toward, 53f, 54, 187t, 220n4 (ch. 3); growth of, 8, 28, 29, 32, 36, 41; levels of, 51t, 53–54, 53f, 61f, 62, 186t; policy preferences by skin tone, 51t, 52–54, 53f, 60–62, 61f, 186–87t; racial identity and status of, 30, 94; sociodemographic shifts and, 8, 32, 36, 41
incarceration, 15, 68–69, 72, 76, 77t, 195t
income: class divides and, 22; colorism and, 36, 68, 160; inequality, 50f, 52, 59–60, 60f, 133–35, 136f, 157, 186t, 197–98t; skin tone and, 4, 15, 25, 29, 32, 39, 47, 49, 62; skin tone identity and, 102, 123, 126
inequality: income, 50f, 52, 59–60, 60f, 133–35, 136f, 157, 186t, 197–98t; political science's focus on, 5; in shared racial categories, 8, 16
In Search of Our Mothers' Gardens (Walker), 14
intersectionality: Black Lives Matter movement and, 79–81, 83; class and, 30, 101, 173; gender and, 6, 30, 65, 72, 76, 89, 101, 139, 173; power and, 11, 45, 166, 191; race and, 6, 11, 30, 45, 65, 89, 101, 162, 166, 173–74, 191; sexual orientation and, 30, 173; skin tone and, 11, 45, 65, 72, 76, 89, 101, 162, 166, 174, 191
interviews. *See* qualitative interviews
intra-group dynamics, 166–68, 171, 173
introjection measures, 115–18, 117f, 120f, 121

Jack and Jill of America, 18, 23, 94
jail. *See* incarceration
Jefferson, Hakeem, 97
jobs. *See* employment

Latinos/Latinas: African American views of, 53f, 54, 187t, 220n4 (ch. 3); on dehumanization by police, 76; racial hierarchy and, 219n2 (ch. 2); skin tone politics and, 7, 28, 36, 170; sociodemographic shifts and, 8, 32, 41

law enforcement. *See* criminal justice system; policing and police brutality
LGBTQ community, 79, 174. *See also* sexual orientation
lighter-skinned African Americans: contextual assessments of, 3, 5, 94; education and, 39; efforts to maintain status, 23; election to political office, 39; employment and, 38; health and, 31; homeownership among, 47; income and, 39, 47; intermarriage among, 23, 93, 99; policing and, 71–79, 75f, 78f, 136, 138–40, 141–43f, 222n3; policy preferences of, 12, 49–56, 50f, 51t, 53f, 56f, 59–62, 60–61f, 134, 136–37f; privilege and, 38, 52, 102, 103, 113, 131, 148, 169; protest participation by, 86–87, 86–87f, 144–46, 145f, 221n8; racial authenticity and, 102, 103, 131, 148; racial identity and, 58, 100; on skin tone as distraction from broader issues of race, 84, 84f; skin tone identity and, 95–96, 100, 102–21, 116–17f, 120f, 131–32, 147–48, 169; slavery and, 3, 16, 19, 24; stereotypes of, 2, 98, 103, 108, 110; stigmatization of, 96; wealth and, 31
linked fate, 26, 39, 57–58, 119, 121, 123, 138, 221n5 (ch. 5)
Lotus Club (Washington, DC), 23
Lucid survey: data comparison with MTurk survey, 220n2 (ch. 3); descriptive statistics from, 73, 184t, 220n3 (ch. 4); measurement of skin tone in, 44, 73, 132; on policing, 73–74, 74t, 75f, 139–40, 143f; on policy preferences, 133, 136f, 197t; on skin tone identity, 114–15, 116f; subgroup sample sizes by skin tone, 222n1 (ch. 6)

Maddox, Keith, 72
Malcolm X, 21–22
marriage, 23, 92, 93, 99, 101
Massey-Martin skin tone scale, 43–44, 43f, 46, 121
MCSUI (Multi-City Study of Urban Inequality), 26–27, 39, 40
media: colorism in, 34, 66, 91, 99, 108, 109; police brutality coverage by, 69–70; protest coverage by, 159; race-based policies and, 65, 162; skin tone identity and, 107–10, 113, 126; social media, 99, 108, 109, 113, 190; stereotypes in, 63, 64, 69, 72, 108
men. *See* African American men; gender
Methodist Church, 24
Middle Eastern/North African (MENA) racial category, 172
mixed-race ancestry. *See* multiracialism
Monk, Ellis, 18, 34, 94
Movement for Black Lives, 174
MTurk survey: on color-based stereotypes, 221nn1–2; data comparison with Lucid survey, 220n2 (ch. 3); descriptive statistics from, 184t; incentives for finishing quickly, 112, 221n2;

measurement of skin tone in, 44; on skin tone identity, 110–12, 114–15, 116f
Multi-City Study of Urban Inequality (MCSUI), 26–27, 39, 40
multiracialism: Census category for, 20, 172, 173; of CMPS respondents, 44; of free Black people, 19–20; growth of, 8, 29, 32–33, 36, 41, 122, 172; health and, 19; privilege and, 219n3 (ch. 2); racial hierarchy and, 20, 122; skin tone and, 3, 14, 19, 24–25, 170–71; slavery and, 3, 19, 24; stereotypes related to, 19; wealth and, 19

National Survey of American Life (NSAL): descriptive statistics from, 184t; on linked fate and racial identity, 58; measurement of skin tone in, 43, 220n5 (ch. 3); on policy preferences, 51t, 55–57, 56f, 190t
National Survey of Black Americans (NSBA), 26–27, 39, 40

Obama, Barack, 4, 54, 189t
one-drop rule, 8, 20–21, 35, 40, 57
optimal distinctiveness theory, 101–2
Ostfeld, Mara, 7, 17, 28, 29

paper bag tests, 23, 92, 94
partisanship, 5, 48, 59–60, 60–61f, 114, 123, 126, 169
Pérez, Efrén, 126
Pew Research Center, 35, 220n5 (ch. 2)
phenotype, 3, 16, 21–23
Phoenix, Davin, 34
pigmentocracy, 34, 168
Plessy v. Ferguson (1896), 17
policing and police brutality: arrests, 3, 15, 25, 68, 77t, 81, 195t; colorism and, 8, 9, 36, 41, 68, 131, 160; dehumanization in, 76–77, 77t, 78f, 135–36, 138, 141f, 157; gender and, 69–73, 75–76, 89, 139–40, 167; movement against, 68, 79–81, 85, 88–90, 128–29, 159–61, 175; murders by police, 70, 159, 190; skin tone and, 2, 4, 12, 18, 32, 38, 68–79, 74t, 75f, 77t, 78f, 85, 89, 153–54, 155f, 162, 167, 175, 195t; skin tone identity and, 13, 135–36, 138–40, 141–43f, 146, 169, 197t, 199–200t; slave patrols as precursor to, 67–68, 88; targeted practices of, 68, 73, 85, 87
policy preferences: affirmative action, 49–52, 50f, 51t, 55–56, 56f, 59, 61f, 134–35, 137f, 162, 185t, 190t, 198t; ANES on, 48–55, 50f, 51f, 53f, 57, 185–89t; conservative, 52, 54; controls in models of, 48–49, 220n3 (ch. 3), 222n2; death penalty, 54; government-guaranteed jobs, 51t, 55–56, 56f, 190t; government spending on services, 50f, 51t, 60, 60f; immigration, 51t, 52–54, 53f, 60–62, 61f, 186–87t; income inequality, 50f, 52, 59–60, 60f, 133–35, 136f, 157, 186t, 197–98t; liberal, 11, 12, 29, 37, 49, 52, 59, 96, 102; NSAL on, 51t, 55–57, 56f,

190t; racial identity and, 133–35, 137f, 197–98t; skin tone identity and, 132–35, 136–37f, 197–98t; welfare spending, 50f, 51t, 52, 59, 60f, 162, 185t; of White Americans, 59–60, 60–61f

politics: cohesion/solidarity, 23, 30, 34, 57, 89, 97, 175; partisanship in, 5, 48, 59–60, 60–61f, 114, 123, 126, 169; public knowledge regarding, 164–65; race and, 5–6, 10, 29–36, 39, 57, 129–30, 157, 165; social identity and, 9, 10, 16, 93, 130, 163. *See also* protest participation; skin tone politics

positionality of researchers, 10–11, 165–66

power: access to, 6, 13, 16, 130, 158; gatekeepers of, 10, 19–20; intersectionality and, 11, 45, 166, 191; political, 173; skin tone and, 5, 11, 17–22, 131, 155–56, 157f, 174; of social identity groups, 97; of social movements, 82; structures of, 15, 165

prison. *See* incarceration

privilege: access to power through, 6; lighter-skinned Blacks and, 38, 52, 102, 103, 113, 131, 148, 169; multiracialism and, 219n3 (ch. 2); of social identity groups, 97; White, 10, 191

protest participation: in anti-police brutality movement, 68, 85, 88, 159–61; gender and, 12, 87–88, 87f, 144; skin tone and, 10, 12, 70, 85–89, 86–87f, 159–62, 167, 175, 221n8; skin tone identity and, 140, 144–46, 145f, 157, 169; in summer of 2020, 82, 87, 88, 159–61

public opinion: Black-White divide in, 34, 59, 62, 162; contemporary research on, 164; skin tone and, 65–66, 132, 158, 175. *See also* policy preferences

qualitative interviews: coding of transcripts from, 193; conversation topics, 45–46, 71, 91, 191, 220n2 (ch. 4); descriptive statistics, 193, 193–94t; feedback from participants, 46, 191, 192, 223n1; methodology for, 11–12, 44–46, 183, 190–93; on movement organizing around colorism, 80–83, 85, 221n7; on policing, skin tone, and gender, 71–73; political knowledge displayed in, 164–65; race and skin tone of interviewers, 11, 45, 165–66, 191; on race-based policies, 62–65, 63t; recruitment process, 45, 183, 190–91; researcher positionality and, 165–66; on skin tone identity, 105–13, 122–23, 128–29

race and ethnicity: boundaries based on, 9, 28, 32–35, 41, 171–73; Census categories for, 20, 32, 92, 161, 168, 172, 173; eugenics and, 3, 15–16, 19, 42; intersectionality and, 6, 11, 30, 45, 65, 89, 101, 162, 166, 173–74, 191; legal definitions of, 17–18, 21, 92; multidimensionality of, 10, 13, 34, 37, 157, 161, 166; one-drop rule and, 8, 20–21, 35, 40, 57; policies based on, 62–65, 63t, 162, 165; politics and, 5–6, 10, 29–36, 39, 57, 129–30, 157, 165; Roots of Race conceptualization, 17, 93; school

suspensions and, 21; skin tone as distraction from broader issues of, 83–84, 84f, 84t; skin tone as marker of, 6, 15, 17, 30, 95, 219n1 (ch. 2); as social constructs, 16, 130, 172. *See also* Blackness; immigrants and immigration; multiracialism; Whiteness; *and specific racial and ethnic groups*

racial authenticity: darker-skinned Blacks and, 4, 16, 18, 94, 98, 100, 102, 109–10; lighter-skinned Blacks and, 102, 103, 131, 148

racial hierarchy: allegiance to fight against, 26, 40; complexity of, 25, 32; multiracialism and, 20, 122; reshaping of, 8–9, 28, 41, 122, 168, 172, 174; skin tone and, 11, 16–17, 41, 219n2 (ch. 2); sociodemographic shifts and, 32, 33, 36, 172; status within, 54, 97; Whiteness as "ideal" in, 130

racial identity: contextual assessments of, 101; dynamic nature of, 94; group boundaries and, 100; importance of, 9, 13, 31, 94, 118, 119t, 121–22; multidimensionality of, 164; people-of-color identity, 169, 170; policy preferences and, 133–35, 137f, 197–98t; politics and, 30, 36, 39, 130, 157; power and status differentials, 100; skin tone and, 5, 40, 57–58, 98, 131; skin tone identity as distinct from, 93, 118, 127, 129, 154, 156, 164

racism: colorism and, 8, 14–16, 21, 102, 130, 155, 165, 174; minimization efforts, 34–35, 42, 122, 131; pseudo-scientific practices and, 42; segregation and, 17; systemic, 34, 192

Rapid and Rigorous Qualitative Data Analysis (RADaR) technique, 193

Reece, Robert, 35

religion, 5, 17, 23–24, 30, 101, 130, 164

reparations for slavery, 55, 56, 190t

Roots of Race conceptualization, 17, 93

#SayHerName campaign, 70, 79

school. *See* education

segregation, 17

self-categorization theory, 100

Seltzer, Richard, 26, 27, 39

sexual orientation: Black Lives Matter movement and, 80; intersectionality and, 30, 173; LGBTQ community, 79, 174; racial identity and, 30, 94

Shelby, Tommie, 31, 89

skin bleaching, 21, 106, 170

skin color. *See* skin tone

skin tone: ANES correlates of, 46–48, 48t; brown paper bag tests of, 23, 92, 94; class and, 11, 22–23, 26, 28, 31–32, 36, 40–41; cognitive constructs associated with, 18, 95; contextual assessments of, 2–5, 16, 18, 94–95, 98, 101–2, 109; criminal justice system and, 4–5, 15, 27, 29, 39, 68–71, 102, 161; dating and, 2, 18, 38–39, 91–92, 94, 107, 128, 160, 162; as distraction from broader issues of race, 83–84, 84f, 84t; education and, 15, 21, 25,

skin tone (cont.)
27, 39, 62; employment and, 12, 25, 29, 32, 38, 39, 62, 152–53, 155f; gender and, 47, 63, 170; health and, 3, 4, 15, 25, 31, 161; hierarchy of, 11, 15, 17, 22–24, 26, 40; homeownership and, 47, 49, 62; income and, 4, 15, 25, 29, 32, 39, 47, 49, 62; intersectionality and, 11, 45, 65, 72, 76, 89, 101, 162, 166, 174, 191; intra-group dynamics and, 166–68, 171, 173; linked fate and, 26, 57–58; as marker of race, 6, 15, 17, 30, 95, 219n1 (ch. 2); multiracialism and, 3, 14, 19, 24–25, 170–71; paradox of, 7, 25–29, 39–42, 49, 55, 66, 85, 89, 122–23, 174; policing and, 2, 4, 12, 18, 32, 38, 68–79, 74t, 75f, 77t, 78f, 85, 89, 153–54, 155f, 162, 167, 175, 195t; power and, 5, 11, 17–22, 131, 155–56, 157f, 174; protest participation and, 10, 12, 70, 85–89, 86–87f, 159–62, 167, 175, 221n8; public opinion and, 65–66, 132, 158, 175; race-based policies and, 62–65, 63t; racial hierarchy and, 11, 16–17, 41, 219n2 (ch. 2); racial identity and, 5, 40, 57–58, 98, 131; in Roots of Race conceptualization, 17, 93; school suspensions and, 21, 25; slavery and, 3, 8, 15–16, 19, 24; stigmatization and, 1–2, 70, 95–96, 103, 131; wealth and, 4, 15, 31, 39, 161. See also color-based stereotypes; colorism; darker-skinned African Americans; lighter-skinned African Americans; skin tone identity; skin tone measures; skin tone politics

skin tone identity: activation of, 128–30, 132, 147–49, 154, 157, 163; affective component of, 98, 99, 111–13, 126; age and, 122–23, 125f, 127, 164; cognitive component of, 98, 105–11, 126; color-based stereotypes and, 92, 95, 100, 102–3, 108–13, 129; correlates of, 121–26, 124–25f; darker-skinned Blacks and, 12–13, 29, 92–103, 106–21, 116–17f, 120f, 126–32, 147, 161, 163, 168–69; data and measures of, 44, 113–21, 116–17f, 119t, 120f, 126–27; education and, 102, 123, 126; experimental design and measures of, 149–56, 151t, 155f, 157f, 205–9f, 213–18t, 222nn5–6, 222n8; formation of, 100, 103, 105; future research needs, 168–71; importance of, 9, 12–13, 40, 93–94, 114, 118–23, 119t, 120f, 125f, 126–28, 163; income and, 102, 123, 126; internalization of, 29, 92, 100, 163; lighter-skinned Blacks and, 95–96, 100, 102–21, 116–17f, 120f, 131–32, 147–48, 169; linked fate and, 123; love and acceptance of, 2, 91; multiracialism and, 171; partisanship and, 114, 123, 126; perceived positionality in society and, 18; policing and, 13, 135–36, 138–40, 141–43f, 146, 169, 197t, 199–200t; policy preferences and, 132–35, 136–37f, 197–98t; protest participation and, 140, 144–46, 145f, 157, 169; psychological attachment to, 9–10, 16, 58–59, 69, 92, 161–64, 168; racial identity as distinct from, 93, 118, 127, 129, 154, 156, 164; shared language and, 105, 111–

13; skin tone politics and, 13, 96, 98–103, 126–47, 146t, 157–58, 163, 168–71, 174–75, 197–204t; socialization processes and, 105–9, 113, 126–27; theoretical framework, 29–30, 92, 103

skin tone measures: advancements in, 26–29, 40; in AmeriSpeak survey, 44, 73; in ANES, 27, 43, 46, 220n1 (ch. 3); in CMPS, 27, 44, 76; in Lucid survey, 44, 73; Massey-Martin skin tone scale, 43–44, 43f, 46, 121; in MTurk survey, 44; in NSAL, 43, 220n5 (ch. 3); pseudo-scientific practices, 42; trichotomized, 220n6; Yadon-Ostfeld Skin Color Scale, 44, 44f, 73–74, 76, 87, 115, 121, 132, 149; in YouGov survey, 44

skin tone politics: class-color linkage and, 31–32, 36, 40–41; color-blindness and, 28, 34–36, 41–42; colorism and, 26–27, 34, 36, 39, 41, 52, 55, 88, 162; controls in models for, 219n4; data and measures of, 11, 42–46, 43–44f; election to office and, 26, 39; literature review, 5–8, 25–29, 31, 39–40; skin tone identity and, 13, 96, 98–103, 126–47, 146t, 157–58, 163, 168–71, 174–75, 197–204t; sociodemographic shifts and, 8–9, 32–34, 36, 40, 41; theoretical framework, 11, 29, 36–37, 37t, 104t, 130. See also policy preferences

slavery and enslaved people: multiracialism and, 3, 19, 24; reparations for, 55, 56, 190t; runaways and slave patrols, 67–68, 88; skin tone and, 3, 8, 15–16, 19, 24

Smith, Robert C., 26, 27, 39
social categorization theory, 12, 96, 97, 126
social identity: activation of, 147; components of, 97–99, 113; defined, 96; optimal distinctiveness theory on, 101–2; politics and, 9, 10, 16, 93, 130, 163; theory of, 12, 96–98, 126. See also racial identity; skin tone identity
socialization processes, 105–9, 113, 126–27
social media, 99, 108, 109, 113, 190
social mobility, 12, 152, 153, 155f, 160, 162, 222n8
sociodemographic shifts, 8–9, 32–34, 33f, 36, 40, 41, 172
socioeconomic status. See class
stereotypes. See color-based stereotypes
stigmatization: attachment to skin tone identity and, 95–96, 103; colorism and, 10, 165, 166, 175; in criminal justice system, 70; skin tone and, 1, 2, 70, 95, 103, 131; of social identity groups, 97, 100
Stokes, Ronald, 21
survey research. See specific names of surveys

Tajfel, Henri, 96
Taylor, Breonna, 70, 159
Tillery, Alvin, 79
Tourgée, Albion, 17–18

unemployment, 15, 31

INDEX

wages. *See* income
Walker, Alice, 14, 22, 25
wealth: access to resources, 17; colorism and, 41; complexion homogamy and, 23; multiracialism and, 19; redistribution of, 27; skin tone and, 4, 15, 31, 39, 161
Weaver, Vesla, 25-26, 35, 39-40, 57-58
welfare programs: perceptions of beneficiaries, 62-65, 63t; spending on, 50f, 51t, 52, 59, 60f, 162, 185t; welfare queen stereotype, 62-64, 72, 162
White Americans: alliances with free Black people, 20; colorism created and perpetuated by, 10-11, 15, 19-22, 165, 192; on dehumanization by police, 76; Democrats, 12, 59, 60, 62; eugenicist views held by, 15-16, 19; as gatekeepers of power, 19-20; incarceration rates for, 69; interactions with Blacks, 18, 38, 128, 153, 155f, 162; partisanship among, 59, 60, 60-61f; perceptions based on skin tone, 109; policy preferences of, 59-60, 60-61f; privileged status of, 10, 191; public opinion divide with Blacks, 34, 59, 62, 162; skin tone politics and, 7, 28, 36
Whiteness: boundaries between Blackness and, 32, 35, 172; as "ideal," 15, 99, 130; legal definitions of, 18, 92; skin tone and proximity to, 5, 15, 38, 95; social characteristics of, 19-20
Wilkinson, Betina Cutaia, 220n4 (ch. 3)
women. *See* African American women; gender
workplace. *See* employment

Yadon-Ostfeld Skin Color Scale, 44, 44f, 73-74, 76, 87, 115, 121, 132, 149
YouGov survey: descriptive statistics from, 184t; on linked fate, 123, 221n5 (ch. 5); measurement of skin tone in, 44, 121; on racial identity, 121-22; on skin tone identity, 114-17, 116-17f, 119-26, 120f, 124-25f

Chicago Studies in American Politics
A series edited by Susan Herbst, Lawrence R. Jacobs, Adam J. Berinsky,
and Frances Lee; Benjamin I. Page, editor emeritus

Series titles, continued from front matter

Accountability in State Legislatures
by Steven Rogers

Our Common Bonds: Using What Americans Share to Help Bridge the Partisan Divide
by Matthew Levendusky

Dynamic Democracy: Public Opinion, Elections, and Policymaking in the American States
by Devin Caughey and Christopher Warshaw

Persuasion in Parallel: How Information Changes Minds about Politics
by Alexander Coppock

*Radical American Partisanship: Mapping Violent Hostility, Its Causes,
and the Consequences for Democracy*
by Nathan P. Kalmoe and Lilliana Mason

The Obligation Mosaic: Race and Social Norms in US Political Participation
by Allison P. Anoll

A Troubled Birth: The 1930s and American Public Opinion
by Susan Herbst

Power Shifts: Congress and Presidential Representation
by John A. Dearborn

Prisms of the People: Power and Organizing in Twenty-First-Century America
by Hahrie Han, Elizabeth McKenna, and Michelle Oyakawa

Democracy Declined: The Failed Politics of Consumer Financial Protection
by Mallory E. SoRelle

Race to the Bottom: How Racial Appeals Work in American Politics
by LaFleur Stephens-Dougan

The Limits of Party: Congress and Lawmaking in a Polarized Era
by James M. Curry and Frances E. Lee

America's Inequality Trap
by Nathan J. Kelly

*Good Enough for Government Work: The Public Reputation
Crisis in America (And What We Can Do to Fix It)*
by Amy E. Lerman

Who Wants to Run? How the Devaluing of Political Office Drives Polarization
by Andrew B. Hall

From Politics to the Pews: How Partisanship and the Political Environment Shape Religious Identity
by Michele F. Margolis

The Increasingly United States: How and Why American Political Behavior Nationalized
by Daniel J. Hopkins

Legacies of Losing in American Politics
by Jeffrey K. Tulis and Nicole Mellow

Legislative Style
by William Bernhard and Tracy Sulkin

Why Parties Matter: Political Competition and Democracy in the American South
by John H. Aldrich and John D. Griffin

Neither Liberal nor Conservative: Ideological Innocence in the American Public
by Donald R. Kinder and Nathan P. Kalmoe

Strategic Party Government: Why Winning Trumps Ideology
by Gregory Koger and Matthew J. Lebo

Post-Racial or Most-Racial? Race and Politics in the Obama Era
by Michael Tesler

The Politics of Resentment: Rural Consciousness in Wisconsin and the Rise of Scott Walker
by Katherine J. Cramer

Legislating in the Dark: Information and Power in the House of Representatives
by James M. Curry

Why Washington Won't Work: Polarization, Political Trust, and the Governing Crisis
by Marc J. Hetherington and Thomas J. Rudolph

Who Governs? Presidents, Public Opinion, and Manipulation
by James N. Druckman and Lawrence R. Jacobs

Trapped in America's Safety Net: One Family's Struggle
by Andrea Louise Campbell

Arresting Citizenship: The Democratic Consequences of American Crime Control
by Amy E. Lerman and Vesla M. Weaver

How the States Shaped the Nation: American Electoral Institutions and Voter Turnout, 1920–2000
by Melanie Jean Springer

White-Collar Government: The Hidden Role of Class in Economic Policy Making
by Nicholas Carnes

How Partisan Media Polarize America
by Matthew Levendusky

Changing Minds or Changing Channels? Partisan News in an Age of Choice
by Kevin Arceneaux and Martin Johnson

The Politics of Belonging: Race, Public Opinion, and Immigration
by Natalie Masuoka and Jane Junn

Trading Democracy for Justice: Criminal Convictions and the Decline of Neighborhood Political Participation
by Traci Burch

Political Tone: How Leaders Talk and Why
by Roderick P. Hart, Jay P. Childers, and Colene J. Lind

Learning While Governing: Expertise and Accountability in the Executive Branch
by Sean Gailmard and John W. Patty

The Social Citizen: Peer Networks and Political Behavior
by Betsy Sinclair

Follow the Leader? How Voters Respond to Politicians' Policies and Performance
by Gabriel S. Lenz

The Timeline of Presidential Elections: How Campaigns Do (and Do Not) Matter
by Robert S. Erikson and Christopher Wlezien

Electing Judges: The Surprising Effects of Campaigning on Judicial Legitimacy
by James L. Gibson

Disciplining the Poor: Neoliberal Paternalism and the Persistent Power of Race
by Joe Soss, Richard C. Fording, and Sanford F. Schram

The Submerged State: How Invisible Government Policies Undermine American Democracy
by Suzanne Mettler

Selling Fear: Counterterrorism, the Media, and Public Opinion
by Brigitte L. Nacos, Yaeli Bloch-Elkon, and Robert Y. Shapiro

Why Parties? A Second Look
by John H. Aldrich

Obama's Race: The 2008 Election and the Dream of a Post-Racial America
by Michael Tesler and David O. Sears

News That Matters: Television and American Opinion, Updated Edition
by Shanto Iyengar and Donald R. Kinder

Filibustering: A Political History of Obstruction in the House and Senate
by Gregory Koger

Us Against Them: Ethnocentric Foundations of American Opinion
by Donald R. Kinder and Cindy D. Kam

The Partisan Sort: How Liberals Became Democrats and Conservatives Became Republicans
by Matthew Levendusky

Democracy at Risk: How Terrorist Threats Affect the Public
by Jennifer L. Merolla and Elizabeth J. Zechmeister

In Time of War: Understanding American Public Opinion from World War II to Iraq
by Adam J. Berinsky

Agendas and Instability in American Politics, Second Edition
by Frank R. Baumgartner and Bryan D. Jones

The Party Decides: Presidential Nominations Before and After Reform
by Marty Cohen, David Karol, Hans Noel, and John Zaller

The Private Abuse of the Public Interest: Market Myths and Policy Muddles
by Lawrence D. Brown and Lawrence R. Jacobs

Same Sex, Different Politics: Success and Failure in the Struggles over Gay Rights
by Gary Mucciaroni

www.ingramcontent.com/pod-product-compliance
Lightning Source LLC
Chambersburg PA
CBHW022045290426
44109CB00014B/990